The Aesthetics
of Care

The Aesthetics of Care

On the Literary Treatment of Animals

Josephine Donovan

Bloomsbury Academic
An imprint of Bloomsbury Publishing Inc

B L O O M S B U R Y
NEW YORK · LONDON · OXFORD · NEW DELHI · SYDNEY

Bloomsbury Academic

An imprint of Bloomsbury Publishing Inc

1385 Broadway	50 Bedford Square
New York	London
NY 10018	WC1B 3DP
USA	UK

www.bloomsbury.com

BLOOMSBURY and the Diana logo are trademarks of Bloomsbury Publishing Plc

First published 2016

Library of Congress Cataloging-in-Publication Data
Names: Donovan, Josephine, 1941- author.
Title: The aesthetics of care : on the literary treatment of animals / Josephine Donovan.
Description: New York : Bloomsbury Academic, 2016. | Includes bibliographical references and index.
Identifiers: LCCN 2015043712 (print) | LCCN 2016002859 (ebook) | ISBN 9781501317194 (hardback : alk. paper) | ISBN 9781501317200 (pbk. : alk. paper) | ISBN 9781501317217 (ePub) | ISBN 9781501317224 (ePDF)
Subjects: LCSH: Animals in literature. | Animal welfare in literature. | Literature, Modern–19th century–History and criticism. | Literature, Modern–20th century–History and criticism. | Ecocriticism.
Classification: LCC PN56.A64 .D66 2016 (print) | LCC PN56.A64 (ebook) | DDC 809/.93362–dc23
LC record available at http://lccn.loc.gov/2015043712

ISBN: HB: 978-1-5013-1719-4
PB: 978-1-5013-1720-0
ePub: 978-1-5013-1721-7
ePDF: 978-1-5013-1722-4

Cover design: Eleanor Rose
Cover image: *Das Schaf*, Franz Marc

Typeset by Integra Software Services Pvt Ltd.
Printed and bound in the United States of America

*If you lie on the earth somewhere you hear a sound
like a vast breath, as though it were the very inspiration
of earth herself, and all the living things on her.*
—Virginia Woolf

CONTENTS

PREFACE

Starting from the feminist ethic of care, I develop in this study an *aesthetics* of care, which I establish as the basis for a critical approach to the representation of animals in literature. The analysis expands necessarily into a discussion of the relationship between ethics and aesthetics, leading to a reconceptualization of key literary critical terms *mimesis* and *katharsis*.

Unlike formalist aesthetics, such as the Kantian, which focuses on the framed, geometric properties of art (lines and shapes), an aesthetics of care emphasizes the emotional meaning of a work—its *mimesis* of what I am calling *emotional qualia*. As Kantian and other formalist aesthetics emerged during the Enlightenment era of modernity, they reflect its privileging of mathematical Newtonian-Cartesian modes of thinking and perceiving. Now, in a postmodern era, which is grounded in new conceptions in physics, such as quantum theory, we need new conceptions in aesthetics, ones that move beyond the privileging of quantifiable properties toward those that recognize that the nonphysical aspects of the universe—the spiritual, the emotional, and the psychic—are at least of equal, if not more, importance than the physical. An aesthetics of care provides such reconceptualization. (A fuller discussion of the new physics appears in Chapter 3.)

In this study, my primary focus is on the treatment of animals in literature, but its theoretical premises are rooted in the above assumptions, which are treated in theoretical discussions of criticism and aesthetics in Chapters 1, 3, and 4, which outline the formalist aesthetics of Kant and others as well as the critiques laid out by Margaret Cavendish and Virginia Woolf, among others. I move on to the consideration of the specific treatment of animals handled by a wide range of authors from Willa Cather

(Chapter 2), Leo Tolstoy (Chapter 5), and the nineteenth-century local-colorists such as Sarah Orne Jewett, George Sand, others (Chapter 6), and J. M. Coetzee (Chapters 7 and 8).[1]

I conclude with two theoretical chapters that focus on the issue of animal sacrifice—a still prevalent literary and cultural formation. Chapter 8, "Metaphysical Meat; 'Becoming Men' and Animal Sacrifice" and Chapter 9, "The Transgressive Sublime, *Katharsis*, and Animal Sacrifice," consider the aesthetics of animal sacrifice seen in contemporary literary examples where vestiges remain of this time-honored ritual access to the sacred. In this discussion, I revisit such ancient texts as *Oedipus Tyrannis*, *Oedipus at Colonus*, and Aristotle's *Poetics*, showing how they prefigure an aesthetics of care. Chapter 10, "Caring to Hear, Caring to See: Art as Emergence," a speculative excursus, proposes the natural physical phenomenon of emergence as the prototype for the cultural phenomenon of literature and art with *mimesis* redefined and reconceived in terms of postmodern conceptions in physics.

This study is built upon the work of innumerable scholars, many of whom are long dead and others of whom I do not know and have never met—Margaret Cavendish, Max Horkheimer, Theodor Adorno, Simone Weil, Carol Gilligan, and other feminist theorists of the ethic of care—but whose work constitutes an ongoing tradition that would restore the ignored marginalized silenced voices of the "different"—whether human or nonhuman— to the public discourse, including that of art and literature. It is an antifascist tradition that repudiates the domination of living subjects in all its forms, whether political, cultural, or aesthetic, and revalorizes despised and derogated "feminine" modes of understanding, such as sympathy and caring attentiveness to what is different from oneself and one's culture. Rather than casting difference as defective and inferior, it regards that which doesn't fit into prescribed social and aesthetic categories as valuable and worthy of moral concern and aesthetic attention. It proposes in

---

[1]Note that in this study I confine myself to Western sources and (mostly) to prose fiction.

the end that we are all linked by an unreifiable subjective chord of ecosympathy. Art as *mimesis* of nature's phenomenon of emergence connects in an aesthetics of care to this chord, linking us all, as seventeenth-century philosopher Margaret Cavendish envisioned, in a "soul in communitie."

Josephine Donovan
Portsmouth, New Hampshire
September 2015

Introduction

The "ethic of care" has established itself as a prominent vein in contemporary feminist ethics. I and several others have extended care theory into the field of animal ethics.[1] Here I propose an *"aesthetics of care"* that is rooted in care theory principles but amplified, modified, and enriched by postmodern reconceptions of physical reality so as to provide a basis for a critical animal ethics approach to literature and art.

The ethic of care was introduced by Carol Gilligan in her now-classic treatise *In a Different Voice* (1982), which was forged in reaction against the Kantian theory of moral development presented by Lawrence Kohlberg. His theory proposed a hierarchical range of "stages" of moral reasoning, with the highest—stages five and six—being those where subjects made moral decisions based on abstract rules and universal principles, rather than particular personal relationships. Gilligan discovered through a series of interviews with adolescent girls that they often exhibited a mode of reasoning that was more particularized and focused on narrative context and relationship—a mode Kohlberg had considered inferior or less well developed than the higher abstract and rationalistic modes. Gilligan, however, valorized the girls' "different voice," casting it as an equally, if not more, valid way of approaching and resolving moral dilemmas.

While the Kohlberg theory might have been the immediate occasion for Gilligan's theory, the ultimate "target of [her] criticism [was] the dominant Kantian tradition" in ethical theory, as Annette C. Baier has pointed out.[2] The Kantian ethical theory, an Enlightenment rationalist formation, emphasized decision-making based on abstract universalizable principles disconnected from particular contexts and

---

[1] See especially *The Feminist Care Tradition in Animal Ethics*, ed. Josephine Donovan and Carol J. Adams (New York: Columbia University Press, 2007).
[2] Annette C. Baier, "The Need for More Than Justice," in *Science, Morality, and Feminist Theory*, ed. Marsha Hanen and Kai Nielsen (Calgary, Canada: University of Calgary Press, 1987), p. 45.

purged of emotional and personal evaluation. Humans are seen as disembodied and autonomous "persons" defined by what they have in common—rationality—abstracted from what makes them unique, different, and particular. The conception is largely mechanistic, such that, as Gilligan noted, moral decision-making done on this model often seems like "a math problem with humans."[3]

As I point out in Chapter 1, this Kantian view reflects the Cartesian-Newtonian ethos pervasive in the early modern period, which constructed nearly every aspect of reality—including aesthetics—along mathematical models. Just as, therefore, the ethic of care was developed as an alternative to the Kantian tradition in ethics, so may an aesthetics of care be fashioned, I propose, as an alternative to the Kantian tradition in aesthetics.[4]

Gilligan offers suggestive literary examples to illustrate her theory, two of which I elaborate in order to point up their aesthetic significance. She opens *In a Different Voice* with a glancing reference to Anton Tchekov's play *The Cherry Orchard* (1904), which involves a confrontation between Lopahin, a capitalist entrepreneur, and Madame Ranevsky, the owner of an orchard he wants to cut down in order to build profit-making summer villas. Gilligan sees the woman's resistance as reflecting a "different" women's perspective; however, she doesn't further expatiate to explain what is different about Madame's values. An ecofeminist approach provides a fuller accounting of Madame's viewpoint, which reflects, I contend, an aesthetics of care.[5]

---

[3]Carol Gilligan, *In a Different Voice: Psychological Theory and Women's Development* (Cambridge, MA: Harvard University Press, 1982), p. 28. Further references follow in the text.

[4]Other feminist critiques of Kantian aesthetics may be found in *Aesthetics in Feminist Perspective*, ed. Hilda Hein and Carolyn Korsmeyer (Bloomington: Indiana University Press, 1993).

[5]The term *ecofeminist* refers broadly to feminist approaches to environmental and ecological issues. I confine its use to the animal ethics branch of ecofeminism that is rooted in care theory, seen in such works as Josephine Donovan and Carol J. Adams, ed., *The Feminist Care Tradition in Animal Ethics* (New York: Columbia University Press, 2007), Carol J. Adams and Lori Gruen, eds., *Ecofeminism: Feminist Intersections with Other Animals and the Earth* (New York: Bloomsbury, 2014), Marti Kheel, *Nature Ethics: An Ecofeminist Perspective* (Lanham, MD: Rowman & Littlefield, 2008), and Greta Gaard, ed., *Ecofeminism: Woman, Animals, Nature* (Philadelphia: Temple University Press, 1993).

"Oh, my orchard!—my sweet, beautiful orchard!" Madame exclaims. "I can't conceive of life without the cherry orchard."[6] Madame's opposition to Lopahin's development schemes is rooted in personal attachment—love, her recognition of the trees' status as living beings, and her appreciation for their role in family and local history. When Lopahin wants to commodify and reshape the land for commercial purposes, seeing it as neutral *space*, the *terra nullius* of the colonizer, Madame sees it as *place*, qualitatively charged with living presences and memory. The orchard is part of Madame's household, her *oikos*, her *Umwelt*.[7]

Madame Ranevsky's particular rootedness in a specific locale positions her thus against abstract exchange-value rationalizations. Her standpoint is therefore embedded in local knowledges or *mētis*, which contrasts to abstract universalizable knowledge in the Kantian mode. *Mētis*, James C. Scott explains, "resists simplification into deductive principles," because it is context-specific and cannot be generalized.[8] Premodern peoples and those uneducated in modern Cartesian logic generally operate according to *mētis*, a form of personal narrative knowledge specific to one's immediate habitat. Lopahin's perspective, on the other hand, reflects the "imperial or hegemonic planning mentality" of modernity, which "excludes the necessary role of local knowledge and know-how" (7).

The trees themselves have ethical claims in the matter, which Madame, appreciating their personal histories, implicitly honors in her attempt to save them. She knows their stories and is linked to them through a bond of sympathy. One might readily postulate, based on Tchekov's own practice, that these are heirloom cherry

---

[6]Anton Tchekov, *The Cherry Orchard*, in *The Plays of Anton Tchekov*, trans. Constance Garnett (New York: Modern Library, n.d.), pp. 115, 97. Further references follow in the text. Tchekov's emphasis in the play is usually interpreted to be primarily on the class dialectic between the upstart peasant entrepreneur and the last of a dying race of effete aristocrats; however, as I here propose, the ecological theme is of paramount importance.

[7]Jakob von Uexküll, *A Foray into the Worlds of Animals and Humans*, trans. Joseph D. O'Neil (Minneapolis: University of Minnesota Press, 2012), p. 139, holds that each animal lives in her own unique "dwelling world" or *Umwelt*. Further references follow in the text.

[8]James C. Scott, *Seeing Like a State: How Certain Schemes to Improve the Human Condition Have Failed* (New Haven, CT: Yale University Press, 1998), p. 316. Further references follow in the text.

trees of considerable vintage. Cherry trees in fact originated in southern Russia in the area of the Black and Caspian Seas where Tchekov was born. It seems likely that Madame's orchard might have included Black Tartarians, an ancient Russian (Circassian) variety of a purplish black color, or Morellos—Tchekov's favorite—dark tart cherries from the same region. We may be sure that her garden was organic and without genetically modified organisms (GMOs). Traditional methods, such as recycling and composting, were likely practiced. Thus, Madame's cherry orchard is to be distinguished from modern industrialized monoculture. Generations of personalized caring labor have gone into its upkeep, labor that worked with nature, rather than against it.

Tchekov himself was an avid gardener. His estate at Melikhovo, where he lived in the 1890s, included cherry trees that he himself planted.[9] After he sold his estate, he was horrified to learn that his beloved trees had been chopped down and sold—a likely impetus for the play. He later moved to Yalta, where his garden included twelve different types of cherry trees.

Tchekov's personal love for trees and the natural environment is reflected in powerful, ecologically sensitive statements made by Dr. Astrov, likely speaking for the author himself, who was a doctor, in another Tchekov play, *Uncle Vanya*; they further enrich our understanding of the playwright's intentions in *The Cherry Orchard*. Astrov, like Tchekov himself, is a gardener and forester by avocation. He "plants fresh trees every year ... [and] tries to prevent the old forests being destroyed."[10]

Astrov decries the ecological destruction he sees around him.

The Russian forests are going down under the axe. Millions of trees are perishing, the homes of wild animals and birds are being laid waste, the rivers are dwindling and drying up.... One must be an unreflecting savage to burn this beauty in one's stove, to destroy what we cannot create ... every day the earth is growing poorer and more hideous (198).

---

[9]Donald Rayfield, "Orchards and Gardens in Checkhov," *SEER* 67, no. 4 (October 1989):531.

[10]Anton Tchekov, "Uncle Vanya," in *The Plays of Anton Tchekov*, trans. Constance Garnett (New York: Modern Library, n.d.), p. 197. Further references follow in the text.

And this in 1899!

Tchekov's evident personal ecological sensitivity, as seen here, thus bolsters the ecofeminist interpretation of *The Cherry Orchard* offered above. Beloved natural creatures and places are being destroyed by the relentless colonizations of modernity. As *The Cherry Orchard* ends (Madame Ranevsky having lost her struggle with Lopahin), one hears "in the stillness...the dull stroke of an axe in a tree, clanging with a mournful lonely sound" (115). It is echoed shortly thereafter by a mysterious "sound...that seems to come from the sky, like a breaking harp-string, dying away mournfully" (115). Perhaps a responsive cry of lamentation from the heavens themselves, a chord of ecosympathy vibrating throughout the universe.

Another literary example Carol Gilligan used to illustrate care theory is Susan Glaspell's celebrated short story, "A Jury of Her Peers" (1917) in which two women informally adjudicate a case involving a neighbor woman who has killed her husband.[11] The women are rooted in the same rural environment as the suspect and, like her, are married and of the same socioeconomic class. They therefore are aware of the contingencies of her situation; as they piece together the contextual details of the event, they come to realize that the woman has endured years of emotional abuse and isolation. When they find her pet canary strangled—a creature who had been the woman's sole emotional companion and, through his daily song, her only access to beauty—they understand the motive, in essence reaching a verdict of justifiable homicide. The real crime here, Gilligan notes, was a failure of relationship—the community's failure to help the woman who endured her suffering alone. The neighbor women indeed adjudge themselves partly responsible, guilty of a failure to care for the woman earlier and of not recognizing the emotional isolation and abuse she was experiencing.

By focusing, therefore, on the narrative context of the issue, the women make an ethical decision (to exonerate the woman) according to the values of an ethic of care that would not be possible

---

[11]Carol Gilligan, "Moral Orientation and Moral Development," in *Women and Moral Theory*, ed. Eva Feder Kittay and Diana T. Meyers (Totowa, NJ: Rowman & Littlefield, 1987), pp. 29–32. My discussion elaborates Gilligan's points somewhat. Susan Keating Glaspell, "A Jury of Her Peers" (1917), in *American Voices, American Women*, ed. Lee R. Edwards and Arlyn Diamond (New York: Avon, 1973), pp. 359–81.

under absolute principles of right and wrong with universalizable "neutral" ethical standards invoked. Through their intimate understanding of the emotional context and attentive perception, these women see a holistic picture whose qualitative details would likely be elided were the situation abstracted or "culled" according to universalizable laws modeled on mathematical formulae. Central to their understanding is the emotional experience of relationship: the woman's love for her bird, which the neighbor women implicitly comprehend and honor; her bleak profane daily life; and the lack of love and caring from the husband and the community, which are seen as relevant factors contributing to the fatal outcome.

These two literary examples point toward an aesthetics of care. In the first, in the Tchekov play, the woman character manifests a resistance to development schemes that would destroy a beloved natural locale and its living inhabitants, replacing it with an imposed homogenous construct. The attitude of Madame Ranevsky is one of caring respect for her environment, a respect rooted in loving attachment to that world and its inhabitants—in this case, cherry trees. She and the trees are intertwined in a web of relationship which constitutes their world and which she wants to preserve and protect. Her philosophy is caring and nondominative, unlike Lopahin's whose development projects reflect the dominative presumptions of Enlightenment modernity, reshaping and "bettering" the world according to uniform mathematized aesthetic ideals.[12]

Madame's preservative attitude may be seen as an expression of what care theorist Sara Ruddick labeled "maternal thinking," which is "governed by the priority of keeping over acquiring, of conserving the fragile, or maintaining whatever is at hand and necessary to the child's life."[13] It contrasts to "scientific thought, as well as ... to the instrumentalism of technocratic capitalism"; as an "ethic of humility," it recognizes "excessive control as a liability" (351), practicing instead caring but nondominative nurturance.

---

[12]See Jonathan Bate, *The Song of the Earth* (Cambridge, MA: Harvard University Press, 2000), pp. 11–12, on a similar resistance to "improvement" landscape development schemes seen in Jane Austen: "Instead of having a responsible, nurturing relationship to the soil, the improver has a purely aesthetic one" (11). Further references to Bate follow in the text.

[13]Sara Ruddick, "Maternal Thinking," *Feminist Studies* 6, no 2 (1980):350–51. Further references follow in the text.

The second example, the Glaspell story, discloses what Jennifer Crawford terms a "post-rational" epistemology,[14] which she posits as a higher stage of development than the rational stage valorized by Kohlberg. It is a form of knowing governed by what Simone Weil called "attentive love," a practice manifest in the attitude of the neighbor women in "A Jury of Her Peers."

Attentive love was defined by Weil in a 1942 essay as

> The love of our neighbor in all its fullness simply means saying to him: "What are you going through?" It is a recognition that the sufferer exists, not only as a unit in a collection, or a specimen from the social category labeled "unfortunate," but as [an individual]... For this reason it is... indispensable, to know how to look at him in a certain way.
> This way of looking is first of all attentive.[15]

The concept of *attention* is central to Weil's thinking and to an ethic and aesthetics of care: that is, paying attention to what is overlooked when the subject is framed according to prescripted value and aesthetic ideals, relegating the overlooked material to insignificance or indeed to nonbeing. As elaborated in her seminal work *La Pesanteur et la grâce* (*Gravity and Grace*) (1948), Weil explained how attention is at the root of an ethical aesthetic.

> The poet produces the beautiful by an attention fixed on the real. Similarly, the act of love. To know that that man who is hungry and thirsty really exists as much as I exist—that is enough, the rest follows automatically.
> Authentic and pure values of truth, beauty, and goodness in the activity of a human being are produced by one sole and the same act, a certain application to the object of complete and full attention [une certain application à l'objet de la plénitude de l'attention].[16]

---

[14]Jennifer Crawford, *Spiritually-Engaged Knowledge: The Attentive Heart* (Aldershot, Hampshire, England: Ashgate, 2005), p. 122. Further references follow in the text.
[15]Simone Weil, "Reflections on the Right Use of School Studies with a View to the Love of God," in *The Simone Weil Reader*, ed. George A. Panichas (New York: McKay, 1977), p. 51.
[16]Simone Weil, *La Pesanteur et la grâce* (Paris: Librarie Plon, 1948), p. 121. My translation. Further references follow in the text.

Attention requires looking directly at an object, suspending imaginative constructs so as to see the object "without interpretation"—an epistemological *ascesis*.

> To try to love without imagining. To love the naked appearance and without interpretation. That which one loves in this way is really God. (60)
> Extreme attention is what constitutes the creative faculty in humans, and such extreme attention is necessarily religious [il n'y a d'attention extrême que religieuse]. (119)

For, "the beautiful is the real presence of God in the material" (115).

Weil, thus, proposes that there is a spiritual dimension (God) that is revealed through intense concentrated caring attention. In other words, focused caring attention reveals presences that are elided when one abstracts, objectifies, and culls. An aesthetics of care is built upon this premise, for the knowledge of these presences is the basis for ethical and aesthetic appreciation. Madame Ranevsky's love for the cherry orchard manifests this aesthetic. Through attentive love she *sees* the moral, emotional, and qualitative significance of the trees, a significance that is stripped away when the trees are viewed through the quantifying, objectifying, affectless gaze of Enlightenment epistemology and capitalist commodification.

Jennifer Crawford rightly emphasizes that Weil's concept entails a "radical empiricism that is not ideologically mediated" (119); seeing a particular reality directly without categorization, without abstraction, "remain[ing] true to the thing itself" (155). It also involves a sympathetic capacity to enter into the experience of another who is seen as a subject, not set apart as an object for ideological or aesthetic manipulation. Attentive love requires a meditative focus within a "non-dominative…discourse that does not want to confine the other within bounds of meaning, but wishes to encounter the other within the transcendent horizon of love" (120). The women in Glaspell's story exemplify this ethic.

British philosopher and novelist Iris Murdoch amplified Weil's conception and applied it to aesthetic matters. Defining "attentive love" as "a just and loving gaze upon an individual reality," Murdoch explained, "the direction of attention…[must be] away from self which reduces all to a false unity, toward the surprising variety of the world, and the ability to so direct attention is love."[17] It is through the praxis of "attentive love" that great writers and artists accomplish their creations, Murdoch maintains. What is involved in the case of writers is a sympathetic understanding of and emotional involvement in the realities of their subjects.

In a little-known early essay "Shakespeare and Hamlet," a young Willa Cather expressed a similar intuition, considering Shakespeare's sympathy for his character as a potent factor in the construction of the play. "He probably read the legend," Cather hypothesized, "and felt sorry for the young prince, and as an expression of his sympathy wrote about him."[18] As Cather biographer Sharon O'Brien notes, "Cather's Shakespeare [thus] erases the boundaries between self and other," "stressing" instead "identification, reciprocity, and interconnection rather than subjugation and domination."[19] Great art and literature, as Murdoch contends, reflect their creators' "realization that something other than oneself is real," expressing thereby "a non-violent apprehension of difference." For "the more the separateness and differentness of other[s]...is realized...the harder it becomes to treat [them] as a thing."[20]

Not surprisingly perhaps, celebrated ecotheorist Rachel Carson has been seen as exemplifying an ethic and aesthetics of care in her books on marine life, which reflect, Marnie M. Sullivan proposes, a praxis of attentive love.

> Decentering human perspective...is a first step toward relating to the "other"—whether human or nonhuman nature—as a subject...Carson's persistent preoccupation with marginal landscapes and their inhabitants model patterns of engagement with the "other" that fosters an ethic of care that avoids domination or exploitation.[21]

---

[17]Iris Murdoch, *The Sovereignty of Good* (New York: Schocken, 1971), pp. 34, 66.
[18]Willa Cather, "Shakespeare and Hamlet" (1891), as cited in Sharon O'Brien, *Willa Cather: The Emerging Voice* (New York: Oxford University Press, 1987), p. 156.
[19]O'Brien, Willa Cather, p. 156. Further references follow in the text.
[20]Iris Murdoch, "The Sublime and the Good," *Chicago Review* 13 (Autumn 1959): 51, 54, 66.
[21]Marnie M. Sullivan, "Shifting Subjects and Marginal World: Revealing the Radical in Rachel Carson's Three Sea Books," in *Feminist Ecocriticism: Environment, Women, and Literature*, ed. Douglas A. Vakoch (Blue Ridge Summit, PA: Lexington, 2012), p. 78.

Two recent landmark works in ecocriticism, Jonathan Bate's *Song of the Earth* (2000) and Lawrence Buell's *Environmental Imagination* (1995), both turn to ecofeminist theories of care as offering the most promising reconceptualizations of our relationship with the nonhuman natural world. Bate notes that the "ecofeminist language of nurture and care" opens up the possibility "for a caring as opposed to an exploitative relationship with the earth" (112).

And, in arguing for "nature's personhood," Buell similarly endorses ecofeminist care modalities as the vehicle through which that *personhood* may be apprehended.

From an ecocentric standpoint the promise of the image of nature's personhood lies in the extent to which it mobilizes what feminist ecological thinkers have come to call an ethics of care... [which] promises to quicken the sense of caring for nature and to help humans compensate for the legacy of mind-nature dualism.[22]

The mentality involved in an aesthetics of care is thus nonviolent, adaptive, responsive, and attentive to the environment, perceiving other creatures as subjects worthy of respect, whose different voices must be attended to, and with whom one is emotionally engaged, interwoven in an ecological and spiritual—subject-subject—continuum. Such a mentality may, it is hoped, foster a moral and ecological sensitivity, as Murdoch argues in *Metaphysics as a Guide to Morals* (1992). "Moral change comes from an *attention* to the world... through an increased sense of the reality of... other people, but also other things."[23] That those "other things" include animals is a central thesis of this study, which offers the consideration that attentive love directed toward animals as moral beings— as subjects—in literature and art (something lacking in most current examples) may lead to a moral awakening—a *metanoia* in Murdoch's conception—enabling a reformulation of their ethical

---

[22]Lawrence Buell, *The Environmental Imagination: Thoreau, Nature Writing, and the Formation of American Culture* (Cambridge, MA: Harvard University Press, 1995), p. 218. Further references follow in the text.
[23]Iris Murdoch, *Metaphysics as a Guide to Morals* (New York: Viking Penguin, 1993), p. 32.

status as beings of comparable dignity and worth to humans and deserving of comparable treatment.

An aesthetics of care, then—unlike the Kantian aesthetics of modernity, discussed in the following chapter, allows—indeed, *enables* ethical concern for the subject matter, which is seen not as dead material available for aesthetic manipulation and framing but as a living presence, one located in a particular, knowable environment, who has a history and is capable of dialogical communication. While my primary focus in this study is on animals, it expands into reflections on human appreciation of and ethical response to the natural world in general, including, indeed, even to physical matter itself, when conceived within a panpsychic universe.

1

The aesthetics of modernity

The aesthetics of modernity reflects the Enlightenment intellectual milieu from which it arose. The Cartesian division between *res cogitans* and *res extensa*, mind and matter—the basis for scientific epistemology—also established the philosophical foundation of modern, Kantian aesthetics. With *res cogitans* postulated by Descartes as radically separate from and ontologically superior to *res extensa*, the groundwork was laid for an ethic and aesthetics of domination. In *Discourse on Method* (1637), Descartes indeed envisaged that through his new "method," which was "based on the rules of Arithmetic,"[1] "we might...render ourselves the lords and possessors of nature."[2] By imposing mathematical paradigms on objectified inert matter, humans may thus bend the physical world to their will and purpose.

Other early modern scientists articulated a similarly dominative view. The English philosopher Francis Bacon, for example, wrote that "the true and ultimate end" of scientific endeavor is "dominion over natural things." Robert Boyle, another early modern English scientist, claimed that a scientific study "teaches us in many cases to know nature, but also ... in many cases to master and command

---

[1]René Descartes, "Discourse on the Method," in *Descartes Selections*, ed. Ralph Eaton (New York: Scribner's, 1927), p. 19. Portions of this chapter appeared in earlier form in my article "Everyday Use and Moments of Being: Toward a Nondominative Aesthetic" in *Aesthetics in Feminist Perspective*, ed. Hilda Hein and Carolyn Korsmeyer (Bloomington: Indiana University Press, 1993), pp. 53–67.
[2]René Descartes, "Discourse on Method," pt. vi, as cited in Basil Willey, *The Seventeenth-Century Background* (Garden City, NY: Doubleday Anchor, n.d.), p. 96.

her."[3] In 1687, Sir Isaac Newton codified the new cosmology in his *Principia Mathematica*, which laid down the governing paradigm of the Enlightenment that the physical universe is governed by a few simple mathematical laws, the keys to the mastery of matter.

The natural world thus under the new Cartesian-Newtonian view was reified as a spiritless object seen to operate mechanically according to this mathematical model. Since the natural world included animals, they too were deemed by Descartes as thoughtless mechanisms. "It is more reasonable," he wrote, "to make earthworms, flies, caterpillars, and the rest of animals move as machines do, than to endow them with immortal souls" (letter to Henry More, 1649).[4] Likewise is the human body but "a machine which moves of itself" (letter to the Marquis of Newcastle),[5] "nothing else than a statue or machine of clay."[6] In short, as he acknowledged, "I have described the earth, and all the visible world, as if it were simply a machine."[7]

In his conception of the material world, Descartes expunged qualities, animation, and spiritual properties, relegating the former to secondary status as sources of knowledge and the latter two to other-worldly status. In discussing, for instance, a piece of bees' wax, his example of *res extensa*, Descartes dismissed the aspects of the wax known through the senses.

> What then did I know so distinctly in this piece of wax? It could be nothing of all that the senses brought to my notices ... [Thus] this wax was not that sweetness of honey, nor that agreeable scent of flowers, nor that particular whiteness ... but simply a body ... Let us ... abstract from all that does not belong to the wax, let us see what remains. Certainly nothing remains except a certain extended thing [*res extensa*].[8]

---

[3]The Bacon quote is from *De sapentia veterum* (1609) and the Boyle quote from *The Usefulness of Experimental and Natural Philosophy* (1661), as cited in Sarah Hutton, "The Riddle of the Sphinx," in *Women, Science and Medicine 1500–1700*, ed. Lynette Hunter and Sarah Hutton (Phoenix Mill, England: Sutton, 1997), pp. 8, 22.

[4]In *Descartes Selections*, ed. Eaton, p. 358.

[5]Ibid., p. 355.

[6]Ibid., p. 350.

[7]Ibid., p. 304.

[8]Ibid., p. 103.

In other words, the only reality acknowledged by Descartes is that measurable by quantitative properties; the qualitative aspects of the wax are dismissed as unreal. As Basil Willey explained in his study of seventeenth-century literature, under this new "Cartesian spirit," "whatever cannot be clearly and distinctly (i.e. mathematically) conceived is 'not true.' ...The criterion of truth which it set up ... [meant that] the only real properties of objects were the mathematical properties."[9]

Such a perspective required that all which did not fit into a mathematical universalizing paradigm was deemed adventitious at best, and at worst it forced to conform to a prescriptive grid (as the case in scientific experiments). This meant that anomalous particulars were either elided and rendered nonexistent or trimmed and reshaped so as to fit into the expected model. Frankfurt School theorists Max Horkheimer and Theodor Adorno note in their critique of modernity, *Dialectic of Enlightenment*, that in the scientific view, "everything— even the human individual, not to speak of the animal—is converted into the repeatable, replaceable process, into a mere example for the conceptual models of the system."[10] Moreover, "in the impartiality of scientific language, that which is powerless has wholly lost any means of expression" (23). Any consideration, for example, of the ethical status of the bees—themselves deemed but inanimate mechanisms—would be considered irrelevant knowledge in Descartes's conception of the wax.

Aesthetic theorists took over the conception of nature as deanimated and spiritless material, to be used, subdued, manipulated, and "improved" by the artist in accordance with universal aesthetic rules that were analogous to the theorems of geometry. Kant's aesthetics, reflecting the mathematizing epistemology of the Cartesian-Newtonian worldview, is prototypical. Art, like the physical universe, operates according to ideal laws that are universally knowable and are disconnected from subjective, sensuous, moral, and emotional knowledge, and from the everyday world of practical use, as well as from its historical and social context. It is indeed through the forms of art that the everyday world is redeemed, just as contingent matter is made significant by

---

[9]Willey, *Seventeenth-Century Background*, p. 92.
[10]Max Horkheimer and Theodor W. Adorno, *Dialectic of Enlightenment*, trans. John Cumming (New York: Continuum, 1988), p. 84. Further references follow in the text.

the coherent order given to it by mathematical construction in the Cartesian-Newtonian view.

Thus, the sleeve on the virgin's dress in early modern painting becomes deemed significant because of its geometrical positioning vis-à-vis other lines in the picture, and not because of its ontic intensity or sacred being, as Erwin Panofsky pointed out in his seminal article "Die Perspektive als Symbolic Form" (1927).[11] The objects in such a painting take significance according to their alignment on a perspective pyramid which orders the elements of the scene. "Their being," Panofsky observes, "is functional but not substantial" (260), and the space within which they lie is a mathematical construction, "fully rational...and homogenous" (261). Panofsky calls this the triumph of a "distancing and objectifying sense of reality" (287). The geometric "spatial perspective," thus, "transforms *being* into *phenomenon* [and] the sacred into a mere content of human consciousness" [die Perspektive Raumanschauung hat die οὐσία zum Φαινόμενον wandelt das Göttliche zu einem blossen Inhalt des menschlichen Bewusstseins] (291).

Similarly, material—both living and inanimate—studied from a scientific viewpoint is of significance only insofar as it provides mathematical quantifiable information. This is the "distancing and objectifying sense of reality" that governs laboratory experimentation. "Nature" thus becomes, Horkheimer and Adorno note, "that which is to be comprehended mathematically" (24).

Kant codified the early modern aesthetic in his *Critique of Judgment* (1790), which conceives of art as a process whereby the artist lifts matter out of its everyday context and organizes it according to ideal aesthetic principles that are essentially geometric in nature, as in the geometric perspective identified by Panofsky. The matter of art is thus seen to operate as matter does in the Cartesian physical universe—mindlessly accordingly prescribed laws and divorced from the unsymmetrical entropy of everyday life with its unpredictable anomalous particularities and eccentricities, and divorced as well from emotional, spiritual, ideological, moral, political, historical, and social interests. Stripped in short, like Descartes's wax, of all nonquantifiable quality, art operates as a

---

[11]Erwin Panofsky, "Die Perspektive als Symbolic Form," in *Vorträge der Bibliothek Warburg Institut 1925-25* (Berlin: B. G. Tuebner, 1927). My translation from the German. Further references follow in the text.

separate self-contained entity according to ideal aesthetic rules. In constructing his work of art, the artist conceives his product through an ideal aesthetic "symbolic form" which orders the elements of his creation.

An art object, as conceived by Kant, then, is that of an autonomous self-referential mechanism. "[T]he agreement of the manifold in a thing with its inner destination, its purpose, constitutes the perfection of the thing."[12] The salient characteristic of a work of art is that it manifests "a merely formal purposiveness, i.e., a purposiveness without purpose" (397)—Kant's celebrated *Zweckmässigkeit ohne Zweck*. The aesthetic judgment is thus confined to the inner dynamic—the *telos*—of the art object, its own inner—largely geometrical—relations. "[T]he teleological judgement serves as the basis and condition of the aesthetical" (423).

This judgment is a "disinterested" one. "Every interests spoils the judgment...and takes from its impartiality" (395). And like Cartesian reason it is universally shared: the "satisfaction...of taste in the Beautiful is...a disinterested and free satisfaction; for no interest...here forces our assent" (379). "[H]e who judges...cannot find the ground of this satisfaction in any private conditions...hence it must be regarded as grounded on what he can presuppose in every other man" (383). "The beautiful is that which pleases universally" (392).

Moreover, the aesthetic judgment "is independent of charm and emotion" (395). By *charm* Kant means colors or any qualitative attributes other than formal "*delineation* [which] is the essential thing." "The colors which light up the sketch belong to the charm; they may...enliven the object...but they cannot make it worthy...or beautiful" (396). In short, "a pure judgment...has for its determining ground neither charm nor emotion" (397). Kant's aesthetic is thus an impassive, impartial, formal judgment stripped of all emotional or qualitative aspects.

Kant considered that it is through the forms of art that the everyday contingent world is redeemed, just as contingent matter is redeemed by the coherence given to it by mathematical laws in the Cartesian-Newtonian view. "We entertain ourselves with [the Imagination] when experience proves too commonplace, and by it

---

[12]Immanuel Kant, "Critique of Judgment," par. 48, in *Kant Selections*, ed. Theodore Meyer (New York: Scribner's, 1929), p. 423. Further references follow in the text.

we remould experience,... so that the material which we borrow
from nature ... can be worked up into something different which
surpasses nature" (426). The great artist lifts "nature" out of the
everyday and endows it with redemptive form. "Genius is the innate
mental disposition (*ingenium*) through which Nature gives the rule
to Art" (418). "Nature" here clearly intends a Newtonian universe
governed by rational laws.

As Walter Sokel suggests, Kant granted the artist "absolute
sovereignty": "He emancipates the artist from all external shackles
and nonartistic considerations. Faithfulness to nature, moral
purpose, empirical truth, religious faith—all are considered irrelevant
to art...The work of art is a universe of its own."[13] Terry Eagleton
proposes that Kant's theory reflects the emergence of capitalism as
the dominant economic system in the West: "The qualities of the
Kantian moral [and aesthetic] law are those of the commodity form.
Abstract universal and rigorously self-identical, the law of Reason
is a mechanism which, like the commodity, effects formally equal
exchanges between isolated individual subjects, erasing the difference
of their needs and desires in its homogenizing injunctions."[14]

Subsequent theorists solidified Kant's notion of art as a
separate, sanitized, dispassionate realm, from which is culled all
nonconforming matters. Following the Kantian tradition, Hegel,
for example, states in the *Aesthetics* (lectures delivered in the 1820s)
that for beauty to exist, "the external shape...must be freed from
every accident of external determinacy, from every dependence
on nature, and from morbidity." Art "casts aside everything in
appearance which does not correspond with the Concept and only
by purification does it produce the Ideal."[15]

Hegel's privileging of the intellectual ideal over the material
informs his aesthetic. "[E]ven a useless notion that enters a man's
head," he asserts, "is higher than any product of nature."[16] As with

---

[13]Walter Sokel, *The Writer in Extremis: Expressionism in Twentieth-Century
German Literature* (Stanford, CA: Stanford University Press, 1959), p. 9.

[14]Terry Eagleton, *The Ideology of the Aesthetic* (Oxford: Blackwell, 1990), p. 83.

[15]Georg Hegel, *Aesthetics* i.483, i.155, as cited in Charles Karelis, Introduction to
Hegel's Introduction to "Aesthetics," trans. T. M. Knox (Oxford: Oxford University
Press, 1979), p. xxxiv.

[16]*Hegel's Introduction to "Aesthetics,"* trans. Knox, p. 2. Further references follow
in the text.

Kant, art performs a redemptive office: "Art liberates the true content of phenomena from the pure appearance and deception of this bad, transitory world, and gives them a higher actuality, born of the spirit" (9). Thus, a landscape painting "acquires a higher rank than the mere natural landscape. For everything spiritual is better than any product of nature" (29). "[A]rt lifts [one]...out of and above imprisonment in nature" (49).

In an important feminist critique of Hegel and neoclassical aesthetics, *Reading in Detail* (1987), Naomi Schor observes how in "the transformation of the so-called insignificant object into an art-object."[17] Hegelian idealism abnegates the contingent material world of living beings. As with Kant, for Hegel "the Ideal implies 'the negation of everything particular'" (*Aesthetics* i.157, in Schor 25); it is "that which escapes the contamination of 'chance and externality'" (*Aesthetics* i.155, in Schor 25).

In *Woman, Nature and Psyche* (1987), Patricia Jagentowicz Mills similarly notes that Hegel's view of the transformation of nature into culture requires the subordination/elision of the natural world, which is feminized, as well as the particular, everyday world of women, which is trivialized. In criticizing Hegel's interpretation of Sophocles' *Antigone* in his *Phenomenology*, Mills interprets it instead as "the revolt of the particular against subsumption under a universal schema." "Antigone rebels against Creon's claim to the right of the universal over the particular and in so doing she refuses to fit neatly into the Hegelian enterprise in which universality ultimately dominates."[18] Schor notes, "Hegel's idealism must...be read as a rejection of the 'nether world' of the Family and the particular in which women...are at home...[There is] a persistent association." She concludes, "of idealist aesthetics with the discourse of misogyny" (5). Underlying Kant's and Hegel's aesthetic theories, Schor points out, is the implicit idea of the male genius imprinting form upon formless, feminine matter, reflecting the age-old Western

---

[17]Naomi Schor, *Reading in Detail: Aesthetics and the Feminine* (New York: Methuen, 1987), p. 36. Further references follow in the text. Hegel's conception of Spirit as an abstract disembodied, colorless transcendent universal is not to be confused with the animating spirit or vitality of "objects" entailed in an aesthetics of care, as further explicated later in this chapter.

[18]Patricia Jagentowicz Mills, *Women, Nature and Psyche* (New Haven, CT: Yale University Press, 1987), p. 36.

equation of form with maleness and formlessness with femaleness, articulated in Aristotle's *Physics* as: "matter longs for form as its fulfillment, as the female longs for the male" (16).

Like Kant, Sir Joshua Reynolds, a major eighteenth-century English aesthetician, conceives of the artist redeeming nature through the imposition of ideal, formal laws of beauty. Reynolds's view, however, as Schor points out, is more explicitly sexist. In the *Third Discourse* (3, 44–45) he stipulates that the great painter "corrects nature by herself, her imperfect state by her more perfect. His eye being able to distinguish the *accidental deficiencies, execrescences*, and *deformities* of things, from their general figures, he makes out an abstract idea of their forms more perfect than any one original" (15, Schor's emphasis added). Thus, the feminized, deficient material world is conceived as *other* to the redemptive male form-giver; and art is conceived as the imposition of a culling masculine form.

This assumption continued well into the twentieth century, seen, for example, in the novel *Nausea* (1938) by Jean-Paul Sartre where the male/form-maker female/formlessness equation still obtains. Indeed, that dyadic assumption pervades his monumental philosophical work *Being and Nothingness*, in which, as feminist critics Margery L. Collins and Christine Pierce have pointed out, the disparaged *en-soi* represents immanence and everyday contingency—feminine attributes—where the valorized *pour-soi*, the transcending, creative consciousness, is masculine.[19] As Frank Kermode notes, for Roquentin, the protagonist of *Nausea*, "contingency is nauseous and viscous [in a figure that is] ultimately sexual. This is unformed matter, materia, matrix; Roquentin's is ultimately the form-giving male role."[20] As I have proposed elsewhere, Roquentin's is a Gnostic response. As in many other works of modern fiction, the natural world is demonized. Characters escape its nefarious control through magical *gnoses*, effected in Sartres's case by imposing controlling symbolic order (whether words—the title of his autobiography, *Les Mots*—or art forms) upon it.[21]

---

[19]Margery L. Collins and Christine Pierce, "Holes and Slime: Sexism in Sartre's Psychoanalysis," in *Women in Philosophy*, ed. Carol C. Gould and Mary W. Warshofsky (New York: Putnam's, 1976), pp. 112–27.

[20]Frank Kermode, *The Sense of an Ending: Studies in the Theory of Fiction* (Oxford: Oxford University Press, 1966), pp. 136–37.

[21]Josephine Donovan, *Gnosticism in Modern Literature: A Study of Selected Works of Camus, Sartre, Hesse, and Kafka* (New York: Garland, 1990), pp. 157–66; 216–26. Sartre's autobiography is *Les Mots* (Paris: Gallimard, 1964).

In her study of nineteenth-century American writer Sarah Orne Jewett, Sarah Way Sherman contrasts the perspective of Roquentin/Sartre for whom the everyday feminine world has no meaning unless redeemed by the male project of imposing form, whether mathematical or aesthetic, with that of Jewett. For Jewett, Sherman notes, "the imposition of geometry is not necessarily redemptive ... Jewett's art offers a vision of transcendence embedded in everyday use ... incarnate in the particular."[22] Jewett thus heralds an important aspect of the aesthetics of care—which I develop further in subsequent chapters.

Literary theory for much of the eighteenth century reflected a Cartesian obsession with "clear and distinct" rules by which the multivarious particulars of reality could be subsumed under generic categories, replicating the deductive species and subspecies of science. Indeed, by then, "any discipline wishing to be accepted as ... serious ... was expected to develop its own body of abstract, theoretical concepts and principles and to present them ... in the form of an axiomatic system."[23] The Cartesian-Newtonian worldview came to be seen as revalidating classical critical axioms, as Alexander Pope noted in 1711.

> Those RULES of old discovered, not devised
> Are Nature still, but Nature methodized.[24]

Thus Samuel Johnson by mid-century could announce in Horatian fashion, "the business of the poet ... is to examine, not the individual, but the species ... he does not number the streaks of the tulip or describe the different shades in the verdure of the forest."[25] Novelist Henry Fielding applied this neoclassical doctrine to

[22]Sarah Way Sherman, *Sarah Orne Jewett: American Persephone* (Hanover, NH: University Press of New England, 1989), p. 274.

[23]Albert R. Jonsen and Stephen Toulim, *The Abuse of Casuistry: A History of Moral Reasoning* (Berkeley: University of California Press, 1988), p. 276.

[24]Alexander Pope, "Essay on Criticism," ll. 88–89, in *Alexander Pope: Selected Poetry and Prose*, ed. William K. Wimsatt Jr. (New York: Holt, Rinehart & Winston, 1961), p. 66. Pope, "Essay on Criticism," ll. 88–89, p. 66.

[25]Samuel Johnson, *Rasselas*, in *Criticism: The Major Texts*, ed. Walter Jackson Bate (New York: Harcourt, Brace & World, 1952), p. 207.

the novel: "I describe not men, but manners; not an individual but a species."[26] As one historian noted, "this is generalized art, from which the local, the temporary, the particular, are almost excluded."[27]

The Kantian view of art was so entrenched that by the twentieth century T. S. Eliot could

Extend the mechanical metaphor to the artist him/herself, reducing aesthetic praxis to a chemical experiment.

When...two gases [oxygen and sulphur dioxide] are mixed in the presence of a filiament of platinum, they form sulphuric acid. The combination takes place only if the platinum is present... The mind of the poet is the shred of platinum...[T]he more perfect the artist, the more completely separate in him will be the man who suffers and the mind which creates.[28]

Following Eliot, the so-called New Criticism of the mid-twentieth century (and structuralism and poststructuralism later in the century) extended his conception of the literary work as a discrete "mechanism" that operates in terms of various objectified structures, which the writer manipulates "disinterestedly" into aesthetic shape (Bate, *Song* 179). Ethical concerns were deemed irrelevant because the matter being manipulated was seen as inanimate, drained of its vital, qualitative juices and extracted from its social, historical, personal, and emotional context, which is simply ignored or considered aesthetically impertinent, just as the wax's qualities were deemed irrelevant to its essential character by Descartes.

The prevailing aesthetics of modernity has thus remained a dominative pseudoscientific one in which the (male) artist reshaped natural materials framed in accordance with universal aesthetic

---

[26]Henry Fielding, *Joseph Andrews*, I.iii, in *The Theory of the Novel*, ed. Philip Stevick (New York: Free Press, 1967), p. 387.

[27]George Clark, *The Seventeenth Century*, 2nd ed. (New York: Oxford University Press, 1961), p. 339.

[28]T. S. Eliot, "Tradition and the Individual Talent," in *Criticism*, ed. Walter Jackson Bate (New York: Harcourt, Brace & World, 1952), p. 527.

"laws"; as such, art is disconnected from particularized everyday life extracted into a disinterested contemplative realm beyond ethical, political, or material concerns.

In her *Women Travelers and the Language of Aesthetics 1716–1818* (1995), Elizabeth Bohls termed this Kantian conception an "aesthetics of colonialism,"[29] because it involves the suppression of all that is deemed *other* to the male subject. Specifically, the "denial of the particular" required by the Kantian aesthetic, Bohls maintains, reflects a repression of the body and all that is associated with it, which is deemed "vulgar" (67). The "second terms" in the dyads "polite/vulgar, man/woman, civilized/savage" (67) "are subordinated as the foils against which the aesthetic subject defines himself" (68). Art, she argues, is thus conceived as a dominative colonialist project, a subdual of the other.

Bohls proposes that several late eighteenth-century women travel writers—among them, Mary Wollstonecraft—offered an alternative, particularistic aesthetic, one that does not exclude the historical and ethical aspects of the subjects treated. Like Dorothy Wordsworth (whose work I consider in Chapter 3), Wollstonecraft in her *Letters Written during a Short Residence in Sweden, Norway and Denmark* (1796), for example, considers the people she encounters as ethical subjects who have worthy stories to tell, not as quaint, colorful objects in an aestheticized landscape whose purpose is—like the virgin's sleeve in the Renaissance painting—to contribute to abstract formal design.

The women writers Bohls treats were by no means the first women thinkers to challenge the colonialist aesthetics of modernity laid out by leading Enlightenment theorists. Indeed, several women philosophers of the seventeenth century contemporaneous to Descartes challenged his fundamental conceptions—at times in direct communication with him.

Anne Finch, Lady Conway, for example, claimed that her philosophy must "truly be called anti-Cartesianism," because it rejected the Cartesian notion "that body is merely dead matter, which lacks life and perception of any kind."

---

[29]Elizabeth Bohls, *Women Travelers and the Language of Aesthetics 1716–1818* (Cambridge: Cambridge University Press, 1995), p. 46. Further references follow in the text.

For truly in nature there are many operations, which are far more than merely mechanical. Nature is not…like a clock, which has no vital principle of motion in it; but it is a living body, which has life and perception, which are much more exalted than a mere mechanism or mechanical motion.[30]

Other early modern women philosophers took issue with Descartes's radical separation of mind and body, with Elisabeth of Bohemia raising in a letter to Descartes the still unanswered question of how the mind relates to the body and vice versa. "I beseech you to tell me how the soul of man (since it is but a thinking substance) can determine the spirits of the body to produce voluntary actions" (letter of May 6/16, 1643).[31] Moreover, "it is…very difficult to comprehend that a soul…can subsist without the body and has nothing in common with it, is yet so ruled by it" (letter of June 10/20, 1643) (16–17). Descartes never supplied an adequate answer.

Afflicted herself with various physical and emotional ills— namely depression—which interfered with her thinking, Elisabeth maintained that it was impossible to detach oneself from bodily and social concerns so as to operate purely in the contemplative realm of abstract ideas—which Descartes counseled in a sympathetic letter to her dated May/June 1645. (His neo-Stoic advice not surprisingly "prescribe[d] detachment from the senses and the imagination, in favour of the pure understanding.")[32]

In addition, Elizabeth complained,

Sometimes the interests of my household, which I must not neglect, sometimes conversations and civilities I cannot eschew, so thoroughly deject this weak mind with annoyances or boredom that it remains, for a long time afterward, useless for anything else. (letter of June 10/20, 1643) (15)

---

[30]Anne Conway, "The Principles of the Most Ancient and Modern Philosophy (1692)," in *Women Philosophers of the Early Modern Period*, ed. Margaret Atherton (Indianapolis: Hackett, 1994), p. 66.

[31]Elisabeth of Bohemia, "Correspondence with Descartes," in *Women Philosophers*, ed. Margaret Atherton (Indianapolis: Hackett, 1994), p. 11. Further references follow in the text.

[32]Jacqueline Broad, *Women Philosophers of the Seventeenth Century* (Cambridge: Cambridge University Press, 2002), p. 33.

Elisabeth conceived of the individual both as embodied and embedded within a social network, anticipating in this, Jacqueline Broad notes, Carol Gilligan's twentieth-century care theory. Elizabeth's "focus," Broad notes, "is not on isolated individuals but on relations between individuals, governed by care and concern."[33]

Catherine Trotter Cockburn, another seventeenth-century English philosopher who took issue with Cartesianism, similarly considered that one must conceive of the individual as connected in a web of relationship, which fosters a moral sense of caring and responsibility to others.

> Mankind [she wrote] is a system of creatures that continually need one another's assistance, without which they could not long subsist. It is therefore necessary, that every one...should contribute his part towards the good and preservation of the whole...For this end they are made capable of acquiring social or benevolent affection.[34]

The most forceful and extended critique of Cartesian premises was elaborated by the redoubtable Margaret Cavendish, the Duchess of Newcastle. Like Lady Conway, Cavendish firmly rejected the idea that physical matter was lifeless and inert, insisting instead that it was alive and informed with subjective consciousness, adopting thus a vitalist, animist, and indeed panpsychist view of nature. It is not therefore, according to Cavendish, only the human mind that is the seat of *res cogitans* but other parts of the body, animals, vegetables, and minerals—all are sentient seats of consciousness and have knowledges unique to their being. "If a Man hath Different Knowledge from Fish, yet the Fish may be as Knowing as Man, but Man hath not a Fishe's Knowledge, nor a Fish a Man's Knowledge."[35] In her early work *Poems, and Fancies* (1653), Cavendish indeed envisages animate atoms.[36]

---

[33]Ibid., p. 34.

[34]Catherine Trotter Cockburn, "Remarks upon Some Writers," as cited in ibid., pp. 148–49.

[35][Margaret Cavendish], The Marchioness of Newcastle, *Philosophical and Physical Opinions* (London: William Watson, 1663), p. 114.

[36][Margaret Cavendish], the Lady Newcastle, *Poems, and Fancies* (London: J. Martin and F. Allestrye, 1653), Brown University Women Writers Project copy, p. 60.

Cavendish seems to have readily understood as well the dominative character of the new Cartesian scientific view. Using the term "Art" to refer to all human intellectual constructs, Cavendish rejects all attempts to impose "Art" upon nature. "Art," she maintains, "is ignorant of Nature, for Mathematical Rules, Measures, and Demonstration cannot rule, measure or demonstrate Nature." Indeed Art should be "but a handmaid to nature, and not her mistress,"[37] thus repudiating the dominative view expressed by Descartes, Bacon, Boyle, and others, which she deplores:

> Mathematicians … endeavour to enchant Nature with Circles, and bind her with lines so hard, as if she were so mad, that she would do some mischief, when left at liberty. Geometricians … measure her so exactly … they almost stifle her … But Chymists torture Nature worst of all; for they extract and distil her beyond substance, nay into no substance, if they could.[38]

Such impositions of abstract form distort natural reality and fail to recognize the extraordinary diversity of the natural world which can, she maintains, only be known through exact attention to particular natural entities and by learning to understand their communications and knowledges.

Cavendish devoted one of her major works, *Observations upon Experimental Philosophy* (1666) to a critique of scientific laboratory experimentation, especially as practiced by members of the fledgling English Royal Society, who, though engaged in empirical studies, embraced "the mathematical metaphysics of Galileo and Descartes [that] the whole world seems to be fundamentally mathematical in structure … involv[ing] … a mechanical conception of its operations."[39] In his *Micrographia* (1665), for example, a prime exposition of Royal Society ideas, Robert Hooke "claimed that nature worked 'Mechanically' … seeds, for example, were

---

[37][Margaret Cavendish], The Marchioness of Newcastle, *Philosophical Letters: Or, Modest Reflections upon Some Opinions in Natural Philosophy* (London: n.p., 1664), p. 111.

[38]Ibid., p. 491.

[39]Edwin Arthur Burtt, *The Metaphysical Foundations of Modern Physical Science*, rev. ed. (1931; Garden City, NY: Doubleday Anchor, n.d.), pp. 172–73.

'little automatons or Engines.' ... The 'structure of Vegetables [was] altogether mechanical.'"[40] "Cavendish," Anna Battigelli notes, "objected to [Hooke's] mechanistic view of the world ... To her mind Hooke was replacing a world governed organically by the force of nature with a mechanistic universe."[41]

Cavendish's critique of Cartesian science informed her aesthetic theory, which rejected what came to be known as Kantian aesthetics *avant la lettre*. The artist or writer should not impose forms upon nature or twist nature to conform to those forms, but rather respond to nature as she is, listening to her voices sympathetically, and replicating them faithfully in her work, allowing them to speak. Aesthetic understanding must be focused justly on the particular, ever-various streaks of the tulip or the different shades in a forest that Johnson would elide. "Every little Fly, and every little Peble, and every little Flower, is a Tutor in Nature's School to instruct the understanding."[42] The greatest degree of truth comes from careful direct unmediated (Weilian) attention to the particulars of the world unobstructed by human technological devices or distortive theory: "those arts are the best and surest informers that alter nature least, and they the greatest deluders that alter nature most, I mean, the *particular* nature of each *particular* creature."[43]

The writer must thus "take a strikt notice of all things,"[44] which requires attentive "Sympathy," which is "but a conforming of the actions of one party, to the actions of the other, as by way of imitation."[45] Cavendish here then offers a theory of art rooted in empathic *mimesis*, an important alternative to the aesthetics of modernity (which we develop further in Chapters 3 and 10). Cavendish believed that the world was unified by an underlying chord of sympathy by which the artist connects to the subject

---

[40]Anna Battigelli, *Margaret Cavendish and the Exiles of the Mind* (Lexington: University Press of Kentucky, 1998), p. 96.

[41]Ibid.

[42]Margaret Cavendish, *The World's Olio* (London: J. Martin and J. Allestrye, 1655), Brown University Women Writers Project copy, p. 100.

[43]Margaret Cavendish, *Observations upon Experimental Philosophy* (1666), ed. Eileen O'Neill (Cambridge: Cambridge University Press, 2001), p. 53, emphasis added.

[44][Cavendish], *World's Olio*, p. 14.

[45][Cavendish], *Philosophical Letters*, p. 292. Further references follow in the text.

matter in question, a participatory epistemology quite at odds with the reifying conception of early modern science.[46]

Nearly three centuries later, Virginia Woolf in *A Room of One's Own* (1927) provided a similar critique of the dominative mentality that informs Cartesian science and Kantian aesthetics, offering an alternative epistemology that does not impose reductive forms upon reality but is instead prediscursively responsive.

Setting up the British Museum as the repository and arch symbol of establishment Enlightenment knowledge, the author, upon entering it, realizes that therein one is expected to "strain off what was personal and accidental... and so reach the pure fluid, the essential oil of truth."[47] In other words, one is expected to practice the Cartesian scientific method of extraction and reduction, according to prescripted formal rules. A student properly trained in this methodology will "no doubt... shepherd... his question past all distractions till it runs into its answer as a sheep runs into its pen" (28). In this crucial perception, Woolf highlights the link between scientific practice, which literally controls and manipulates natural entities—here the sheep, and the mental practice which coerces the matter of reality into preestablished redemptive categories. Horkheimer and Adorno succinctly, if less poetically, similarly propose: "domination in the conceptual sphere is raised up on the basis of actual domination" (14); "the deductive form of science reflects hierarchy and coercion" (21). The student sitting by Woolf's side in the British Museum, who is "copying assiduously from a scientific manual," is, she feels, undoubtedly engaging in such a deductive Cartesian method and thereby "extracting pure nuggets of essential ore every ten minutes or so" (28).

Woolf's resistance to forcing reality into man-made conceptual categories is further exemplified in her ruminations on the swamp that she imagines having been supplanted by the construction of Oxford and Cambridge universities (which she collapses under the term *Oxbridge*). "Once, presumably, this quadrangle with its smooth lawns, its massive buildings, and the chapel itself was marsh

---

[46]See Josephine Donovan, "Participatory Epistemology, Sympathy, and Animal Ethics," in *Ecofeminism: Feminist Intersections with Other Animals and the Earth*, ed. Carol J. Adams and Lori Gruen (New York: Bloomsbury, 2014), pp. 75–90.

[47]Virginia Woolf, *A Room of One's Own* (New York: Harcourt Brace, 1957), p. 25. Further references follow in the text.

too, where the grass waved and the swine rootled" (9). In reflecting on the construction of the university, Woolf imagines an "unending stream of gold and silver" (9), thus connecting the patriarchal institution with capitalism. "Hence the libraries and laboratories; the observatories; the splendid equipment of costly and delicate instruments which now stands on glass shelves, where centuries ago the grasses waved and the swine rootled" (10). There is clearly the suggestion here that we might be better off with just the wild grasses, the prepatriarchal swamp—a point developed more extensively in *Three Guineas* (1938), where Woolf connects the rise of civilization with women's subordination and the concomitant rise of fascism and militarism. Without women's historic subordination to men, without their having poured their energies into men, "without that power probably the earth would still be swamp and jungle. The glories of all our wars would be unknown... The Czar and the Kaiser would never have worn their crowns or lost them" (*Room* 36).

As Woolf proceeds with her inquiries in the British Museum, she finds herself "glancing with envy at the reader next door who was making the neatest abstracts, headed often with an A or a B or a C, while my own notebook rioted with the wildest scribble of contradictory jottings. It was distressing, it was bewildering, it was humiliating. Truth had run through my fingers. Every drop had escaped" (31).

In this state, Woolf begins to fantasize a Professor von X. who is "engaged in writing his monumental work entitled *The Mental, Moral, and Physical Inferiority of the Female Sex*" (31). Using once again an image of the domination and destruction of a natural creature to explain the mentality behind such research, Woolf says the professor "jab[s] his pen on the paper as if he were killing some noxious insect as he wrote, but even when he had killed it that did not satisfy him; he must go on killing it"(31). Here again, as with the swamp image, Woolf connects Oxbridge epistemology with the repression-destruction of the natural world. It is a matter of dominator/dominated. Such objectification and control serve, moreover, to fortify the professor's ego and secure his identity. When confronted with new, anomalous evidence, the professor reaches "for his measuring-rods to prove himself 'superior'": he must tame it, control it, shepherd it into pens, objectify it, and kill it.

Woolf developed her own aesthetic theories in the context of Bloomsbury discussions of the subject. Two of her Bloomsbury friends, Clive Bell and Roger Fry, both developed formalist aesthetic theory in the tradition of autonomous art established by Kant and in England by Samuel Taylor Coleridge. In his work *Art* (1913), Clive Bell coined the term "significant form" to explain his Kantian view of the art object as an end in itself. "[H]aving seen [art] as pure form, having freed it from all causal and adventitious interests, from all that it may have acquired from its commerce with human beings, from all its significance as means, [one] has felt its significance as an end in itself."[48]

Roger Fry's *Vision and Design* (1920) proposed a Kantian aesthetic theory not far removed from Bell's. "We must," he urged, "give up the attempt to judge the work of art by its reaction on life, and consider it as an expression of emotions regarded as ends in themselves."[49] "The aesthetic emotion," he maintains, is "as remote from actual life and its practical utilities as the most useless mathematical theory" (302).

In elaborating on the notion of "significant form" Fry brings out the imperialistic impulse behind it. Significant form, he notes, "implies the effort of the artist to bend to our emotional understanding by means of his passionate conviction some intractable material which is alien to our spirit" (302). Here again we sense the colonialist view of Kant et al., seeing the artist as one who wrenches reality, who forces reality to behave in accordance with a redemptive order, calling to mind the mentality of Professor von X.

Bell's view of art as "pure form" disconnected from "adventitious interests," as well as Fry's dominative view, is clearly repudiated by Woolf in *A Room* where she rejects the idea that it is possible to "strain off" the "personal and accidental and so reach the pure fluid, the essential oil of truth" (25). There and elsewhere she insists that truth and beauty ("moments of being") are embedded, contextual, and in process, not something that can be extracted and distilled from the "suffering human beings" (44) who create and experience them.

"On Re-reading Novels" (1922), in which she reviews Percy Lubbock's *Craft of Fiction*, further indicates Woolf's discomfort

---

[48]Clive Bell, *Art* (New York: Frederic A. Stokes, 1913), p. 53. Further references follow in the text.
[49]Roger Fry, *Vision and Design* (London: Chatto and Windus, 1920), p. 29. Further references follow in the text.

with traditional formalism, in particular Lubbock's insistence that "form" be considered the constitutive element of great literature. Woolf argues that the concept "form" comes between the reader and the emotions of a text as a kind of "alien substance" "imposing itself upon emotions which we feel naturally, and name simply."[50] Rather, she suggests, our sense of the meaning of a work as a whole comes to us in "moments of [emotional] understanding" that enable us to see what the overall point of a work is. "Therefore the 'book itself' is not form which you see, but emotion which you feel." And it is the writer's own feelings that are expressed in the work's style: "the more intense the writer's feeling the more exact ... its expression in words." The work of literature is thus the site of an emotional exchange between writer and reader. Lubbock's focus on form fails to appreciate this emotional communication; indeed, "whenever Mr. Lubbock talks of form it is as if something were interposed between us and the book as we know it" (126).

Woolf's resistance to forcing reality into a preconceived order, shepherding it into a pen or extracting its generic essence, is further illustrated in a comment she made about narrative structure in "Modern Fiction" (1925). "Let us record," she urged, "the atoms as they fall upon the mind in the order in which they fall, let us trace the pattern, however disconnected and incoherent in appearance which each sight or incident scores upon the consciousness."[51] Thus, rather than seeing form as redemptive of a threateningly chaotic reality (as Roquentin does in *Nausea*), Woolf asks that the artist be faithful to that reality, not eliding its anomalies in a rush to preconceived pattern, echoing thus the Duchess of Newcastle.

Woolf impugns, therefore, the dualistic compartmentalization and objectification that the Oxbridge Cartesian-Kantian epistemology and aesthetics entail. Rather her vision is holistic: one cannot separate art and life, nor mind and body. Indeed, it is women's impoverished material circumstances that have crippled them intellectually and spiritually—the central thesis of *A Room of One's Own*. "The human frame being what it is, heart, body, and brain all mixed together, and not contained in separate compartments ... a

---

[50]Viriginia Woolf, "On Re-Reading Novels," in *Collected Essays*, vol. 2 (London: Hogarth, 1966), p. 126. Further references follow in the text.
[51]Virginia Woolf, "Modern Fiction," in ibid., p. 107.

good dinner is of great importance to good talk. One cannot think well, love well, sleep well, if one has not dined well" (*Room* 18). Elisabeth of Bohemia would have readily concurred.

Nor is art is disconnected from material reality but rather attached

> like a spider's web...to life at all four corners. Often the attachment is scarcely perceptible...But when the web is pulled askew...one remembers that these webs are not spun in midair by incorporeal creatures, but are the work of suffering human beings, and are attached to grossly material things, like health and money and the houses we live in. (43–44)

Woolf also redefines reality, seeing it not as inert *res extensa* but as informed with an ontic intensity—"moments of being"[52]—which the perceptive artist or writer seeks to transmit in her work.

> What is meant by "reality"? It would seem to be something very erratic, very undependable—now to be found in a dusty road, now in a scrap of newspaper in the street, now in a daffodil in the sun. It lights up a group in a room and stamps some casual saying. It overwhelms one walking home beneath the stars and makes the silent world more real than the world of speech—and there it is again in an omnibus in the uproar of Piccadilly...Now the writer...has the chance to live more than other people in the presence of this reality. It is [her] business to find it and collect it and communicate it to the rest of us (*Room* 113–14).

In a later, more recently published article, "A Sketch of the Past," Woolf gives as an example of a "moment of being" an occurrence in her youth: "I was looking at the flower bed by the front door; 'that is the whole,' I said. I was looking at a plant with a spread of leaves; and it seemed suddenly plain that the flower itself was part of the earth; that a ring enclosed what was the real flower; part earth part flower" (71). Elaborating on this idea of interconnected wholeness, Woolf explains, these "moments of being" reveal that

---

[52]Virginia Woolf, "A Sketch of the Past," in *Moments of Being*, ed. Jeanne Schulkind (San Diego, CA: Harcourt Brace Jovanovich, 1985), pp. 70, 78. Further references follow in the text.

there is "some real thing behind appearances; and I make it real by putting it into words. It is only by putting it into words that I make it whole" (72). For,

> behind the cotton wool [of daily life] is hidden a pattern; that we—I mean all human beings—are connected with this; that the whole world is a work of art; that we are parts of a work of art. *Hamlet* or a Beethoven quartet is the truth about this vast mess that we call the world. But there is no Shakespeare; there is no Beethoven; certainly and emphatically there is no God; we are the words; we are the music; we are the thing itself. (72)

Or, as Woolf intuited in an early reflection, "If you lie on the earth somewhere you hear a sound like a vast breath, as though it were the very inspiration of earth herself, and all the living things on her."[53] Like Tchekov and Cavendish, Woolf seems here to intuit a reverberating chord of ecosympathy echoing through the natural orders, which we may hear if we are attuned through focused attention.

Thus, unlike the dominative view of the artist who stamps his form upon reality, redeeming it, civilizing it, Woolf sees the writer as one who is immersed in that reality, is a part of a larger underlying wholeness, and who allows or enables its being to be expressed. The artist connects us to that wholeness—that "hidden pattern," that "some real thing behind appearances"; by putting it into words she makes it come real by making it knowable. Like Cavendish, then, Woolf envisages a world in which all—artist, reader, and subject matter—are linked through an invisible chord of sympathy. It is the artist's job to make that manifest.

Intuitions that would seem to resonate with those proffered by Woolf and Cavendish have been put forth in recent years by the New Materialists, who propose that there is an active presence within the material world that is occluded by classical physics and

---

[53]Virginia Woolf, *A Passionate Apprentice: The Early Journals 1897–1909*, ed. Mitchell A. Leaska (New York: Harcourt, 1990), p. 203. See also Louise Westling, "Participatory Knowledge and the World in Virginia Woolf," in *Engendering Rationalities*, ed. Nancy Tuana and Sandra Morgan (Albany, NY: State University of New York Press, 2001), pp. 245–58, and L. Elizabeth Waller, "Writing the Real: Virginia Woolf and the Ecology of Language," *Bucknell Review* 44, no. 1 (2000):137–57.

epistemology. Offering a "post-Cartesian" rejection of the view that matter "is mechanical, inorganic,"[54] these thinkers no longer conceive matter as "passive or inert" but rather recognize the "emergent, generative (or agentic) capacities even within inorganic matter" (9), positing that there is, in short, something "vibrant" or even "mind-like" about material reality.

The impetus for this new materialist theoretical turn stems largely from revolutionary discoveries in early twentieth-century science, notably in quantum physics, which destabilized the concept of object, because of the indeterminacy of the most primordial "objects" of nature, quantum wave/particles, thus calling into question subject-object dualism. I further discuss these developments in Chapters 3 and 10.

Jane Bennett, one of the foremost proponents of the New Materialism, describes how a "moment of being," not unlike Virginia Woolf's, inspired her to write *Vibrant Matter* (2010), one of the key texts in the field. "My book," she writes,

> Was... quite literally, a reply to a call from matter that had congealed into "things." In particular, some items of trash had collected in the gutter of a street in Baltimore—one large black workglove, one dense mat of oak pollen, one unblemished dead rat, one white plastic bottle cap, one smooth stick of wood— and one sunny day as I walked by, they called me over to them. I stood enchanted by the tableau they formed, and for a few surreal moments thought I caught a glimpse into a parallel world of vibrant powerful things.[55]

While the New Materialist view and other deconstructions of subject-object dualism would seem then to point in the direction of an aesthetics of care, in that they allow for an agency in the subject matter that is denied in Kantian aesthetics, Bennett's anecdote points up the problematics of this association. In her recollection

---

[54]*New Materialisms: Ontology, Agency, and Politics*, ed. Diana Coole and Samantha Frost (Durham, NC: Duke University Press, 2010), p. 9. Further references follow in the text.

[55]Jane Bennett, "Powers of the Hoard: Further Notes on Material Agency," in *Animal, Vegetable, Mineral: Ethics and Objects*, ed. Jeffrey Jerome Cohen (Washington, DC: Oliphaunt Books, 2012), pp. 238–39. Further references follow in the text.

of the gutter tableau, which included an "unblemished" rat and a white plastic bottle cap, Bennett implies an ontological and aesthetic ("unblemished"/"white") equivalency among the items.[56] But surely there is a difference to be made (something the New Materialists often fail to do) between a living or formerly living being and a manufactured commodity. To the former is owed, I would contend, respect and ethical attention, unlike the latter. (One might indeed be moved, under an ethic of care, to bury the rat, offering her a measure of final dignity, in honor of her past existence as a presence with whom a caring, dialogical relationship had been possible.)[57]

In *Vibrant Matter*, in elaborating on her reaction to the rat, Bennett recalls that she saw it of interest, first, as an example of an impressed "human activity": "the rat-poisoner's success." On second reflection she "was repelled by the dead (or was it merely sleeping?) rat" (4). In the end, these reactions are superceded by her equal ascription to all the items in the tableau a certain "energetic vitality" which she labels "thing-power" (5).

At first, Bennett clearly demonizes the rat as a monstrous *other*, construing it thus within prescripted (and erroneous) constructions of rats as dangerous enemies. The dead body is initially deemed thus a token of humanist triumph—"the rat poisoner's success." The second reaction—of revulsion and fear—seems to stem from the possibility that the rat is alive. If so, the animal's ethical status—and Bennett's ethical responsibility—changes dramatically. Under an ethic of care, Bennett would have an obligation to help the animal to recover, to return her to her natural environment.[58] Instead, we have

---

[56]In *Vibrant Matter* (Durham, NC: Duke University Press, 2010), pp. 116–17, Bennett envisages "an ontological field without any unequivocal demarcations between human, animal, vegetable or mineral." Further references follow in the text. A further discussion of New Materialism may be found in my article "Animal Ethics, the New Materialism, and the Question of Subjectivity," in *Critical Animal Studies*, ed. John Sorenson and Atsuko Matsuoka (Rowman & Littlefield, forthcoming).
[57]Humans can and do form strong loving bonds with rats. See Joan Dunayer, *Animal Equality: Language and Liberation* (Derwood, MD: Ryce, 2001), pp. 35–36. Also Tai Moses, "Rat Race," in *Zooburbia: Reflections on the Wild Animals among Us* (Berkeley, CA: Parallax Press, 2014), pp. 37–41.
[58]Further elaborations on an ethic of care applied to animals may be found in *The Feminist Care Tradition in Animal Ethics*, ed. Donovan and Adams. All its contributors would agree that humans have ethical responsibilities to care for injured individual animals—whether wild or domestic.

the assumption that the animal is dead, of interest and significance as part of a vibrant assemblage, an aesthetic tableau. Ironically, we find here rescripted the aesthetics of modernity in which the "unblemished" (aesthetic ascription) rat's body has significance only as part of an interesting, if vibrant, aesthetic composition. New Materialism, therefore, though it offers stimulating new perspectives on *physical* matter, fails to provide a significantly new understanding of *living* matter. Any ontological equation between the two is ethically untenable.

While Woolf's critique of Enlightenment aesthetics is largely on epistemological grounds, it implies an ethical dimension in that the mentality she deplores and the methodology it entails involve a coercive and destructive praxis toward the natural world—driving sheep, stabbing at insects.[59] A more pointed ethical critique has been developed in recent years, beginning with Horkheimer and Adorno in the 1940s and 50s and intensifying in the early twenty-first century, especially among critics who approach aesthetics from the standpoint of animal ethics.

The traditional Kantian view of art as a privileged realm divorced from ordinary human activity means that it is considered immune from ethical critique. The ethical status of the subject matter, the ethical positioning of the artist or writer, and the moral effect of the art upon reader or viewer all are in the Kantian formalist view deemed irrelevant. Viewing nature as inert and lifeless matter available for artistic form-giving enabled the ethical agnosticism inherent in the Kantian view, because if there is no life there, there would seem to be no ethical obligation. A similar logic governs scientific experimentation where the subjects—living animals—are deemed lifeless automatons to whom no ethical obligation is owed.

The Cartesian view has indeed legitimized atrocious animal experimentation. An early critic revealed its horrific consequences.

The scientists administered beatings to dogs with perfect indifference and made fun of those who pitied the creatures as

---

[59]Woolf's empathetic sensitivity to living creatures is dramatized in her brilliant essay, "The Death of a Moth" (1942), in *Collected Essays*, vol. 1, ed. Leonard Woolf (London: Chatto & Windus, 1966), pp. 359–61.

if they felt pain. They said the animals were clocks that the cries they emitted when struck were only the sound of a little spring that had been touched, but that the whole body was without feeling. They nailed the poor animals up on boards by their four paws to vivisect them to see the circulation of the blood.[60]

The animals are thus viewed as mechanistic automatons—inert matter—who, having no ethical status, may be used and abused as the scientist sees fit. In their critique of behaviorist animal experimentation, Horkheimer and Adorno note how, ironically, the scientists in question who coerce quantifiable data "from defenseless animals in their nauseating physiological laboratories" are themselves operating as mechanistically as their subjects' "mutilated bodies." "The professor at the dissecting-table defines these spasms scientifically," but he himself "functions as mechanically, as blindly and automatically as the twitching limbs of the victim" (*Dialectic* 245). For, as the celebrated vivisector Claude Bernard once explained, in his defense, "the physiologist... does not hear the cries of animals. He does not see their flowing blood, he sees nothing but his idea."[61] Thus, Horkheimer and Adorno observe, Cartesian "Reason, mercilessly advancing, belongs to man. The animal, from which he draws his blood conclusion, knows only irrational terror and the urge to make an escape from which he is cut off" (*Dialectic* 245).

An artist depicting the above scene of laboratory torture would be immune likewise from ethical critique in the Kantian view, just as the scientist performing the above experiment would be held blameless under Cartesianism. But when the objects of scientific experimentation or aesthetic treatment are regarded as living subjects, ethical questions arise. Considering aesthetics from an ethical standpoint, the moral perspective of the artist, as well as the moral status of the subject matter, are pertinent questions.

---

[60]As cited in Tom Regan, *The Case for Animal Rights* (Berkeley: University of California Press, 1983), p. 5. The practice of vivisection is, unfortunately, not an antiquated anomaly; 64,361 dogs were used in research experiments in 2012 in the United States alone, according to a USDA Animal and Plant Inspection Service report.

[61]Claude Bernard, as cited in John Vyvyan, *In Pity and in Anger: A Study of the Use of Animals in Science* (Marblehead, MA: Micah Publications, 1988), p. 44.

Indeed, an ethical analysis of this example would hinge on the question of artistic intent: whether the artist of such a scene were exploiting the material for the voyeuristic or perverse pleasure of the viewer, considering torture material as *aesthetically interesting* (the case with significant examples of contemporary art) or whether the depiction were intended dialectically to provide an ethical or political critique. (However, even in the latter case, the artist or photographer must be held ethically liable, in my view, if he staged the torture scene or, in the event of a live happening, did nothing to stop it.) The intent of the artist is therefore a key issue: when the artist has a *critical* intent, she has in mind the ethical status of the principals, considering them as *subjects*, whereas in the case where the artist is providing the scene for pornographic titillation or aesthetic gratification, the subjects are reduced to aesthetic *objects* with no ethical status. The Kantian view would support the latter objectifying practice, since it holds that the matter being treated is passive, inert, and available to the human subject, who is reshaping it in accordance with prescripted rules, laws, and ideals. The treated matter has no ethical status of its own.

Contemporary liberal rights theory largely follows the Kantian privileging sanctification of the artist and his work. Thus, no matter how ethically repugnant the subject matter, the artistic process under this view remains shielded from ethical critique. An example may be made of so-called crush videos. In these pornographic films, small animals—mice or chicks—are tortured and crushed to death by (usually) stiletto heels.[62] A formalist view of the matter would exempt all concerned from ethical responsibility: the status of the video as "art" trumps everything else. While crush videos may be an extreme example, they dramatically raise the question of the ethical status of the subject matter in art and literature, a consideration of which necessarily challenges the Kantian aesthetics of modernity.

The issue has been addressed by feminist critics of pornography. Susanne Kappeler, for example, notes in her critique of the genre, that what is required in such representation is the effective (and sometimes literal) death of the subject, her transformation

---

[62]See Catharine A. MacKinnon, "Of Mice and Men," in *Feminist Care Tradition*, ed. Josephine Donovan and Carol J. Adams (New York: Columbia University Press, 2007), pp. 322–23.

into an object.[63] Indeed, as Margaret C. Jacob has pointed out, pornography as a genre arose in the Enlightenment and is rooted in the mechanistic premises of Cartesian science.

The universe of the bedroom created by the materialist pornographer stands as an analogue to the physical universe of the mechanical philosophers. In both, bodies were stripped of their texture, color, smell, of their qualities, and encapsulated as entities in motion, whose very being is defined by their motion.[64]

In other words, like Descartes' wax, porn bodies are stripped of particularizing quality and reduced to mechanistic quantity, thus becoming "an abstraction divorced from the everyday...where nothing matters but the force of projectiles, the compulsive pushing and pulling of bodies" (122).

As Kappeler notes, such framing abstraction involves objectification of a live subject. "Looking at the scene, framing it, taking a picture ensures [a Kantian] disinterestedness by imposing a structure of representation" (46), in which the subject is reified and thus rendered powerless and voiceless before the viewer. It is an exercise in domination where the living, feeling reality of the subject is excised. For, as Theodor Adorno perceived, "it is part of the mechanism of domination to forbid recognition of the suffering it produces."[65]

In one of her last articles, "Regarding the Torture of Others" (2004), Susan Sontag linked the horrific photographs of American torture of prisoners at the Abu Ghraib prison in Iraq, which had just come to light, with the dominative aesthetics of pornography whose normalization through ubiquitous internet availability seems to have blocked any "recognition of the suffering" involved.

Most of the pictures [Sontag notes] seem part of a larger confluence of torture and pornography: a young woman leading

---

[63]Susanne Kappeler, *The Pornography of Representation* (Minneapolis: University of Minnesota Press, 1986), p. 46. Further references follow in the text.
[64]Margaret C. Jacob, "The Materialist World of Pornography," in *The Invention of Pornography: Obscenity and the Origins of Modernity 1500–1800*, ed. Lynn Avery Hunt (New York: Zone Books, 1996), p. 164. Further references follow in the text.
[65]Theodore Adorno, *Minima Moralia: Reflections from Damaged Life*, trans. E. F. N. Jeffcott (London: Verso, 1954), p. 67. Further references follow in the text.

a naked man around on a leash is classic dominatrix imagery. And you wonder how much of the sexual tortures inflicted on the inmates of Abu Ghraib was inspired by the vast repertory of pornographic imagery available on the Internet.[66]

Sontag concludes grimly, "It is hard to measure the increasing acceptability of brutality in American life, but its evidence is everywhere, starting with the video games of killing that are a principal entertainment of boys" (28).

Intervening in the Abu Ghraib photos means regarding them in a way differently than the photographers/artists intended. Instead of identifying with the torturer and taking sadistic pleasure in the humiliation of dehumanized, objectified, and aestheticized victims, an ethical perspective recognizes the subjectivity of the victims, imagining their feelings empathetically, and deploring thus their treatment. In this way, the ethical status of the subjects of abuse is established. Such a process is what art critic Griselda Pollock (following Israeli artist Bracha Ettinger) has termed "wit(h)nessing," where the viewer or reader views the traumatic subject matter *with* the subjects being treated, not looking (down) *at* them from a distance. The artistic encounter, she writes, should "enjoin a co-subjectivity...so that...something of the other is processed by the viewer."[67] Wit(h) nessing requires that the sacrificial victim be seen as a *subject* who has feelings and with whom one respectfully engages, not simply cast off and distanced as an aesthetically interesting *object*.

Analyzing a Holocaust photo of a Nazi soldier shooting a woman and child point blank, Pollock notes further how the images fit into a prescribed mythic or ideologically determined narrative trajectory. "It reiterates some deeper, mythic troping of gender and death: normalising the aggression of male violence, and the suffering of women as the perpetually dying" (220). This "predetermined aesthetic" deflects "the full horror" of the event

[66]Susan Sontag, "Regarding the Torture of Others," *New York Times Magazine*, May 23, 2004, p. 27. Further references follow in the text. See also Sontag's *Regarding the Pain of Others* (New York: Farrar, Straus & Giroux, 2003).

[67]Griselda Pollock, "Dying, Seeing, Feeling: Transforming the Ethical Space of Feminist Aesthetics," in *The Life and Death of Images: Ethics and Aesthetics*, ed. Diamuid Costello and Dominic Willsdon (Ithaca, NY: Cornell University Press, 2008), p. 235. Further references follow in the text.

"by the normalisation" of feminine "vulnerability and dying" (221). In other words, just as prescriptive mathematical paradigms shape how the scientist views nature, so to do prescriptive mythic paradigms shape how cultural forms are produced and perceived; they are filtered through a conceptual lens, which organizes reality according to patterns that have become normalized in a given culture. Thus sexist assumptions—that women are normally the victims of brutality; that indeed to be a victim is to be feminized—shape how one responds to the Holocaust photo; similarly, pornographic sadomasochistic imagery organized how the Abu Ghraib photos were shaped and received; and likewise speciesist assumptions (as seen in Bennett's perception of the dead rat as dangerous vermin) govern how animals are conceived and perceived in cultural representations of them—the subject of Part II of this book. As Horkheimer and Adorno explain in *Dialectic of Enlightenment*, "the conceptual apparatus determines the senses even before perception occurs... *a priori*. Kant foretold what Hollywood consciously put into practice... images are pre-censored according to the [cultural] norm of understanding." (84). To disrupt this "mythic troping," Pollock calls for a "non-fascist feminist ethico-aesthetical intervention," which involves the process of "wit(h)nessing," disrupting the "Orphic voyeurism" (230) of the "genocidal gaze" (222).

Often the subject victims themselves offer resistance, Adorno notes, through their expressions (obvious in the Abu Ghraib photos) or vocally. But the perpetrators override and repress such expression by imposing upon them a legitimizing generic concept, as the Americans did the Islamic prisoners, as the Nazis did the Jews—Adorno's concern; and just as laboratory scientists and slaughterhouse workers do animals ("the physiologist... does not hear the cries of animals... he sees nothing but his idea"—Claude Bernard). Thus, as Adorno argues, in the case of torture and brutality to humans, the resistance of the subject to reification has to be denied, silenced, and repressed by the torturer in order for the brutality to proceed. So that "when the gaze of a fatally-wounded animal falls on a human being" it must be "repel[led]" with "defiance"—"after all it's only an animal," a logic that ultimately reduces the creature to "a thing, so that its stirring can no longer refute the manic gaze" of the perpetrator. This logic is also applied to other humans who are analogized to animals and thence to things, thereby distancing them from the perpetrator. "Indignation over cruelty diminishes in proportion as the victims are less like normal readers" (*Minima Moralia* 105). Aestheticization of violence and cruelty depends upon a similar distancing, reifying logic.

The most caustic critic of the aestheticization of atrocity in contemporary culture is French theorist Paul Virilio, who goes so far as to claim that contemporary art operates under what he calls an "aesthetics of Auschwitz," because of its "pitiless and emotionless" treatment of objectified subjects.[68] As a result of twentieth-century mass atrocities, such as the Holocaust, humans have become desensitized and art and aesthetic criticism have consequently become dispassionate and incapable of sympathetic emotion. Contemporary art has become but "a lethal presentational art of scientific voyeurism" (4). Thus the mentality of "Auschwitz inhabits us all," such that we are heirs to a "pitiless art" (3). "Hasn't," he concludes, "the universality of the extermination of bodies as well as of the environment from AUSCHWITZ to CHERNOBYL, succeeded in *dehumanizing us from without* by shattering our ethic and aesthetic bearings?" (16).

Speaking in the throes of the Serb-Croatian-Bosnian conflict in the mid-1990s, which engendered much atrocious behavior, Dzebad Karahasan similarly deplored "contemporary indifferent art,"[69] seeing it as an important contributor to a cultural mentality that allows and condones atrocity. In an article, "Literature and War" (1995), Karahasan asserts that while literature is an important articulator and determinant of a culture's values, recent developments have corrupted literature's time-honored ethical contribution. Especially destructive trends include politicized nationalist literature, which foments hatred for an enemy, and "art for art's sake," which "perceives literally everything as an aesthetic phenomenon" (7). The latter reduces literature "to play" that is "free from any ethical questions," which are turned into "aesthetic" issues (6). Like Virilio, Karahasan fears that contemporary readers and viewers have become "aestheticized people" "who watch

---

[68]Paul Virilio, *Art and Fear* (New York: Continuum, 2006), p. 11. Further references follow in the text.
[69]Dzebad Karahasan, "Literature and War," *Agni* 41 (1995):7. Further references follow in the text.

violence and the worst suffering [aesthetically] in order to feel something for the moment" (7).

The peculiar conjunction of violence and brutality with dispassion and rationality has been seen by many as a hallmark of modernity, a conjunction that unites atrocious behavior with aesthetic disinterestness—enabling what Hannah Arendt famously, if controversially, termed the "banality of evil." In her recent analysis of literature and film from an animal ethics standpoint, *Creaturely Poetics* (2011), Anat Pick, for example, notes how modern institutions that torture and destroy animals reflect this conjunction, as revealed in documentaries that feature slaughterhouses and laboratories engaged in animal experimentation (notably the films *Le Sang des bêtes* [1949] by Georges Franju and *Primate* [1974] by Frederick Wiseman). These films critically depict "institutionalized violence against animals" in "institutional sites [that] ... disclose the fusion of rationality and violence as paradigmatically modern."[70] They reveal that the mentality which governs in such places is *aesthetic*. "Both films" perceive "modern instrumentalism and technoscience as forms of surrealist art" (132). *Primate,* in particular, "can be seen ... as an extended exposition, not just of the banality (or rationality) of evil but of the *aesthetics of evil*" (147). *Primate* depicts cruel manipulative operations—including vivisection— on monkeys in the Yerkes Primate Laboratory. It does so with no explanatory voice-over; it simply witnesses in silence—thus forcing the viewer to see what is actually happening prediscursively, so to speak, before being shaped into obfuscating, ideologically determined, explanatory reduction.

The reification inherent in the formalist aesthetics of modernity occasions not just, however, a disinterested, dispassionate, "banal" bureaucratic response but the dominative process itself may engender a sadistic response, for the matter being reshaped and controlled is necessarily seen as an inferior object over which the manipulator has power. The exercise of such power—coercing matter into agreeable shapes—can arouse sadistic pleasure. Indeed, there is a sadistic element in the very experience of disinterestedness,

---

[70] Anat Pick, *Creaturely Poetics: Animality and Vulnerability in Literature and Film* (New York: Columbia University Press, 2011), p. 131. Further references follow in the text.

which requires self-mutilation, a cutting off of the emotions. Val Plumwood aptly terms the process the "sado-dispassionate gaze," whereby "the object of attention is passive and othered as 'object.'"[71] Not only hard core pornographers, however, produce sadistic images of atrocious violence in art and literature, but many highly regarded modern writers also indulge in an aestheticization of violence—especially against animals—enabled thus perhaps because consideration of animals as ontologically inferior and as exploitable matter is the accepted ideological norm in modern culture within which these writers operate. Such an ideology enables them to use animals aesthetically and to guilelessly exploit the titillating shock value animal torture and death affords.

Marian Scholtmeijer makes this point in her critique of a scene in Jerzy Kozinsky's novel *The Painted Bird* in which a character cruelly daubs paint on a live bird to watch the bird be killed by other birds confused by the coloring. The bird's treatment is thus used to exemplify human wartime sadism, but it is also used by the author, Scholtmeijer contends, because it is aesthetically interesting. "The victimization of animals is not explored for the animal's sake...[Instead,] what should be inexplicable—violence against animals—becomes all too intelligible when one looks at artistic motivations."[72] Especially objectionable, she says, is "Kozinski's pornographic interest in the events [of human and animal cruelty] he describes" (229).

Another example Scholtmeijer singles out as a blatant example of the artistic practice of exploiting animal cruelty is Hemingway's treatment of bulls in *The Sun Also Rises*. "The bulls," she notes, "are only animate objects in an artistic spectacle. Seen as art, the spectacle in the bullring does not merely override animal pain; it in fact causes that pain to disappear, since the whole event is just a geometric interplay of abstract forces" (264). In *Beasts of the Modern Imagination* (1985), Margot Norris likewise proposes that in *Death in the Afternoon*, Hemingway conceives the bullfight as an

---

[71]Val Plumwood, "The Concept of a Cultural Landscape: Nature, Culture and Agency in the Land," *Ethics and the Environment* 11, no. 2 (2006):124. Further references follow in the text.

[72]Marian Scholtmeijer, *Animal Victims in Modern Fiction: From Sanctity to Sacrifice* (Toronto: University of Toronto Press, 1993), p. 229. Further references follow in the text.

art form with the "artist as sadist," the "matador literally creat[ing] 'art' out of torture and killing."[73]

In a recent critique of Alain Renaut's aesthetic justification of bullfighting, French critic Luc Ferry links such aestheticization of animals to Enlightenment hubris, noting that the aesthetics of modernity and art conceived under its theory is rooted in a Cartesian will to dominate. Renaut argued that in a bullfight, the bull is essentially an art object and that in the matador's control of the bull's movements "resides the true aesthetic dimension of bullfighting," seeing "artistic creation" as connected to "the submission of unreasoning matter to a will that gives it form"—a reprisal of the Kantian-Hegelian view that grounds the aesthetics of modernity. Criticizing this idea, Ferry notes that in this humanist world-view "man [sic] is defined by this 'breaking away' from a natural state to which the animal remains prisoner...it is the enactment of this difference, the foundation of modern humanism, that we are witnessing in the bullfight." "[N]ature, in this case the living being, is relegated to the status of an object to be dominated or 'civilized.'"[74] Such a view overrides and represses the living subjecthood of the bull relegating him to the status of inert matter to be manipulated and shaped according to aesthetic constructs. This is the formalist aesthetics of modernity.

Similarly, egregious aestheticization of living animals has become commonplace in contemporary avant-garde art (see Amy Youngs for a catalog of atrocious examples).[75] Eduardo Kac, for example, has labeled as art a transgenic rabbit he created which "glows bright green when she is illuminated with blue light." He did so by combining "an enhanced version of the green fluorescent gene found in jellyfish" with the "unborn rabbit's DNA." Kac calls this

---

[73]Margot Norris, *Beasts of the Modern Imagination: Darwin, Nietzsche, Kafka, Ernst, and Lawrence* (Baltimore: Johns Hopkins University Press, 1985), pp. 11–12.

[74]Luc Ferry, "Neither Man nor Stone," in *Animal Philosophies: Essential Readings in Continental Thought*, ed. Matthew Calarco and Peter Atterton (New York: Continuum, 2004), pp. 152, 153.

[75]Amy Youngs, "Creating, Culling and Caring," in *The Aesthetics of Care? The Artistic, Social and Scientific Implications of the Use of Biological/Medical Technologies for Artistic Purposes*, Symposium, Perth Institute of Contemporary Arts, August 5, 2002, ed. Oron Cutts (Perth: University of Western Australia, 2002), p. 72. Further references follow in the text.

"transgenic artwork": "the artwork consists of the rabbit herself."[76] What is offensive about Kac's practice from the point of view of an ethics and aesthetics of care is not only does it violate the animal's bodily integrity and thereby its inherent dignity, it also necessarily denies the subjecthood of the animal (who was named "Alba") cruelly reducing her to the status of object to be manipulated for human aesthetic purposes.

Moreover, as Youngs points out, creating transgenic rabbits involves killing the mother rabbit, as well as the babies who are not transgenic (which is 97 percent of the offspring); these are but the "failed culled animals of the experiment" (72). The "art" is thus created by selecting according to a prescripted idea—a "culling process": all that do not fit into this aesthetic model are rejected and killed as being inferior and defective. It is a fascist genocidal operation.

Some might claim that Kozinsky's painted bird and Kac's fluorescent rabbit are justified on the grounds that they are "aesthetically interesting." That is, they engage the reader's or viewer's attention, drawing it to otherwise taboo or socially prohibited scenes of violence. Such vicarious, distanced encounters give the reader safe exposure to transgression, an experience that may be linked to the aesthetics of the sublime, which I discuss in Chapter 9. But, as noted by Youngs, such focusing of the attention on the "aesthetically interesting" requires the elision of attention on the suffering being, an excision of ethical attentiveness, an attitude consonant with the disinterested framing entailed in the aesthetics of modernity, which is situated, as Plumwood notes, within an ideology of "sado-dispassionate rationality" ("Concept" 123).

In literature, one of the most common devices that exploit animal pain for aesthetic effect is the animal metaphor, or, more specifically, the animal "stand-in" or surrogate, where the animal acts as a substitute for a human and/or is employed as an objectified vehicle through which to reveal or express human feelings. Using animal death and agony to dramatize, symbolize, or comment upon the emotional state of the human protagonists continues to be a standard fictional device. A random sample of short stories

---

[76]As cited in Steve Baker, *Picturing the Beast: Animals, Identity, and Representation* (Urbana: University of Illinois Press, 2001), p. xxviii.

published in the United States in recent years by highly regarded contemporary writers reveals its pervasive use. In Alice Munro's story "Runaway" (2003), for example, a goat serves as scapegoat for the woman protagonist; in "Measuring the Jump" (2003) Dave Eggers has the protagonist identifying with stockyard cows whom he imagines shooting because their lives, he thinks, are pointless. In a Don Chaon story (2003), it is a macaw; Junse Kim (2003), a raccoon; Richard Mausch (2003), an elephant (the latter three Pushcart Prize stories); William Trevor (2006), a dog; Samantha Hunt (2006), a horse; Roberto Bolaño (2007), rabbits; Callan Wint (2012), fifty cats battered to death or poisoned. [77] All of these writers fail to imagine the suffering of the animals, whose pain is thereby trivialized and effaced. Animals in these stories figure only insofar as they amplify or symbolize aspects of the human characters' relationships or situations; the moral reality of the animals' own suffering is elided. The circumstantial realities of the animals themselves are largely ignored so that the perceived pathos of their condition may be used to illustrate the mental state or moral condition of the humans. In short, the moral reality of the animals' suffering is overridden in the interests of creating an aesthetic effect. Were, indeed, the authors to include focus on the animals' suffering, it would upset the anthropocentric aesthetic design of the works.

The use of the animal metaphor may at times be aesthetically justified, morally innocuous, and creatively productive. For example, the statement, "the ballerina leaped with gazelle-like grace" applies attributes of the gazelle to characterize the graceful movements of the ballerina. Such a figure is morally innocuous. But would one say "the gazelle leaped as gracefully as a ballerina"? Probably not, because it upsets our hierarchical view

---

[77]Roberto Bolaño, "The Insufferable Gaucho," *The New Yorker*, October 1, 2007; Don Chaon, "I Demand to Know Where You're Taking Me," in *The Pushcart Prize XXVII*, ed. Bill Henderson (Wainscott, NY: Pushcart Press, 2003), pp. 227–48; Dave Eggers, "Measuring the Jump," *The New Yorker*, September 1, 2003; Samantha Hunt, "Three Days," *The New Yorker*, January 16, 2006; Junse Kim, 2003, "Yangban," in *Pushcart Prize XXVII*, ed. Henderson, pp. 448–62; Richard Mausch, "The Weight," in *Pushcart Prize XXVII*, ed. Henderson, pp. 562–78; Alice Munro, "Runaway," *The New Yorker*, August 11, 2003; William Trevor, "Folie à Deux." *The New Yorker*, July 24, 2007; Callan Wint, "Breathariano," *The New Yorker*, October 22, 2012. Further references follow in the text. An earlier version of this section appeared in my "Aestheticizing Animal Cruelty," *College Literature* 38, no. 4 (Fall 2011):207–22.

that humans are not to be exploited aesthetically to characterize animals. Indeed, such a simile invites a comic response. However, a metaphor concerning a gazelle would become morally objectionable if, for example, a hunter, whose wife has just left him, willfully shoots the gazelle in different parts of her body so as to force a slow tortured death upon her, the purpose of this episode being to show the anguish of the hunter over his wife's decision, using the animal in short as a surrogate for the wife. A scene of this type in fact occurs in Tim O'Brien's Vietnam novel *The Things They Carried* (1990) in which a G.I., upset over the death of his buddy, tortures a baby water buffalo in this way. The point of the episode is to show how upset the G.I. is and/or how war brings out the worst in everyone. In each case, the animal's suffering is exploited to make a point about the human character. Such episodes are aesthetically satisfying (to some) because they provide an effective way to dramatize human emotions. But in their transposition of an ethical subject into an aesthetic object, they require the sacrifice of the animal as an independent being to human aesthetic interests. To anyone who pays attention to the animal's suffering, however, these episodes are not aesthetically pleasurable and are not cathartic (as the depiction of human suffering is held to be in classical Aristotelian theory), because they are gratuitous, to no redemptive purpose (the justification for human suffering offered in many religious and ethical theories). (I discuss the O'Brien novel and Aristotelian *katharsis* more extensively in Chapters 8 and 9.)

Using animal cruelty to dramatize human feelings about or behavior toward other humans is a standard fictional practice. In the Munro story noted above, for example, a husband kills his wife's pet goat as a way of acting out his feelings toward her. The goat, Flora, seems to symbolize the wife's free wayward soul, which the husband seeks to kill. Trevors's "Folie à Deux"concerns a shameful secret shared by two men: their cruel childhood treatment of a lame dog, Old Jericho. Trevor heightens the pathos of the dog's drowning thusly: "The old dog, limping behind them when they carried it to the sea, his tail wagging madly, head cocked to one side" (63). The point of the story is how this episode has continued to haunt the men. As in the Munro story (and scores of others), the animal's death is of interest only for its effect on the human characters and/ or as a vehicle to dramatize human relations and feelings. In these cases, the author is using the pathos of the death of an innocent animal to create a powerful aesthetic effect.

Note I am not suggesting that the authors necessarily condone their characters' behavior; nevertheless, they are using instances of cruelty toward animals and exploiting animal suffering for their own aesthetic purposes. And, while the short story examples cited above are by no means pornographic, the operation whereby the ethical reality of the actual existing being is subordinated to an other, aesthetic purpose remains similar to that in pornography. In the Bolaño story noted above, for example, which concerns the deterioration of civil society in Argentina and an elderly patriarch's attempt to cope with it, there are numerous references to wild rabbits who come to represent a degenerated uncivilized human world. The first image the protagonist has of the rabbits is from a train window where he sees several rabbits gang up on another and tear him or her apart. Later a character is bitten by a rabbit. That gauchos are reduced to trapping rabbits rather than tending cattle is seen as a sign of the country's deterioration and feminization. Throughout the story, rabbits are treated as antagonistic pests who are taking over the pampas, signifying entropy; they are of use only when dead, as skins or as food for humans (several rabbit meals are described). Nowhere is the actual reality of real rabbits allowed to intrude, nor is the rabbit viewpoint anywhere expressed; they are quite simply subordinated to their symbolic use. Similarly, in Hunt's "Three Days" story (noted above), a horse's drowning symbolizes the destruction of rural life by development. (He dies in a shopping mall that has grown up around the family farm.)

As Stephen Webb notes, "our use of language incorporates animals as symbols and metaphors...while real animals disappear...[I]n most literature where they appear at all, animals are nothing but figures, rhetorical embellishments or marginal tropes; they are not to be taken literally on their own terms."[78] "As a general rule," he notes further, "animals vanish in the signs that represent them" (89).

In *The Sexual Politics of Meat* (1990), Carol J. Adams notes that as in literary texts so in the "cultural text" of meat-eating animals

---

[78]Stephen H. Webb, *On God and Dogs: A Christian Theology of Compassion for Animals* (New York: Oxford University Press, 1998), p. 87. Further references follow in the text.

exist only as "absent referents," transformed through slaughter from living creatures into dead meat. "Through butchering, animals become absent referents. Animals in name and body are made absent *as animals* for meat to exist."[79] When the referent (real animal) is commodified and objectified, whether as metaphor or meat, it is inserted in a human chain of signifiers so as to circulate in a symbolic exchange system: as the vehicle of a metaphor in the linguistic exchange of literature; as "live" stock ("pork bellies") and meat in commodities, stock, and futures markets, as well as in supermarkets. In all of these exchanges, the living animal is eclipsed, deadened, exploited, and discarded. The slaughterhouse is the scene, in short, of a dominative transaction similar to that enacted bloodlessly in the literary metaphor. The living animal (the vehicle) is objectified, cannibalized, and discarded, its living properties, its *anima* transferred into the entity *meat* (the tenor), which when consumed conveys those properties into the consumer. As Webb points out, "the linguistic eclipse of animals is correlated to (both preparing and made possible by) their annihilation in the meals we serve, so that practice and discourse shape each other" (87).

The aesthetics of modernity, established under Cartesian Kantian premises, which vaunts the human subject over the natural "object," remains an aesthetics of domination—whether in the field of science or in the cultural fields of art and literature, legitimizing the exploitation of animals for human use and pleasure—from slaughterhouses and laboratories to artistic production. Numerous postmodern ethicists have called for an alternative ethic that, as Jennifer Crawford puts it, "challenges the dualism and mastery that lie at the heart of modernity" (13). Enabling this ethical awareness is a reconceived epistemology, which Crawford terms "spiritually-engaged knowledge," the title of her 2005 groundbreaking book. Such knowledge requires "a radical empiricism that is not ideologically mediated" (119) and which "collapses subject-object duality" (4) in the dialogical mode of "conversation" (7)—with *who*s, not *what*s on both ends of the communicative line. Crawford's postmodern epistemology, which we develop further in Chapter 3, establishes the basis for an aesthetics of care.

---

[79]Carol J. Adams, *The Sexual Politics of Meat: A Feminist-Vegetarian Critical Theory* (New York: Continuum, 1990), p. 40.

2

Willa Cather's
aesthetic transitions

Perhaps the most extreme assertion of an equation between Cartesian scientific methodology and artistic practice was made by French writer Emile Zola in his celebrated essay "The Experimental Novel" (1880), which served as a kind of theoretical manifesto for the naturalist movement in literature, of which he was a prime member and which flourished in the latter nineteenth century in Europe and the early twentieth century in the United States.

Zola takes as his model Claude Bernard, a notorious exponent and practitioner of vivisection in the manner excoriated, as noted in Chapter 1, by early critics of Cartesian experimentation. In his *Introduction à l'étude de la médicine expérimentale* (1865), which "treats of practical experiments on living beings, of vivisection,"[1] and lays out a theoretical justification for his experimental method, vivisection (the cutting open of living, unanesthetized beings), Bernard explains that the object of his method "is to study phenomena in order to become their master" (as cited in Zola, 24)— echoing the dream of mastery articulated by Descartes, Bacon, and other early modern scientists, discussed in Chapter 1. The profile he adopts in his vivisection research, Bernard explains in a later work, *La Science expérimentale* (1878), is one of "conqueror and dominator" (*conquérant et dominateur*).[2]

In his essay, Zola repeatedly emphasizes that he sees literature as joining in this scientific enterprise of domination, echoing Bernard's

---

[1] Emile Zola, "The Experimental Novel," in *The Experimental Novel and Other Essays*, trans. Belle M. Sherman (New York: Haskell House, 1964), p. 4. Further references follow in the text.

[2] As cited in Vyvyan, *Pity and Anger*, p. 46. My translation from the French.

words at times almost verbatim. "Our goal is…to know the determinism of phenomena and to make ourselves master of these phenomena" (19), "to make ourselves masters of nature" (27), to "dominate and control" (31). Our "great object [is] the conquest of nature and the increase of man's power a hundredfold" (31). The matter of literature is analogized by Zola to the laboratory victim and the writer to the vivisector. "Continuing…the work of the physiologist…we [novelists] should operate on the characters…in the way the chemist and the physicist operate on inanimate beings, and as the physiologist operates on living beings" (18). Living beings are thus objectified as mechanisms upon which the writer *cum* vivisector operates. "Our naturalistic works…experiment on man, and…dissect piece by piece this human machinery" (25), subscribing thus to the Cartesian idea that inanimate and animate matters operate as machines. "The body of man is a machine, whose machinery can be taken apart and put together at the will of the experimenter" (16), as well as the writer.

Implicit in Zola's rhetoric of mastery is a gender inflection, a recapitulation of the age-old notion of the male master controlling/ redeeming abject feminized matter. "Here is our rôle as intelligent beings: to penetrate to the wherefore of things, to become superior to these things, and to reduce them to a condition of subservient machinery" (25). Indeed, Zola praises Bernard's work for its "manly" tone (41).

Willa Cather came of age as a writer during the heyday of naturalism. In her youth, she practiced vivisection in a "makeshift laboratory" as a kind of hobby in the basement of the family home in Red Cloud, Nebraska, where she dissected "toads and frogs" and eventually "cats and dogs."[3] In her 1890 high school graduation address, "Superstition versus Investigation," Cather defended the practice as progress that should not be impeded by regressive prejudices. "Has any one a right to destroy life for scientific purposes?" she asked.[4] Her answer was a resounding "yes." "The young orator" of the commencement address thus "placed herself in a tradition of experimenters…Bacon, Newton, and Harvey," seeing herself as "the descendent of [these] powerful forefathers" (O'Brien 113).

---

[3]O'Brien, *Willa Cather*, p. 89. Further references follow in the text.
[4]E. K. Brown, *Willa Cather: A Critical Biography* (New York: Knopf, 1953), p. 45.

Cather was "dressed as a boy" for the occasion (O'Brien 113), reflecting her youthful male identification. She often signed her name "William Cather M.D." and, in addition to emulating male scientists in her vivisection hobby, expressed a desire to become a doctor, which she saw as a commanding male role, whose opposite was the weak, enervated figure of the feminine patient, something she determined herself never to become.

> In choosing to be a doctor, the adolescent girl was thus ... choosing not to be a defective female patient, aspiring [rather] to the role she associated with power, health, and wholeness, shunning the one she associated with weakness, sickness, and mutilation. (O'Brien 93)

Not surprisingly, then, Cather's early conception of writing was not unlike that envisaged in Zola's "Experimental Novel," with which she was undoubtedly familiar. Though she disliked what she saw as Zola's fatalism and pessimism, she expressed admiration for "the virility of [Zola's] epic manner" (Cather's words, cited in O'Brien 153). In her first critical writings in the early 1890s, one finds, Sharon O'Brien notes, "a set of metaphoric equivalences—weapon/pen/penis—that reveal her equation of creativity both with paternity and with an aggressive, phallic masculinity" in which "the dissector's knife, the surgeon's scalpel and the writer's pen" are assimilated (148). Her early aesthetic theory was thus "infused with the late nineteenth-century ideology of masculinity" (151), imagining "the creative process ... as a struggle to subdue intractable subject matter" (151) or "the artist [as] a conqueror ... [and] the reader his colonized subject" (151); equating "technology's victory over nature" with "the 'virile' writer's praiseworthy triumph over recalcitrant subject matter" (389). It thus seems that the young Cather had taken over Zola's ideas almost whole cloth.

In the early years of the twentieth century, however, as Cather matured as a writer and as a person, her aesthetic began to shift away from this dominative conception toward an aesthetics of care. Heavily influenced in this respect by Sarah Orne Jewett, the clearest statement of her revised views came, fittingly, in her 1925 Preface to Jewett's *Country of the Pointed Firs*, which O'Brien classifies as the "major statement of the mature writer's aesthetics" (158).

Here we find a conception of the artist and artistic process that is diametrically opposed to the Zola model Cather earlier embraced. Instead of a male master sadistically dominating recalcitrant subject matter, forcing it into preconceived aesthetic shape, the writer now is seen in more conventionally "feminine" terms as one who engages dialectically with the material, giving in to it emotionally, following its lead, following its natural contours, allowing it to shape and inform the resulting artwork. The artist thus listens responsively to the subject matter, allowing its voice to help guide in the shaping of the art. Art thus is not disconnected and set apart as an aesthetic object, as in the Kantian view, but rather connects to, remains rooted in, the living material—be it people and their everyday life, animals, or the land—that it grows out of.

In her Jewett preface, Cather repudiates the "common fallacy" that the writer achieves greatness "by improving upon his subject-matter, by using his 'imagination' upon it and *twisting it* to suit his purpose."[5] The result of such an effort, she claims, is but a "brilliant sham...like a badly built and pretentious house" (7). Instead, she advocates, if the writer is to achieve anything worthwhile, it

> must be by giving *himself absolutely to his material*. And *this gift of sympathy* is his great gift...He *fades away into* the land and people of his heart, he dies of love only to be born again. (7, my emphasis)

Cather had intuited this concept in an early story "The Resurrection" (1897), where she described how in relating to the natural world—in this case a river—one experiences "*that intimate sympathy with inanimate nature*" that informs genuine literature.

> To all who follow [the river] *faithfully*, and not for gain but from inclination, the river gives a certain simpleness of life and freshness of feeling and *receptiveness of mind* not to be found among the money changers of the market-place...It gives him,

[5]Willa Cather, Preface to *The Country of the Pointed Firs and Other Stories* by Sarah Orne Jewett (New York: Doubleday Anchor, 1956), p. 7. Further references follow in the text.

no matter how unlettered he may be, something of that *intimate sympathy with inanimate nature that is the base of all poetry.*[6]

Unlike those who perceive the natural world instrumentally as a commodity to be exploited (as Lopahin in *The Cherry Orchard*), which requires a deadening of emotional, sympathetic connection, ethical and aesthetic appreciation is rooted, Cather maintains, in a receptive emotional interchange with an animate other. Jewett's stories, Cather writes in her preface, exemplify this quality: "they melt into the land and the life of the land until they are not stories at all, but life itself" (6). This seems to be the essence of Cather's new theory that art should remain connected, as Woolf puts it, like a spider's web, "attached to life at all four corners" (*Room* 43). Not just attached, in Cather's view, but infused with and informed by the vital spirit of living subject matter, rooted in particular place. "Jewett wrote of the people who grew out of the soil and the life of the country near her heart, not about exceptional individuals at war with their environment" (9).

To write on this level requires acute attentiveness that the writer "take strikt notice" (as Margaret Cavendish enjoined) of the details of her subject world. Then she tries "to get these conceptions down on paper exactly as they are to [her] and not in conventional poses supposed to reveal their character" (8). Here Cather thus urges the writer to brush aside what Griselda Pollock terms "mythic troping," ideological preconceptions, prefabricated organizing aesthetic shapes dictated by cultural norms: rather the writer should avoid such screens and get to the matter directly in as unmediated a fashion as possible.

Jewett was able to do this. "She early learned to love her country for what it was. What is more important, she saw it *as it was*" (10, my emphasis). Not only were her visual descriptions thus realistic, so too were her oral representation of the way people of rural Maine actually spoke—reflecting Jewett's local knowledge, her *mētis*.

The language her people speak…is a native tongue…made in…communities where language has been undisturbed

---

[6]Willa Cather, "A Resurrection," in *Willa Cather's Collected Short Fiction, 1892–1912*, rev. ed., ed. Virginia Faulkner (Lincoln: University of Nebraska Press, 1970), p. 433.

long enough to take on color and character from the nature and experiences of the people...imply[ing the community's]...history...its attitude toward the world, and its way of accepting life. (10).

In order to accurately transmit the character of this dialect, rooted as it is in a historically and geographically specific community and natural environment, the writer "must be able to think and feel in that speech—it is a gift from heart to heart" (10). The writer must thus be personally and emotionally immersed in and conversant with the world she transcribes.

Jewett herself advocated the kind of realism Cather here describes. On numerous occasions when giving advice to aspiring writers she would say, "My dear father used to say to me very often, 'Tell things just as they are!'...The great messages and discoveries of literature come to us, they *write us*, and we do not control them in a certain sense."[7] Jewett thus conceived of the writer as a transmitter of "things as they are" who imposes as little artifice as possible, allowing thus the material to help shape the art. In pertinent advice she gave directly to the young Willa Cather, Jewett counseled her to avoid shaping her material so as to conform to norms currently fashionable in popular journals.

Write it as it is, don't try to make it like this or that...Don't try to write the kind of short story that this or that magazine wants—write the truth, and let them take it or leave it.[8]

In other words, don't mold the material according to some preconceived notion of proper aesthetic form. Don't "write a '*story*,'" she counseled another writer, "but just *tell the thing*!" (*Letters*, Cary

---

[7]*Sarah Orne Jewett Letters*, enl. and rev. ed., ed. Richard Cary (Waterville, ME: Colby College Press, 1967), p. 52. In *The Environmental Imagination* Buell notes how numerous nineteenth-century women writers practiced this kind of detailed attention to the environment, which he terms "extrospection" using "zero-degree interference" (81). Such writers include, in addition to Jewett and Cather, especially Susan Fenimore Cooper and Celia Thaxter.

[8]Interview with Willa Cather, *Philadelphia Record*, August 9, 1913, in *The Kingdom of Art: Willa Cather's First Principles and Critical Statements, 1893–1896*, ed. Bernice Slote (Lincoln: University of Nebraska Press, 1966), p. 449.

ed. 120). Jewett here comes close to the New Materialist idea that the "things" have a vibrancy of their own that a writer by focused attention can perceive or intuit. (Elsewhere, Jewett expressed an animist view of nature, which I discuss further in Chapter 3.)

Cather's first novel *Alexander's Bridge* (1912) presents a protagonist who in many respects exemplifies the dominator artist extolled in the aesthetics of modernity, as envisaged by theorists from Kant to Zola. Bartley Alexander is a celebrated architect, a Faustian engineer, characterized as "a tamer of bridges" whose mind was "as hard and powerful as a catapult," having excelled in school "in higher mathematics."[9] He is, in short, a cross between a scientist and an artist. His projects involve developmental reforms such as "drainage and road-making" (197)—Enlightenment schemes of reshaping the natural environment, not unlike those of Tchekov's Lopahin. In the course of pursuing his successful career, however, he has become a feelingless robot himself, governed by commercial interests: "a powerful machine," a "mechanism useful to [commercial] society; [to] things that could be bought in the market" (299).

The central plot of the novel involves his infatuation with a reencountered youthful amour, the Irish actress Hilda Burgoyne, who exemplifies the passionate vitality missing in his life. (His wife Winifred is a proper Bostonian and their relationship lacks ardor.) However, what makes the work of interest in terms of Cather's evolving aesthetics is that the novel marks her final disavowal of the aesthetics of dominance she embraced early in her career, representing, as O'Brien notes, "a deconstruction of masculine aesthetics" (389).

The collapse of a fatally flawed bridge and Alexander's consequent death indicate that the aesthetics according to which the bridge work was constructed is itself fatally flawed, "a brilliant sham...like a badly built...house," which results from the artist's misguided attempt to "twist" nature "to suit his purpose" (as Cather explained in the Jewett preface). The use of logic and mathematics to control and reshape nature is thus doomed to fail because it does

---

[9]Willa Cather, "Alexander's Bridge," in *Willa Cather: Stories, Poems, and Other Writings*, ed. Sharon O'Brien (New York: Library of America, 1992), p. 287. Further references follow in the text.

not work *with* the natural world, negotiating with and incorporating its energies; rather it tries to control, "tame," and dominate them, coercing them according to man-made aesthetic design.

A powerfully symbolic image in the novel supports this interpretation. Not long before his death, Alexander reminisces about the moment in his youth when he walked on his first bridge.

And always there was the sound of rushing water underneath, the sound which, more than anything else meant death; the wearing away of things under the impact of physical forces which men could direct but never circumvent or diminish. (339)

He comes to the realization that "under the moon, under the cold splendid stars, there were only those two things...death and love, the rushing river and his burning heart" (340).

Alexander's epiphany comes too late, however, for the aesthetics under which he has operated throughout his career denies both love and "death, the only thing as strong as love" (340). In other words, the hubris of Enlightenment aesthetics is the belief that one can control and reshape life and nature according to artificial formulae, as Alexander has done with his bridge and dam-building. But such an aesthetic fails to deal with the "rushing water," entropy, mortality, and the passions of the body. Instead, it distances itself from them, casting them as *other* against which it sets itself as master and dominator. Such a modality is doomed to fail, Cather implies in this novel. In denying death, the aesthetics of modernity becomes, ironically, an aesthetics *of* death. In subsequent works, Cather will embrace an aesthetics of life, which incorporates rather than attempts to control "the rushing water," embodying its resurrectory energies.

In *The Song of the Lark* (1915), one of the first novels Cather wrote under the influence of her new aesthetic theory, art is reconceived as a vehicle for disclosing what Virginia Woolf called "moments of being" that inhere in, as a sacred dimension of, the everyday and the natural world. The novel concerns the growth and development of a woman artist, Thea Kronberg, an aspiring opera singer. Pursuing her career as a "new woman" in the big city (Chicago), Thea becomes dispirited and discouraged by the careerist path she must follow in order to achieve success. In this she resembles Bartley Alexander who also became a "mechanism" in a reified commercial system. With her enthusiasm on the wane and seeking reinspiration, Thea visits Panther Canyon, an ancient Cliff Dwellers settlement, in the southwestern United States. There through meditating on the lives and art of these premodern peoples, she comes to conceive of art and her profession in a new way and is thereby reinspired to continue her life-calling as a singer.

> On the first day Thea climbed the water trail she began to have intuitions about the women who had worn the path, and who had spent so great a part of their lives going up and down it. She found herself trying to walk as they must have walked, with a feeling in her feet and knees and loins which she had never known before...She could feel the weight of an Indian baby hanging on her back as she climbed.[10]

Thus, through a kind of bodily empathy—through the "gift of sympathy"—Thea seems to almost merge with the ancient women, absorbing thereby their ways of being. She bathes regularly in a stream where they washed, immersing herself thus in its water, which expressed "a continuity of life that reached back into the old time." The bathing has a "ceremonial" aspect, part of the "ritualistic" character of the canyon itself (304). Thus, by direct connection with a premodern community that she envisages as in sync with natural rhythms, Thea is reborn, baptized into a new way of seeing and being and a new artistic creed.

Her aesthetic epiphany occurs while meditating on the Indian women's pottery, which she sees as itself directly connected to and infused with the natural world—unlike the Kantian conception of art as a discrete, dominative reshaping—"twisting"—of that world. Their pottery, she reflected, was "their most direct appeal to water, the envelope and sheathe of the precious element itself" (303). "What was any art," she thought, "but an effort to make a sheath, a mould in which to imprison for a moment the shining, elusive element which is life itself...The Indian women had held it in their jars" (304). Art is thus seen as connected to and infused with evanescent "moments of being"—"shining, elusive...life itself," embedded in the Indian women's art. As O'Brien notes, in the

---

[10]Willa Cather, *The Song of the Lark* (Lincoln: University of Nebraska Press, 1978), p. 302. Further references follow in the text.

Southwest Indian culture Cather saw the "dichotomy between 'art' and 'life' erased" (414). The Indians "seem not to have struggled to overcome their environment...They accommodated themselves to it, interpreted it and made it personal...they built themselves into it" (415). In other words, they worked *with* nature, not against it, in what Val Plumwood has characterized as a "collaborative" mode in which the "agencies" of the natural world and its creatures are acknowledged and engaged ("Concept" 125, 130).

The Indian women's pottery is then an integrated women's art of "everyday use," as termed by Alice Walker in her celebrated story (1973) of that title where the art in question is a quilt and where the pivotal question is what constitutes aesthetic value.[11] Is an old family quilt of value as an autotelic art "object" that can be hung on the wall of a museum and is worth big bucks as a commodity in the commercial art market? Or is it of value because it is imbued with personal and local history, because it has a story of its own—a spiritual vitality—and is embedded in a familiar everyday place where it is used to sheathe and warm the body, an object of care?

The former view is that of Dee, a young African-American woman who has left her rural home for the city where she has learned the ways of modernity. She returns home as an outside observer, framing her old house and her mother aesthetically in terms of commodity values. On arrival, for example, she takes photos of the house and of her mother knowing they will be seen by others of her urban class as "quaint" commodities. The mother resists this objectification which she implicitly feels Dee is imposing upon her and her world.

The pivotal clash in the story is over the old quilt. Dee looks at it—along with other craft items in the house, such as a butter churn—with Kantian eyes. She sees it as an autotelic art object that has prize commodity value; it is something to be hung on the wall. Her mother, on the other hand, sees it as an object of everyday use, one that is infused with personal, emotional value—in this sense like Madame Ranevsky's cherry orchard; therein lies its significance. She therefore decides to give the quilt to her other daughter who appreciates its family history and plans to use it on her bed. Thus,

---

[11]Alice Walker, "Everyday Use," in *Women and Fiction*, ed. Susan Cahill, pp. 364–72 (New York: Mentor, 1975).

Walker implicitly rejects in this story the idea of art as a discrete masterpiece to be isolated from the real world—and therefore rejects a body of aesthetic theory that since Kant has dominated Western thinking. Rather she proposes an art that is embedded in the everyday, that is infused with personal family and local history, and whose interest lies in these so-called adventitious matters.

Walker amplifies this idea in her essay "In Search of Our Mother's Gardens" (1974), which considers her mother's garden as a work of art: "Whatever rocky soil she landed on, she turned into a garden. A garden so brilliant with colors, so original in its design, so magnificent with life and creativity, that to this day people drive by our house ... and ask to stand and walk among my mother's art." For her mother, Walker realizes, "being an artist has still been a daily part of her life."[12]

In an article on "non-colonising" gardening, Val Plumwood proposes the model of an "adaptive garden," one that works in "negotiation or dialogical relationship with surrounding elements" in "collaboration with nature and place."[13] One can posit that Walker's mother's garden—like Tchekov's cherry orchard—was of this type. Such a garden allows and enables indigenous flora, recycles vegetal matter as compost, is organic, welcomes wildlife who happen to enter the garden area, and does not excise "weeds," but works with and around spontaneous growth. Of course, we don't know if Walker's mother hewed to these policies but as a rural African-American gardener in the early to mid-twentieth-century South, she might well have used these traditional practices.

Thus, in "Everyday Use" and the garden essay, Alice Walker articulates a nondominative aesthetic theory complementary to Plumwood's eco-ethics, where art remains embedded in and arises out of conversation with the contingent, everyday world. Quilts, for example, are often made from pieces of old dresses or curtains—in other words, of recycled, not new material. Different patches have different histories and evoke different emotional memories: a prom dress evokes one set, Grandmother's apron another. This cluster of memories goes into the aesthetic experience of a family quilt. The

---

[12]Alice Walker, "In Search of Our Mothers' Gardens," *Ms.* 2, no. 11 (May 1974):105.

[13]Val Plumwood, "Decolonising Australian Gardens: Gardening and the Ethics of Place," *Australian Humanities Review* 36 (July 2005):3, 2, 1.

artistic praxis envisaged is one that does not deny the qualitative essence of the environmental "material" but honors its "voice." Art is not extracted from the environmental material but works with it in a dialogical fashion, enabling a recognition of those qualitative moments of being, of beauty, that inhere in the everyday world. Under an aesthetics of care, then, while art inevitably modifies the natural environment, as in a garden, a quilt, Indian pottery, it does so by reworking the natural material in such a way as to preserve or enhance its inherent character or value, its local web of relations, and, insofar as possible, without harming the natural material or context. Art is not transcendent; it does not deny death, but remains rather part of the mortal process. The mother's quilt in "Everyday Use" will be worn out; it will not achieve immortal status but, like all women's domestic craft, will erode in the process of time. Yet, the moments of beauty and meaning captured in this work remain as a "negative critique" (to use Adorno's term) of the reified world of commodity exchange, as a utopian glimpse of an other, sacred, ontological world, which Woolf holds is brought to life by the artist. Homemade quilts and pottery are not, therefore, just deanimated mechanistic *objects* hanging in space; they are aesthetic *subjects*, embedded in place, identified and defined by attentive love.

In a later novel, *One of Ours* (1922), Cather introduces an episode concerning quilts similar to that in Walker's story. Here a servant woman in the Wheeler family, Mahailey, refuses to bequeath her mother's quilts to one of the Wheeler sons, Ralph, knowing that as an entrepreneurial capitalist he will sell them as commodities. As in Walker's story, the quilts and Mahailey represent the domestic world of personal relationship, of care, as opposed to the capitalist public world of commercial transaction.

The protagonist of the novel, Claude Wheeler, is like Dee in the Walker story, an ambitious youth who leaves home to attend the state university, a site, like the British Museum, of the knowledges of modernity. There Claude learns that scholarship is an exercise of the logos, of rationalist deduction; one must purge it of personal qualitative feelings. In working on a paper on Joan of Arc, Claude prides himself "that he had kept all personal feelings out."[14]

---

[14]Willa Cather, *One of Ours* (New York: Knopf, 1922), p. 61. Further references follow in the text.

Claude finds, however, "that after all his conscientious study he really knew little more about the Maid of Orleans than when he first heard of her from his mother, one day when he was a boy" (62). He found "a picture of her in armour, in an old book," and had taken it "down to the kitchen where his mother was making apple pies ... and while she went on rolling out the dough and fitting it to the pans, she told him the story" (62). Thus, it is not Enlightenment knowledge derived from the objective modes of university learning that Claude finds most powerful; rather it is the tradition of oral feminine storytelling that has remained persuasive in his memory.

A subsequent novel, *The Professor's House* (1925), amplifies the idea that knowledge and art are not something discrete and strained off of everyday familial matter; rather they are rooted in it, intertwined in a web of relationship with it; and infused with its local qualitative energies.

The central issue in the first section of the novel is Professor Godrey St. Peter's reluctance to leave his old study, which is located in an attic he shares with his wife's seamstress, Augusta, who stores her dressmaker forms therein. A successful scholar, St. Peter has bought a new house with some award money, but when the time comes to move, he finds he can't leave his old niche. He realizes that his world and Augusta's, however disparate, have by circumstance grown together. "I see," he tells her, "we shall have some difficulty in separating our life work, Augusta. We've kept our papers together a long while now."[15] St. Peter's attitude reflects respect for things "as they are," as they have happened to fall together historically, not wishing to reorganize them according to logical schema.

In a later conversation with Augusta, she happens to mention that the "Blessed Virgin composed the Magnificat" "just as soon as the angel had announced to her that she would be the mother of our Lord" (100). The notion elates St. Peter and he repeats it to himself: "(Surely she had said that the Blessed Virgin sat down and composed the Magnificat!)" (100). The idea appeals because of the unmediated character of the creation process it assumes. The creation of the song came directly from Mary, a prime participant in the subject matter; art is here seen as directly connected to and an

---

[15]Willa Cather, *The Professor's House* (New York: Knopf, 1925), p. 23. Further references follow in the text.

unobstructed outgrowth of the event and personality it expresses. Nor are critical categories imposed to reconceive the process. Rather the flow from actual event to art is unimpeded.

In reflecting on his attachment to his attic world, St. Peter recollects how sounds from the domestic world below had filtered up, helping to keep him in touch with that world and thereby interweaving his work with its matter.

Just as, when Queen Mathilde was doing the long tapestry now shown at Bayeux,—working her chronicles of the deeds of knights and heroes,—alongside the big pattern of dramatic action she and her women carried the little playful pattern of birds and beasts that are a story in themselves: so, to him, the most important chapters of his story were interwoven with personal memories (101).

Thus, just as Queen Mathilde surreptitiously slipped into the Bayeux tapestry, "the little playful pattern of birds and beasts"— the "little stories of everyday domestic existence" that Hegel held in contempt (Schor 32), requiring their elision in the construction of great art—so the professor realizes his best work is interwoven with domestic matter. Like Claude Wheeler's study of Joan of Arc, the professor finds that "his most important chapters" are those informed with the personal.

That Cather saw her own work in similar terms is clear from several comments she made about it. In a recently published letter dated November 28, 1918, shortly after the publication of her novel *My Ántonia*, for example, she complained about a critic's characterization of the novel, that "it exists in…an atmosphere of pure beauty." "Nonsense," Cather exclaimed, "it's the atmosphere of my grandmother's kitchen and nothing else."[16] In an earlier (also recently published) letter, she remarked of *The Song of the Lark*: "If I had written a preface to the book I would have said '…I don't want to be 'literary.' Here are a lot of people I used to know and love; sit down and let me tell you about them" (letter of January 31, 1916).[17]

---

[16]*The Selected Letters of Willa Cather*, ed. Andrew Jewell and Janis Stout (New York: Knopf, 2013), p. 261.
[17]In ibid., p. 215.

Literature thus conceived is a matter of domestic oral storytelling, which grows naturally out of the domestic matter it transcribes. Cather indeed once explained that she wrote *O Pioneers!* (1913), the first novel she composed under Jewett's clear influence, as if she were telling it to her Maine mentor.

> I dedicated O Pioneers! to Miss Jewett because I had talked over some of the characters in it with her one day in Manchester, and in this book I tried to tell the story of the people as truthfully and simply as if I were telling it to her by word of mouth.[18]

While the connection of art to domestic matter is, as we have seen, a key issue in *One of Ours* and *The Professor's House*, in what is perhaps Cather's greatest work, *O Pioneers!* (1913), the central issue is how humans may nondominatively know, relate to, and interconnect with, the natural world. That the *mētis* or local knowledges practiced in the domestic world may serve as a model for an eco-sensitive epistemology is at the heart of Cather's view. For, as O'Brien notes, in contrast to Bartley Alexander, Alexandra Bergson, the protagonist of *O Pioneers!* "achieves her creative designs by letting them emerge from the soil not by seeking to subdue nature by force" (392).

Alexandra's mentor in this respect is Crazy Ivar, an eccentric Norwegian hermit who lives in a sod hut, a "clay bank," not far from Alexandra's farm, dwelling therein "without defiling the face of nature any more than the coyote that had lived there before him."[19] Ivar espouses an animist religion, saying the Bible "seemed truer" in his natural environment, where one senses the presence of living, nonhuman radiance.

> If one stood in the doorway of his cave, and looked at the rough land, the smiling sky, the curly grass white in the hot sunlight; if one listened to the rapturous song of the lark, the drumming of the quail, the burr of the locust against the vast silence, one understood what Ivar meant. (381)

---

[18]Interview, "Philadelphia Record," August 9, 1913, in *Kingdom of Art*, ed. Slote, p. 448.
[19]Willa Cather, *O Pioneers!* (Boston: Houghton Mifflin, 1941), p. 36. Further references follow in the text.

Ivar has a sympathetic understanding of animals and is often consulted as a kind of unofficial veterinarian in the region, because of his ability to enter into their subjective points of view. When a neighbor's horse

> ate green corn and swelled up most as big as the water-tank[,] he petted her just like you do your cats...he kept patting her and groaning as if he had pain himself, and saying, "there now, sister, that's easier, that's better!" (33)

His doctoring works. "He cured their horses," Alexandra notes, "he understands animals" (33), giving as another example, a situation where Ivar removed the injured horn from a panicked cow, showing how his caring aura managed to pacify the terrified animal.

> Didn't I see him take the horn off the Berquist's cow when she had torn it loose and went crazy? She was tearing all over the place, knocking against things. And at last she ran out on the roof of the old dugout and her legs went through and there she stuck, bellowing. Ivar came running with his white bag, and the moment he got to her she was quiet and let him saw her horn off and daub the place with tar. (34)

Alexandra's younger brother, Emil, who has been listening intently to this story, responds empathetically. "His face reflecting the sufferings of the cow," he asks, "and then didn't it hurt any more?" Alexandra pats him reassuringly. "No, not any more. And in two days they could use her milk again" (34).

Ivar relates to the animals empathetically as fellow subjects. In describing a seagull who had recently visited his pond he observes,

> My! What a voice she had! She came in the afternoon and kept flying about the pond and screaming until dark. She was in trouble of some sort, but I could not understand her. She was going over to the other ocean, maybe, and did not know how far it was. She was afraid of never getting there. She was more mournful than our birds here; she cried in the night...Next morning, when the sun rose, I went out to take her food, but she flew up in the sky and went on her way. (40)

Emil wants to know, "Do the birds know you will be kind to them, Ivar? Is that why so many come?" Ivar responds by presenting the birds' point of view.

See, little brother, they have come from a long way, and they are very tired. From up there where they are flying our country looks dark and flat. They must have water to drink and to bathe in before they can go on with their journey. They look this way and that, and far below them they see something shining, like a piece of glass set in the dark earth. This is my pond. They come to it and are not disturbed. Maybe I sprinkle a little corn. They tell the other birds, and next year more come this way. They have roads up there, as we have down here. (42–43)

Needless to say, Ivar is a vegetarian (43) and abhors hunting and killing birds and animals. "I hope you boys never shoot wild birds?" (40). He enjoins Alexandra's brothers, and he refuses to allow guns on his property.

Alexandra consults with Ivar about how she should keep her pigs. She's worried because many neighbors' pigs are dying. Ivar says it's because they're kept in "a stinking pen... I tell you, sister, the hogs in this country are put upon!" (44). He counsels her to give them a larger space to live in—"a little sorghum patch, maybe?" (44), provide them with a shed for shade, give them plenty of clean water and feed. While Alexandra's brothers ridicule such attentiveness— "She'll be for having the pigs sleep with us, next" (45)—Alexandra proceeds to follow Ivar's advice and provides the pigs with a more humane living environment.

From the point of view of a feminist ethic of care[20] Alexandra's raising of pigs and cows, presumably for slaughter (though Cather doesn't mention this), is, of course, problematic. However, at least she does display a caring attitude when she adapts her treatment so as to be responsive to the animals' own needs and habits. And the fact that Cather gives such prominent attention to Ivar's animal-sensitive vegetarianism provides a critical perspective on

---

[20]See Josephine Donovan, "The Voice of Animals: A Response to Recent French Care Theory in Animal Ethics," *Journal of Critical Animal Studies* 11, no. 1 (2013):8–23.

commercial farming practices that commodify animals, which he implicitly deplores, leading Alexandra, as seen, to modify her own practices.

Later, when Ivar—stigmatized by society as an uncivilized hermit, a wild man-outcast—is threatened with confinement in an asylum—another institution of modernity that condemns and erases eccentric particularities ("they have built the asylum for people who are different, and they will not even let us live in the holes with the badgers" Ivar says [93]), Alexandra takes him in and gives him a place on her farm, thus embracing difference and including it within her fold.

Alexandra's philosophy of life is pragmatic and dialogical; that is, she works with people, as well as with the land and environment in a responsive way. Her praxis is one which involves working with one's materials *as they are* and adapting to contingencies *as they arise* in an ad hoc, trial-and-error manner. In explaining her decision to put up a silo, which her brothers question, she says, "Well, the only way we can find out is to try ... Lou [her brother] can learn by my mistakes and I can learn by his" (89). She is also willing to compromise. In an earlier confrontation with a brother she refuses to run over him but pulls back when he protests. But when she backs off, he relents (69), thus she achieves her purpose nonviolently (and nonmanipulatively, because her backing off is sincere, not a manipulative ruse). Later, dealing with her neighbor Frank, who is threatening to sue a woman whose hogs keep getting into his wheat, Alexandra counsels a non-confrontational approach, namely that he simply fix the neighbor's fence for her: "I've found it sometimes pays to mend other peoples' fences" (140), she observes.

Alexandra's approach to farming is likewise nonconfrontational. It is not a matter of conquering matter, twisting it to one's purpose, but rather adapting and responding to it, following its contours where they go, letting it evolve in its own way. When after many years of such labor, her farm is rich and productive, Alexandra claims it was just a matter of letting the land express itself. "We had n't any of us much to do with it ... The land did it ... nobody knew how to work it right," but once we did, "all at once it worked itself" (116). Perhaps her success is due to the fact that "for the first time ... since that land emerged from the waters of geologic ages, a human face was set toward it with love and yearning" (65). Alexandra's attitude of attentive love toward the land is one of ecosympathy.[21]

> She had never known before how much the country meant to her. The chirping of the insects down in the long grass had been like the sweetest music. She had felt as if her heart were hiding down there, somewhere, with the quail and the plover and all the little wild things that crooned or buzzed in the sun. (71)

Alexandra's attitude (and perhaps Cather's) thus is animist, like Ivar's. The land and its creatures are subjects whom she loves. It is a nondominative caring relationship sustained by a chord of sympathy. For Alexandra is really an artist operating according to an aesthetic of care: "You feel that...it is in the soil that she expresses herself best" (84). There were days in which she was so "close to the flat, fallow world about her" that she "felt...in her own body the joyous germination of the soil" (204).

One of her happiest memories concerns a solitary wild duck, whom she and Emil happened to notice one day, "swimming and diving and preening her feathers, disporting herself very happily in the flickering light and shade" (204). "No living thing had ever seemed to Alexandra as beautiful as that wild duck" (205). While there is a suggestion here of a metaphoric connection, that Alexandra is like the duck, living happily in solitude, it is important to realize that the duck really is a duck, and Alexandra relates to her emotionally and empathetically—feeling her beauty, manifesting thus an aesthetics of care.

As a boy, Emil was "tender-hearted" (54), as we have seen. Indeed, the opening scene of the novel concerns five-year-old Emil's despair over his frightened freezing kitten who has climbed a telegraph pole and refuses to come down. As the cat is rescued, a neighbor, the Bohemian girl Marie Tovesky, joins him in warming her up (11). Marie remains "tender-hearted" into adulthood, retaining an

---

[21]In "Biophilia and the Conservation Ethic," in *The Biophilia Hypothesis*, ed. Stephen R. Kellert and Edward O. Wilson (Washington, DC: Island Press, 1993), p. 31. E. O. Wilson claims that there is an "innately emotional affiliation of human beings to other living organisms"—a "biophilia." Alexandra's feelings seem to reflect this connection.

animist empathy with wild creatures and nature. She tells Emil that in the old country "Bohemians...were tree worshippers before the missionaries came" (152) and that although "a good Catholic," she retains an animist faith. "I think I could get along with caring for trees, if I hadn't anything else...I feel as if this tree knows everything I ever think of when I sit here. When I come back to it, I never have to remind it of anything; I begin just where I left off" (153).

Emil, however, in his progress into adulthood seems to have left his tender-heartedness behind, following a typical male maturation process which, as I argue in Chapter 8, involves learning to accept and practice animal sacrifice. In a pivotal scene with Marie, Emil shoots five ducks. At first, Marie "laughed delightedly" (127) but when Emil brings the ducks to her, "dangling [them] by their feet" and dropping them in her apron, "her face changed" (128) as she realizes what they've done, belatedly empathizing with the birds.

I didn't think [she says]. I hate to see them when they are first shot. They were having such a good time, and we've spoiled it all for them...Ivar's right about wild things. They're too happy to kill. You can tell just how they felt when they flew up. They were scared, but they did n't really think anything could hurt them. (128)

The scene seems to foreshadow the violent deaths Marie and Emil are to endure at the hands of Frank, Marie's husband, who shoots them under the mulberry tree Marie had earlier related to animistically. In the classical Pyramis and Thisbe legend, which this episode recapitulates, the blood of the dead lovers is absorbed by the tree, turning its white berries to red. In Cather's handling, "the white mulberries that had fallen in the night...were covered with dark stain" (268).

But...the darkened mulberries...told only half the story. Above Marie and Emil, two white butterflies...were fluttering in and out among the interlacing shadows; diving and soaring, now close together, now far apart; and in the long grass by the fence the last wild roses of the year opened their pink hearts to die. (270)

With these resurrectory images, Cather connects death with the agricultural cycle of the seasons, the eternal return. Marie herself had earlier intuited that in the depth of winter, "down under the frozen crusts, at the roots of the trees, the secret of life was still safe, warm as the blood in one's heart; and the spring would come again! Oh, it would come again!" (202).

Alexandra herself, when her father died at the beginning of the novel, imagines going into the grave with him and "let[ting] the grass grow back over everything" (16). And so Cather concludes this great novel with a final image of death and resurrection, the Demeter-Persephone cycle, of life emerging from death.[22]

> Fortunate country, that is one day to receive hearts like Alexandra's into its bosom, to give them out again in the yellow wheat, in the rustling corn, in the shining eyes of youth! (309)

---

[22]See Josephine Donovan, *After the Fall: The Demeter-Persephone Myth in Wharton, Cather, and Glasgow* (University Park, PA: Pennsylvania State University Press, 1989).

3

The aesthetics of care

The aesthetics of care is rooted in an alternative epistemology to the dominative "I-it," "sado-dispassionate" conception offered in the Cartesian–Kantian constructions of Enlightenment modernity. Art and literature created under an aesthetics of care are conceived through a participatory epistemology—an "I-thou" relationship, in which the natural world and its multivarious creatures are recognized as subjects who have stories of their own. Such subjects are qualitatively particularized, embedded in specific locales— their unique physical bodies and historically and geographically specific environments. The knowledge of these subjects' ways of being requires experiential attentiveness to their unique shapes, expressions, and patterns, as well as to their contextual habitats. It requires listening to their diverse voices. Because it operates through what Simone Weill termed "attentive love," which *sees* the qualitative value in the subjects being treated (value elided in Kantian culling aesthetics), an aesthetics of care enables ethical concern for those subjects.

Aesthetics in this construction requires emotional interaction with living entities—alive agents, hearing those voices, responding to them with ethical care, and transmitting their realities with minimal intervention. Such conversations and knowledges come about through the varied practices of "attentive love"—empathy, sympathy, wit(h)nessing subjects' experiences. A new and different participatory form of empathic *mimesis* is called for, one that, as Jennifer Crawford specified, "collapses subject-object duality in conversation," "challeng[ing] the dualism and mastery that lie at the heart of modernity" (4, 13), and affording access to a sacred, other dimension, without the use of violent sacrifice. Such a mode, which Theodor Adorno labels "mimetic comportment" in *Aesthetic Theory*, requires, he notes, "an attitude toward reality distinct from the fixated antithesis of subject and object."[1]

Ironically, classical physics and Cartesian conceptions—upon which the dominative aesthetics of modernity is based—have been undermined from within science itself by discoveries in quantum physics. Cartesian constructions nevertheless persist in behaviorist biology, zoology, and the social sciences, as well as in common law and popular culture, which continue to construe animate life as inanimate and mechanistic, as objects available for human exploitation.

In the early twentieth century, however, the premises of classical physics and its attendant "I-it" epistemology were destabilized and disrupted by new knowledges of subatomic particle behavior, which challenged the traditional distinction between subject and object, observer and observed. In particular, physicists came to realize that the act of measurement or observation causes the quantum wave-particle phenomenon to "collapse" into a definite state. "The act of measurement ... forces a system into a definite state and place at a given time ... [such that] the initial mixed wave function 'collapses' into a precise state,"[2] a phenomenon that is referred to as the "collapse of the wave function." Before the "collapse," the wave function—a mathematical equation—indicates but probabilities of time and location; it is only upon interaction with the measuring instrument and observer that a precise entity in time and space is determinable (or exists).

That the observing self and the measuring instruments are necessarily implicated thus in the material being observed or measured is the so-called Copenhagen Interpretation of quantum physics proposed by Danish physicist Niels Bohr. In his "Discussion

---

[1] Theodore W. Adorno, *Aesthetic Theory*, ed. Gretel Adorno and Rolf Tiedemann, trans. Robert Hullot-Kentor (Minneapolis: University of Minnesota Press, 1997), p. 110. Further references follow in the text.

[2] Leon M. Lederman and Christopher T. Hill, *Quantum Physics for Poets* (Amherst, NY: Prometheus, 2011), pp. 189, 225; see also Karen Barad, *Meeting the Universe Half-Way: Quantum Physics and the Entanglement of Matter* (Durham, NC: Duke University Press, 2007), p. 280. Further references to Barad follow in the text. Portions of this discussion appear in my article "Participatory Epistemology, Sympathy, and Animal Ethics," in *Ecofeminism*, ed. Adams and Gruen, pp. 75–90.

with Einstein" (1949) Bohr explained, "*we are just faced with the impossibility, in the analysis of quantum effects, of drawing any sharp separation between an independent behavior of atomic objects and their interaction with the measuring instruments which serve to define the conditions under which phenomena occur.*"[3] As Karen Barad explains in *Meeting the Universe Half-Way: Quantum Physics and the Entanglement of Matter and Meaning* (2007), there is an "ontological entanglement [between] objects and agencies of observation" (309). "Our knowledge-making practices are material enactments that contribute to, and are part of, the phenomena we describe" (249). In short, "we are not outside observers of the world ... [W]e are part of that nature we seek to understand" (184). Quantum physics therefore requires a "participatory epistemology,"[4] because an observer's consciousness *participates* in the realization or emergence of a particular reality (*realization* in two senses—the becoming real of the entity [ontological] and the understanding of and knowledge of the entity [epistemological]).

A pioneering atomic physicist, Sir Arthur Eddington, maintained that these quantum enigmas are due to the fact that physical sciences are based upon "measures" that register "measurable" phenomena—that is, material phenomena that have features— objective data—that can be detected by instruments and observation. "The physical atom," in other words, "is ... a schedule of pointer readings." But, he specifies further, "the schedule is ... attached to an *unknown background*."[5] What we detect through our instruments and observations are "measure-groups resting on a shadowy background that lies outside the scope of physics" (152). Mathematics and physics are "extracted out of the broader reality," which is not physical but rather mental. "It is in this background that our own mental consciousness lies" (282); indeed "consciousness has its roots in this background" (330).

Simone Weil in her little-known essays on quantum physics came to a similar conclusion. In "Classical Science and After"

---

[3] As cited in Barad, *Meeting*, p. 308.
[4] Christian de Quincey, *Radical Nature: Rediscovering the Soul of Matter* (Montpelier, VT: Invisible Cities Press, 2002), p. 18. Further references follow in the text.
[5] A. S. Eddington, *The Nature of the Physical World* (New York: Macmillan, 1928), p. 259, emphasis added. Further references follow in the text.

["La Science et nous"] (1941), Weil invokes the concept of attention (later developed in her ethical theorizing about "attentive love") to claim that physics fails to pay attention to the "negligible," which is "nothing other than what has to be neglected in order to construct physics,"[6] "for physics is essentially the application of mathematics to nature at the price of an infinite error" (34). In another undated piece, "Fragment: Foundation of a New Science" ["Du fondement d'une science nouvelle"], Weil returns to "the notion, fundamental in physics, of the *negligible*." "[S]omething is missing in these images [detected by scientific instruments]—and that something...is the presence of the whole surrounding universe," for the images "are not existing things but abstractions."[7] "To the Enlightenment," thus, as Horkheimer and Adorno put it, "that which does not reduce to numbers...becomes illusion" (*Dialectic* 7). Eddington, however, maintains that the background behind the objective images detected by science is real and is accessible through the mental phenomenon of consciousness. "[C]onsciousness" is "the only avenue to what I have called *intimate* knowledge of the reality behind the symbols of science" (340). There is, in other words, both Weil and Eddington maintain, a nonphysical realm of existence to which all conscious creatures connect and through which they may communicate; "behind the cotton wool," Virginia Woolf divined, "is a hidden pattern" ("Sketch" 70).

More recently, twenty-first-century physicist Lee Smolin remarks how the mathematical model necessarily abstracts and extracts from the complexities of the natural environment, eliminating all that does not fit into the simplifying quantitative grid: "to apply mathematics to a physical system, we must first...isolate it and...separate it out from the complexity of motions that is the real universe."[8] A similar process of extraction occurs, as we have seen, in Kantian aesthetics.

In his classic *A Mathematician's Apology* (1940), G. H. Hardy established, indeed, how integral mathematics and Kantian

[6]Simone Weil, "Classical Science and After," in *On Science, Necessity, and the Love of God*, ed. and trans. Richard Rees (London: Oxford University Press, 1968), p. 31.
[7]Simone Weil, "Fragment: Foundation of a New Science," in *On Science*, ed. and trans. Rees, p. 81.
[8]Lee Smolin, *Time Reborn* (Boston: Houghton Mifflin, 2013), p. 38. Further references follow in the text.

aesthetics are to one another. "A mathematician [is] a maker of patterns... [B]eauty and seriousness [are] the criteria by which his patterns should be judged";[9] Thus, "great mathematics" is defined by the fact that it has "permanent aesthetic value" (chap. 25). Significantly, Hardy notes how mathematical beauty eliminates the anomalous, the particular, the inadventitious: in a beautiful pattern "there are no complications of detail... We do not want... 'variations'... [or] 'enumeration of cases'" (chap. 18). But as Smolin warns, "simplicity and beauty... are the signs not of truth but of a well-constructed approximate model of a limited domain of a phenomenon" (112).

Other leading contemporary theorists have likewise come to the conclusion that there is an invisible communicative informational medium that cannot be explained by classical physics. Jane Bennett, for example, the New Materialist theorist, proposes that there is "a subterranean 'sympathy' between bodies that we normally segregate: life/matter, person/thing, animal/vegetable/mineral" ("Powers" 259). Molecular biochemist Candace Pert in *Molecules of Emotion* (1997) asserts that chemical molecules attach to physical cells in the body and vibrate information which stimulates an emotional response, thus connecting mind and matter. But this information transmission occurs outside traditional realms of matter and mind, "some realm beyond the physical,"[10] "a whole new realm... which science has yet to explore" (261). "The mind, the consciousness, consisting of information, exists first, prior to the physical world, which is... an out-picturing of consciousness" (257).

This nonphysical, nonquantifiable, non-objectifiable realm is expressed through *qualia*—all the properties Descartes dispensed with in his analysis of bees' wax. A still unexplained phenomenon in the Cartesian–Newtonian epistemology of classical physics is how *qualia* (qualities experienced by a subject, such as colors, tastes,

---

[9]G. H. Hardy, *A Mathematician's Apology* (1940) (Cambridge: Cambridge University Press, 2012), chap. 13 (no pages given). Further references follow in the text.
[10]Candance B. Pert, *Molecules of Emotion: Why You Feel the Way You Feel* (New York: Scribner's, 1997), p. 257. Further references follow in the text. French theorist Bruno Latour uses the term *plasma* for this vast subterranean unarticulated reality which occasionally takes form. See Graham Harman, *Prince of Networks: Bruno Latour and Metaphysics* (Melbourne: re. press, 2009), p. 133. On this "silent background" also see Graham Harman, *Tool-Being: Heidegger and the Metaphysics of Objects* (Peru, IL: Open Court, 2002), p. 5 et passim.

feelings, etc.) emerge from or relate to *quanta*, objective physical properties. Since how *qualia* are transmitted via inexpressive physical objects is not explained in classical physics, such transmission implies an *other* nonphysical medium through which such communication occurs, as Pert suggests. I have argued elsewhere that ethical knowledge is conveyed through what I called *emotional qualia*,[11] which come alive or become apparent in communicative encounters between living entities. Just as qualitative properties, such as taste, smell, or feel, of a physical entity arise or emerge when a subject encounters that object, so emotional qualia emerge in one's encounter with another subject. The knowledge thus conveyed necessarily includes an ethical dimension. A dog's whine, a cow's bellow, a horse's shying, a spider's flight, a snake's flinch, a bird's screech are emotional qualia whose ethical message is unmistakable.

In his *magnum opus, Negative Dialectics*, which elaborates his critique of the dominative modes of Enlightenment epistemology, Theodor Adorno proposes that *qualia* may be appreciated through the mode of intense "yielding" attention to the subject matter being perceived. "Yielding" to the object enables one to appreciate and understand its qualitative dimension.

> To yield to the object means to do justice to the object's qualitative moments. Scientific objectification, in line with the quantifying tendency of all science since Descartes, tends to eliminate qualities and to transform them into measurable definitions.[12]

The Cartesian mode—"abstract unification"—requires a process whereby "to aggregate what is alike means necessarily to segregate it from what is different. But what is different is the qualitative" (43). Thus, through attention to emotional qualia one sees what is dismissed as different and irrelevant in the classical (Kantian) scientific reductionism. Alternative to this mode is one where "the experience of the object [is] turned into a form of subjective reaction," requiring an "elective affinity between knower and the known" (45).

A panpsychist explanation of this communicative ontology is proposed by Eddington; namely, that there is a mental substrate to

[11] In "Participatory Epistemology" (2014).
[12] Theodor W. Adorno, *Negative Dialectics*, trans. E. B. Ashton (New York: Continuum, 2007), p. 43. Further references follow in the text.

all reality, that "mind, or some mind-like quality, is present in all parts of the natural world, even in matter itself."[13] That matter on the quantum level responds to or reacts in some sense to our knowing or measuring it means that there is something mental inherent in matter. Both ends of the communicative link—observer/experiencer and observed/experienced—reside in a mental matrix through which communication occurs. And it is through the communicative link itself—the moment of connection of being—that a new reality emerges. "Perhaps everything," Lee Smolin muses, "has external and internal aspects" (270).

Freya Mathews, a contemporary philosopher who espouses a panpsychist position aligned with the process philosophy of Alfred North Whitehead and Charles Hartshorne, proposes that we must reconceive reality as a "subject-subject continuum" instead of a "subject-object dualism."[14] "Subjectivity," she argues, "is fundamental to the nature of reality" (7). As opposed to objectifying scientific knowledge, what is needed, she contends, is "a dialogical and participatory relation to the world" (6). Like many other theorists in this vein, Mathews derives an ethical mandate from this participatory epistemology. "It is through encountering the world, making contact with its subjectival dimensions that we ... acquire a sense of spiritual kinship, which ... provide[s] the basis for a respectful and sympathetic attitude" (79)—one that is "nonintrusive" and doesn't "dismantle" the world and "rebuild it according to ... abstract designs" (79).

Barbara McClintock, a Nobel-prize-winning geneticist known for her intense involvement with the plants she studied, exemplifies the dialogical participatory practice called for by Mathews as others. Her studies, which yielded an extraordinary knowledge of the intricate workings of corn-plant genetics, led her to see the plants she worked with as subjects, as "ensouled."[15] "Over the years," Evelyn Fox Keller notes, "a special kind of sympathetic

---

[13]David Skrbina, *Panpsychism in the West* (Cambridge, MA: MIT Press, 2005), p. 2.
[14]Freya Mathews, *For Love of Matter: A Contemporary Panpsychism* (Albany: State University of New York Press, 2003), p. 170. Further references follow in the text.
[15]Evelyn Fox Keller, *A Feeling for the Organism: The Life and Works of Barbara McClintock* (San Francisco: W. H. Freeman, 1983), p. 204. Further references follow in the text.

understanding grew in McClintock, heightening her powers of discernment, until finally, the objects of her study have become subjects in their own right" (200). An "organism" for her became seen as "a living form…object-as-subject" (200). In explaining her method to Keller, McClintock noted that while examining the minutest of living particles—chromosomes,

> I found that the more I worked with them the bigger and bigger [they] got, and when I was really working with them I wasn't outside, I was down there. I was part of the system. I was right down there with them…It surprised me because I actually felt as if I were right down there and these were my friends…As you look at these things, they become part of you. (117)

One begins to feel a "real affection" for them (117).

In emphasizing the "subjecthood" of the plants, McClintock stressed that for the scientist it is a matter of being receptive to what the living tissue is telling one—not forcing it to behave in prescribed ways. Rather one must be patient and attentive, following Adorno's "yielding" practice: one must "let it come to you"; one must "hear what the material has to say to you" (198). When McClintock states, "You let the material tell you where to go" (125), she, like Adorno, is expressing an aesthetics of care.

Attentiveness to each individual organism—*qua* individual—another attribute of a caring aesthetics is also a hallmark of McClintock's method. One has to be attentive to each particular organism and get to know it individually, she maintains, since plants even in the same species differ widely and have their own unique characteristics.

> No two plants are exactly alike. They're all different, and as a consequence, you have to know that difference…I start with the seedling, and I don't want to leave it. I don't feel I really *know the story* if I don't watch the plant all the way along. So I know every plant in the field. I know them intimately, and I find it a great pleasure to know them. (Keller 198, emphasis added)

Each organism is thus perceived to have a narrative history, a story of its own that is worthy of attention. McClintock's kind of "intimate knowledge," Keller notes, entails a "feeling for the organism" (198) that is intellectual, emotional, and visceral—a shared participatory knowledge stemming from the fact that both observer and observed are living beings who operate within the same communicative medium and can therefore connect and exchange information on that basis. McClintock thus operates within the subjective qualitative dimension that is deemed "negligible" (to reprise Weil's term) in classical Cartesian epistemology.

The philosophical groundwork for such a participatory epistemology was laid out in the twentieth century by Martin Buber, Mikhail Bakhtin, and Iris Murdoch, in addition to Weil, Horkheimer, and Adorno. The idea of grounding ethical and aesthetic judgments in the I-thou relationship was first fully developed by Buber, an existentialist theologian, in his seminal work *I and Thou* (1923). One of the most compelling examples Buber uses to illustrate the dialogical *I-thou* relationship is an experience he had as a boy with a horse.

When I was eleven years of age, spending the summer on my grandparents' estate, I used...to steal into the stable and gently stroke the neck of my darling, a broad dapple-grey horse. It was not a casual delight but a great, certainly friendly, but also deeply stirring happening...[W]hat I experienced in touch with the animal was the Other, the immense otherness of the Other, which, however, did not remain strange...but rather let me draw near and touch it.

Buber recalls that in stroking "the mighty mane" and feeling "the life beneath my hand, it was as though the element of vitality itself bordered on my skin, something that was not I...and yet let me approach, confided itself to me, placed itself elementally in the relation of *Thou* and *Thou* with me."[16]

In his important study of Buber's aesthetics, *The Text as Thou* (1992), Steven Kepnes notes that Buber felt narrative was the

---

[16]Martin Buber, *Between Man and Man*, trans. Ronald Gregor Smith (New York: Macmillan, 1965), p. 23. Further references follow in the text. Portions of the following discussion appeared in my article "Ecofeminist Literary Criticism: Reading the Orange," *Hypatia* 11, no. 2 (Spring 1996):161–82.

most effective means of revealing the I-thou relationship. This is because narrative not only focuses upon specific details (and the I-thou encounter is always a specific existential event—a moment in time—between two individuals), it shows those details in relation. In the example cited above of the boy's relationship with the horse, as Kepnes notes, the details of his touching the horse's "mighty mane"—that it was "sometimes marvelously smooth-combed, at other times just as astonishingly wild" (Buber 23)—are essential to comprehending the nature of the relationship.[17] Narratives, in short, are able to "say things that concepts cannot. Narratives capture, express, 'hold' the complex mix of I and thou and world that cannot be clearly summed up in a philosophical concept ... Only story can hold within it the web of relationships within which the I-thou occurs" (Kepnes 87).

Literature and other forms of art can be a primary means of expressing or disclosing the *thou*, which is always revealed in concrete embodiments. Buber, indeed, presents an incarnational theory of art. The artist embodies the *thou*, which he or she experiences in the creative process, in form; the viewer or reader brings the *thou* to life in the encounter with the work of art. Buber uses the term *geistige Wesenheiten* to encompass creative works; while variously translated as "spiritual beings" or "forms of the spirit," Buber suggested "spirit in phenomenal forms" as an appropriate English translation (Kepnes 23). Thus, the work of art, though an object in concrete form, becomes alive as a *thou* in the encounter with the viewer: "a *geistige Wesenheit*, a work of art or form of spirit, although, an *It*, can 'blaze up into presentness,' into the status of a Thou, again" (Kepnes 24). Unlike the I-it relationship, which Buber sees as a means of "'conquering' the world,"[18] the I-thou relationship is dialogical: both terms of the relation are seen as spiritual presences that have a reality of their own to communicate, which must be respected and attended to. Art is the medium by which that reality is transmitted from subject to subject. In his pioneering work of

---

[17]Steven Kepnes, *The Text as Thou: Martin Buber's Dialogical Hermeneutics and Narrative Theology* (Bloomington: Indiana University Press, 1992), p. 86. Further references follow in the text.

[18]Martin Buber, *I and Thou*, trans. Walter Kaufman (New York: Scribner's, 1970), p. 91.

ecocriticism, *The Song of the Earth* (2000) Jonathan Bate amplifies Buber's theory. In ecopoetics, he writes,

> the italicized *thou* strives to replace the dialectic of subject and object with an intercourse of I and thou. Where the subject/object relationship is one of power, the I/thou is one of love. Bond and tie replace mastery and possession. (112)

Bate concludes, "an ... ecofeminist language of nurture and care, as against male technological exploitation, ... is apposite" (112).

The principal literary theorist who emphasized the importance of subject-subject dialogue is Mikhail Bakhtin, a Russian critic significantly influenced by Martin Buber.[19] Bakhtin esteemed literature in which the author preserves the subjectivity of characters and doesn't reduce them to aesthetic or ideological objects. In his early work, *Problems of Dostoievsky's Poetics* (1929), Bakhtin valorized the Russian writer for his "struggle against the *materialization* of [people], and of all human values under the conditions of capitalism."[20] "In Dostoievsky's works [humans] overcome ... [their] 'thingness'" (70). Dostoievsky's work is in this way "dialogical. It is not constructed as the entirety of a single consciousness which absorbs other consciousnesses as object, but rather as the entirety of the interaction of several consciousnesses, of which no one fully becomes the object of any other one" (14).

As an example, Bakhtin analyzes the character Devushkin in Dostoievsky's early novel, *Poor Folk*. This character, himself a poor man, resents all attempts to fix him, to stereotype him, and to objectify him in short, as a "poor person." "Dostoievsky shows how the hero himself revolts against literature in which the 'little man' is externalized and finalized without being consulted." Devushkin is *"personally* deeply insulted ... and outraged" by the characterization of poverty in Gogol's *Overcoat*; he felt that "he had been defined totally once and for all" (47). In short, Devushkin had been erased as a person, as a *thou* by being abstracted and signified a "poor person"—a generic category—in someone else's ideological text.

---

[19]Nina Perlina, "Mikhail Bakhtin and Martin Buber: Problems of Dialogic Imagination," *Studies in Twentieth-Century Literature* 9, no. 1 (1984):13–28.
[20]Mikhail Bakhtin, *Problems of Dostoievsky's Poetics*, trans R. W. Rotsel (N.p.: Ardis, 1973), p. 51. Further references follow in the text.

Throughout his work, Bakhtin resisted what he called "theoretism" or what authors Gary Saul Morson and Caryl Emerson term "semiotic totalitarianism,"[21] namely pseudoscientific linguistic systems that eradicate the particularized living subject, who should be understood, according to Bakhtin in a "chronotopic" context, that is, in specific historical time and geographical environment or place (366–69). In opposition to theoretism, Bakhtin proposed an ethical and aesthetic focus he terms a *prosaics*, which concerns itself with "quotidian events that...elude reduction to...laws or systems" (33).

One of the Enlightenment projects of reductive homogenization that ignored and erased particular locales, Bakhtin recognized, was the eradication or domination of regional dialects by official "standard" national languages, a process that occurred throughout the Western world during the seventeenth through nineteenth centuries. The imposition of standard English versus the affirmation of regional dialects became a central literary issue in the United States in the nineteenth century. The so-called local-color school, of which Sarah Orne Jewett was a member, offered points of resistance to the colonization of their regional discourse by the centralized "standard" language. Jewett's story "A White Heron" (1886) reflects this regional resistance to cultural imperialism: the girl Sylvia refuses to be co-opted by an ornithologist, who as a scientist, represents the homogenizing discourses of modernity, and saves the heron from taxidermy.[22] She therefore affirms the heron as living subject, whom she (like McClintock and her corn plants) sees as a friend who shares with her a unique eco-neighborhood in rural Maine.

In important, pioneering articles Patrick Murphy extended Bakhtin's dialogical theories to nonhumans. Picking up from Bakhtin's study of Dostoievsky and combining it with his theorizing

---

[21]Gary Saul Morson and Caryl Emerson, *Mikhail Bakhtin: Creation of a Prosaics* (Stanford, CA: Stanford University Press, 1990), p. 28. Further references follow in the text. See further discussion in Josephine Donovan, *Women and the Rise of the Novel, 1405–1726*, 2nd. rev. ed. (New York: Palgrave Macmillan, 2013), chap. 1.
[22]Sarah Orne Jewett, "A White Heron," in *The Country of the Pointed Firs and Other Stories*, ed. Cather, pp. 161–71. See Josephine Donovan, "Breaking the Sentence: Local-Color Literature and Subjugated Knowledges," in *The (Other) American Traditions*, ed. Joyce Warren (New Brunswick, NJ: Rutgers University Press, 1993), pp. 226–43.

about dialect, Murphy suggests that in dialogue the speaker works to render what one might call the idiolect of the other. A writer such as Dostoievsky, for example, is "a renderer of the 'other' as speaking subject."[23] Murphy goes beyond Bakhtin, however, to extend the idea of the speaking other to nonhuman entities such as animals, suggesting that their "language" be considered a form of dialect which must be revalidated and heard, not erased by theoretistic discourses that elide the speakers. "The point is not to speak for nature but to work to render the signification presented us by nature into a verbal depiction by means of speaking subjects" (152).

That such metahuman dialects can and should be learned by humans is a point made by Jewett in her essay "River Driftwood" (1881).

> Who is going to be the linguist who learns the first word of an old crow's warning to his mate...? How long we shall have to go to school when people are expected to talk to the trees, and birds, and beasts in their own language!...It is not necessary to tame [them] before they can be familiar and responsive, we can meet them on their own ground.[24]

Because each dialogical encounter with a perceived subject is unique and particular, the communications transmitted from the subjects being considered by the artist or writer will vary according to the subject of the enunciation. The communicative meaning expressed by a quilt or an ancient family cherry tree will differ from those expressed by a conscious subject, such as a water buffalo or a rat or a human being. Ethical obligation will therefore vary according to the content of the message and the ethical status of the subject. My purpose here, however, is not to extrapolate on the ethics of the matter but to establish aesthetic modalities (alternative to the Kantian) that enable the "voices"—the emotional meaning— of the various subjects to be registered, regardless of the degree of ethical obligation that may be entailed. In other words, while

---

[23]Patrick Murphy, "Ground, Pivot, Motion: Ecofeminist Theory, Dialogics, and Literary Practice," *Hypatia* 6, no. 1 (1991):252.
[24]Sarah Orne Jewett, "River Driftwood," in *Country By-Ways* (Boston: Houghton Mifflin, 1881), pp. 4–5.

the degree of ethical responsibility one has for preserving a family quilt is not to be equated with that for tending an injured animal (with one's obligation in the latter case being considerably greater), an emotional attentiveness is required in both cases, and it is this caring aesthetic attentiveness to emotional qualia that awakens one's ethical concern, however different the degree of ensuing obligation may be.

Such attentiveness often leads one to understand another's localized and particularized story, which can be represented in a "chronotopic" discourse (such as seen in the novel), or to use Jim Cheney's term, a "bio-regional narrative."[25] Sylvia understands the heron's story; she "hears" his voice. And such personal narrative knowledge is the basis of her ethical appreciation of the bird and her refusal to sacrifice his life. As Carol Bigwood notes, "To really encounter difference on its own terms rather than on terms of the dominant faction there is a need for theories and stories that emerge from localized places and continually bend back to it so as to never to fly off into fleshless abstractions and subjugating universals,"[26] such as reducing the heron to a scientific object as the ornithologist intends to do.

Cheney proposes the concept of "contextual discourse" as a participatory epistemological mode that enables a genuine reciprocity of information sharing, where the subject is not objectified but listened to, as a fellow being. Unlike what he calls "totalizing language," which "assimilate[s] the world to it," contextual language "assimilates language to the situation, bends it, shapes it to fit" (120). It operates in Adorno's mode of yielding. "Responding in this way to the whim of the moment" Kathryn Rabuzzi explains in her study of the aesthetics of domestic labor, "is markedly different from imposing your own will...The passivity so induced is that of a light object thrown into the water; it is not the object that determines its direction, but the movement of the water."[27]

---

[25]Jim Cheney, "Postmodern Environmental Ethics: Ethics as Bioregional Narrative," *Environmental Ethics* 11 (1989):117–34. Further references follow in the text.
[26]Carol Bigwood, *Earth Muse: Feminism, Nature and Art* (Philadelphia: Temple University Press, 1993), p. 270.
[27]Kathryn Allen Rabuzzi, *The Sacred and the Feminine: Toward a Theology of Housework* (New York: Seabury, 1982), p. 153.

Being thus responsive to one's immediate environment is a form of the practical, "local knowledge" known as "*mētis*."[28] It is a craft-based knowledge rooted in one's unique habitat, transmitted orally and through local dialects and by manual practice—learning by doing—and through personal experience and apprenticeship. Sylvia's knowledge of her woodland neighborhood is a form of *mētis*. She knows the forest paths and patterns, the location and habits of native creatures, from personal experience. It is indeed her particularized knowledge of the locale that the ornithologist hopes to exploit in his vain quest for the heron. It requires attentiveness to the particulars of one's environment and timely adjustment to them.

Domestic labor—housework, as traditionally practiced—is another example of *mētis*. The housewife has to be responsive to the vagaries of her immediate environment, adjusting her labor according to the needs of her family and the conditions of the day. She has to keep an eye on the sky if she wants to do a wash, canceling plans if it rains. She has to respond to illness and injury of those around her. She has to adjust her cooking to the availability of certain produce, and so forth. Any worker who deals with the elements—weather, land, and sea—has to operate adaptively according to the pragmatics of *mētis*. A harbor pilot who knows the currents and tides of his particular harbor operates through *mētis*, as does an herbalist who knows the plants and soils of her particular region. Writers operating through an aesthetics of care know their subject matter through the praxis of *mētis*.

The particularized adaptive knowledge of *mētis* requires a personal chronotopic understanding of the inhabitants of one's unique physical environment. One must know their history, their personal eccentricities and relationships, their habitual behavior, and understand their language. One must know them, as McClintock knew her corn plants, as Alexandra her land, and Sylvia the heron, as fellow beings, as friends.

Environmental ethicist Paul Taylor sees this kind of responsive sensitivity as a basis for ethical environmental awareness. We must, he says, be "'open' to the full existence and nature of the organism come before us."

---

[28]See Scott, *Seeing Like a State*, pp. 316–24.

As one becomes more and more familiar with the organism being observed one acquires a sharpened awareness of the particular way it is living its life. One may become fascinated by it and even get to be involved in its good and bad fortunes. The organism comes to mean something to one as a unique, irreplaceable individual...The progressive development from objective, detached knowledge to a recognition of individuality...to a full awareness of an organism's standpoint, is a process of heightening our consciousness of what it means to be an individual living thing.[29]

The caring attentiveness to other, different beings proposed by Taylor and others is a form of "attentive love," "a recognition that the sufferer exists, not only as a unit in a collection, or a specimen" but as an individual (Weil "Reflections," 51). It therefore requires ethical acknowledgment of—rather than elision of—suffering, when the subject is in pain.

One of the *qualia* elided in Cartesian constructions is emotion, the feeling experience of the living body. In particular, Horkheimer and Adorno emphasize that scientific objectification fails to register the experience of suffering, for, as Adorno notes in *Aesthetic Theory*, suffering cannot be conceptualized by objective quantification. "Suffering remains foreign to [rational] knowledge; though knowledge can subordinate it...suffering conceptualized remains mute and inconsequential" (18). In returning to the example of vivisection, Horkheimer and Adorno cite another French scientist, Pierre Flourens, who argued that surgery on humans should be done without anesthesia because the latter causes one to forget the pain. Horkheimer and Adorno endorse the idea (sardonically) because it would expose people to the suffering vivisection inflicts on animals and also reveal that science depends upon "oblivion for suffering."

Perennial domination over nature, medical and non-medical techniques, are made possible only by the process of oblivion. The loss of memory is a transcendental condition for science. All objectification is forgetting (*Dialectic* 230).

---

[29]Paul W. Taylor, *Respect for Nature: A Theory of Environmental Ethics* (Princeton, NJ: Princeton University Press, 1986), pp. 120–21.

The elision of the suffering of the particular creature involved in abstract, "deductive" thinking is ethically corrupt, according to Adorno: "this tacit assent to the primacy of the general over the particular... constitutes its inhumanity" (*Minima Moralia* 74).

Art, by contrast, as envisaged by Adorno, "participates in... suffering" (*Aesthetic Theory* 344), providing access to the nullified experiential body and thereby offers an alternative to the forgetting and repression required in the epistemology and aesthetics of modernity. "Art," Adorno enjoins in *Aesthetic Theory*, must not "forget the suffering that is its expression and in which form has its substance" (260). Art and literature, indeed, are the primary means by which the suffering body finds expression. And "the need to lend a voice to suffering is a condition of all truth" (*Negative Dialectics* 17–18).

Art, therefore, articulates "needs, mute in themselves that await the expression that artworks fulfill" (*Aesthetic Theory* 345). In particular, it is a matter of giving voice to the expressions and feelings of nature. "If the language of nature is mute, art seeks to make this muteness eloquent" (*Aesthetic Theory* 78); "art wants... to attain what has become opaque to humans in the language of nature" (*Aesthetic Theory* 77).

In *Eclipse of Reason*, Horkheimer offers a similar view of the purpose of art and literature, that it be the voice of the natural world and her creatures, a purpose he claims has been lost in the literature and art of modernity.

> Once it was the endeavor of art, literature and philosophy... to be the voice of all that is dumb, to endow nature with an organ for making known her sufferings... Today nature's tongue is taken away.[30]

Indeed, he contends, "nature's text... if rightly read, will unfold a tale of infinite suffering" (126).

Adorno's prophetic vision imagines a "utopia of the *qualitative*— the things which through their difference and uniqueness cannot be absorbed into the prevalent exchange relationships" of modern commerce and science (*Minima Moralia* 120, emphasis added)—in

---

[30]Max Horkheimer, *Eclipse of Reason* (New York: Continuum, 1987), p. 101.

other words, a utopia of the nonassimilable, the noncategorizable. He envisages a world where "people could be different without fear" (103)—where difference would not be forced to conform, on the one hand, or elided as nonexistent, on the other. Art points in the direction of, and provides a glimpse of, this liberated utopian world. It does so by providing a negative critique of the reification and domination that pervade the practices and institutions of modernity.

In a 1964 conversation with Marxist Ernst Bloch, a theorist of utopia, Adorno defined utopia as a "determined negation" which "always points at the same time to what should be."[31] In other words, art forms by their very nature constitute a counter, anticipatory reality to the commodified culture of modernity.

> The iridescence that emanates from artworks ... is the appearance of the affirmative *ineffabile*, the emergence of the nonexisting as if it did exist ... yet what does not exist, by appearing, is promised. (*Aesthetic Theory* 233)

In an earlier article, "Reconciliation under Duress" (1958), Adorno explained that by engaging dialectically with the subjective quality of the materials of the world, art establishes a counter image—and therefore a negative critique—of their reification.

> In the form of an image, the object is absorbed into the subject instead of following the bidding of the alienated world and persisting in a state of reification. The contradiction between the object reconciled in the subject ... and the actual unreconciled object in the outside world, confers on the work a vantage-point from which it can criticize actuality.[32]

While Adorno's aesthetic theory would seem to include all art regardless of subject matter, even including works governed by a Kantian dominative aesthetic, he in fact stresses that the utopian

---

[31]Ernst Bloch, *The Utopian Function of Art and Literature* (Cambridge, MA: MIT Press, 1988), p. 12.
[32]Theodor Adorno, "Reconciliation under Duress," in *Aesthetics and Politics*, by Ernst Bloch et al. (London: Verso, 1980), p. 160.

dimension can be achieved only through a nondominative "mimetic comportment." Indeed, art thus conceived, "negates the spirit that dominates nature" (*Aesthetic Theory* 118). "Brutality...the subjective nucleus of evil—is a priori negated by art" (*Aesthetic Theory* 232). But art, by providing "images of gentleness, promises of a happiness cured of domination over nature" (*Minima Moralia* 224).

Mimetic comportment, the praxis at the heart of Adorno's aesthetic theory, involves a yielding to the subject matter, listening to its voice, following where it leads—in other words, it requires a practice of "attentive love," a caring, responsive receptivity to the unique particulars of one's environment, paying attention to emotional qualia: "Mimetic comportment," he explains in *Aesthetic Theory*, is "the unimpeded corrective of reified consciousness" (330), because "mimetic power is...the power of qualitative distinction" (331). "Art's mimetic element [is] incompatible with what is purely a thing" (*Aesthetic Theory* 17). Unlike Kantian dominative aesthetics in which "artworks are to dissolve everything that is heterogenous to their form" (*Aesthetic Theory* 109), the nondominative art he envisages embraces the subjective other, allowing it its own expression and vitality.

> Aesthetic comportment assimilates itself to that other rather than subordinating it. Such a constitutive relation of the subject to objectivity in aesthetic comportment joins eros and knowledge. (*Aesthetic Theory* 331).

Adorno's concept of *mimesis* is surprisingly similar to that articulated by Margaret Cavendish centuries ago. The "strikt" "imitation" of nature, which Cavendish deemed the artist's task, is accomplished through a praxis of empathic *mimesis* or attentive "sympathy," which is, she wrote, "but a conforming of the actions of one party, to the actions of the other, as by way of Imitation" (*Philosophical Letters* 292).

Following an ontology similar to that espoused by modern theorists Eddington, Mathews, Woolf, Buber, and others (as well as Cavendish), Adorno conceives of a nonphysical subjective spirit residing in the objective world. "What is waiting in the objects themselves needs...intervention to come to speak" (*Negative Dialectics* 29). Just as the subatomic particle becomes realized in conjunction with an observer, so the material of art comes to be realized—emerges—as Woolf and Buber perceived—through the artist's articulation. Its spirit comes alive in the responsive artistic process of caring aesthetic comportment.

Richard Wolin explains that in Adorno's aesthetics,

> through their reliance on the mimetic faculty, works of art preserved the idea of a radically different relation of man to nature, a relation that ceases to be based on the principles of domination and control, and instead seeks to give expression to spirit in conformity with the delicate contours of nature. By virtue of their mimetic side, works of art *seek to meet nature half way*, and therefore foreshadow the ideal of a noncoercive, reconciled relation of species to nature.[33]

In conceiving art, thus, within an aesthetics of care, art is seen as providing a consoling office. Adorno in fact gives a caring image to illustrate how art exemplifies the process of reconciliation, of the modeled dialectical interweaving of spirit and matter and the emergence of the former from the latter in art.

> The comforting motherly hand that strokes one's hair gives sensuous pleasure. Extreme spirituality reverses into the physical...Without the harmonious sonority of a string quartet, the D-flat major passage...of Beethoven's op. 59, no. 1, would not have the power of consolation...Essential to artworks is that their thingly structure...makes them into what is not a thing; their reity is the medium of their own transcendence. (*Aesthetic Theory* 277)

To summarize then, an aesthetics of care entails a "mimetic comportment" wherein the writer or artist engages with her subject matter in an I-thou relationship where the other is perceived as a subject, not an object, as in the I-it construction. Such engagement requires paying emotional as well as intellectual attention to the particular other and his or her milieu. It means *being with* the

---

[33]Richard Wolin, "The De-Aesthetization of Art: On Adorno's *Aesthetische Theorie*," *Telos* 41 (1979):118.

subjects, seeing through their eyes, feeling through their bodies. It also means being part of their environment as an indigene, as embodied and as embedded in their everyday world, known through *mētis*, not standing apart as an outside observer but integrated into the same world as the "observed." Mimetic comportment involves communicating with the other through emotional *qualia*, hearing the voices of nature thus expressed. It means transmitting those voices as literally as possible, mimetically, with as little intervention as possible, not twisting and manipulating the subject material according to one's own imposed aesthetic design. The receptive epistemological modes of attentive love and mimetic comportment enable the artist or writer to see the qualitative value that inheres in the subjects under consideration—whether quilt or pottery, corn plant or tree, animal or person—value that is elided in the culling objectifications and extractions of Kantian aesthetics.

This aesthetics of care relies then on a recognition of the mysterious ontological interweaving of the spiritual and the material. Art thus in this view may be seen as participating in the transubstantive phenomenon of "emergence" where spirit arises out of matter, where "moments of being" erupt in the mundane, providing a negative critique of reification—processes that deaden and deny the animate world—and offering a utopian glimpse of a nondominative world in which the sacred may be accessed through means other than through violent sacrifice.

4

Animal ethics and literary criticism

In recent years—prompted no doubt by the "animal rights" movement—literary critics have begun reexamining the status of animals in literature, identifying ideologically driven representation, questioning the ubiquitous aesthetic exploitation of animal pain and suffering, and seeking alternative forms of representation either in existing but neglected texts or by calling for new modes that do not, as Philip Armstrong puts it, "reduce the animal to a blank screen for the projection of human meaning."[1] For, as Marian Scholtmeijer noted, in much extant literature "animals are ... scarcely animals at all but schematic elements in an aesthetic or psychological design" (*Animal Victims* 259).

In her important article "Animals and Spirituality" (2000), Scholtmeijer laid out the basic tenet of a critical animal ethics approach to literature: "We can ask of a work of literature that it deconstruct habitual ways of thinking about animals ... [so that] the animal is no longer amenable to exploitation, ideational or otherwise."[2]

Disrupting "habitual ways of thinking about animals" means disrupting ideologically driven "mythic troping" about animals, removing anthropocentric perspectives and adopting an animal-centric point of view. An animal ethics approach to literature may thus be labeled "animal-standpoint criticism." Let us take

---

[1]Philip Armstrong, *What Animals Mean in the Fiction of Modernity* (London: Routledge, 2008), p. 3. Portions of this chapter appeared in slightly different form in my article "Aestheticizing Animal Cruelty."
[2]Marian Scholtmeijer, "Animals and Spirituality: A Skeptical Animal Rights Advocate Examines Literary Approaches to the Subject," *LIT* 10, no. 4 (2000):380.

an example. Here is a seventeenth-century poem about animals, Thomas Carew's "To Sexham" (ca. 1640):

> The willing ox, of himself came
> Home to the slaughter, with the lamb
> And every beast did thither bring
> Himself to be an offering[3]

The poem depicts farm animals obligingly going to their slaughter, reflecting an obviously anthropocentric bias, distorting the desires and interests of the animals so as to have them unrealistically and improbably conform to the interests of the human/farmer. Such a viewpoint is subtended by the ideology of *speciesism*—which holds that in terms of their moral worth and ontological status, animals are inferior to and subservient to humans. Like Marxist and feminist criticism—its predecessors in the field—animal-centered criticism often requires what Paul Ricoeur termed a "hermeneutic of suspicion,"[4] one that critiques and demystifies normalizing ideologies embedded in texts (classism for Marxist criticism, sexism for feminist criticism, speciesism for animal-standpoint criticism). Cary Wolfe sees animal-centered criticism as following in the footsteps of earlier political criticisms.

> Given what we have learned in recent decades about many non-human animals—the richness of their mental and emotional lives, the complexity of their forms of communication and interactions—many scholars now think that we are forced to make the same kind of shift in the ethics of reading and interpretation that attended taking sexual difference seriously in the 1990s (in the form of queer theory) or race and gender seriously in the 1970s and 1980s.[5]

---

[3]As cited in Erica Fudge, *Perceiving Animals: Humans and Beasts in Early Modern Culture* (Urbana: University of Illinois Press, 2002), p. 3. Fudge analyzes the poem to slightly different purposes than I do there.

[4]Fredric Jameson, *Marxism and Form: Twentieth-Century Dialectical Theories of Literature* (Princeton, NJ: Princeton University Press, 1971), p. 119.

[5]Cary Wolfe, "Human, All Too Human: 'Animal Studies' and the Humanities," *PMLA* 124, no. 2 (2009):567–68.

Most political criticisms are rooted in what has come to be called standpoint theory, which attempts to identify and articulate the point of view or standpoint of a silenced, oppressed group. The original formulation of standpoint theory was presented by Hungarian Marxist Georg Lukács in his *History and Class Consciousness* (1923). Lukács singled out industrial workers (the proletariat) as a subjugated group which, because of its commodification or reification in the capitalist production process, held a particular and privileged view of the system. This critical awareness arose as the workers, who were, of course, subjects, were treated as objects. In assembly-line production, Lukács noted, the worker "is turned into a commodity and reduced to a mere quantity." But beneath the "quantifying crust," lies a "qualitative living core." "[T]he process by which the worker is reified and becomes a commodity dehumanizes him... [but] it remains true that precisely his humanity and soul are not changed into commodities."[6] Care theory may be seen as a standpoint theory. As the proletariat is posited as the repository of a suppressed perspective or standpoint on its oppression, so Carol Gilligan's adolescent girls evinced a critical consciousness—a "negative critique" in Adorno's dialectical conception—toward the system suppressing their dissident voices.

The suppressed standpoint or voice is held under these theories to be privileged because it offers perspectives, unnoticed by the governing ideologies, on the suffering being inflicted. As these perspectives are rooted in the oppressed person's or creature's own situation, they are necessarily subjective, particularized, and situational, adapted to the circumstances of the case. As *political* theories which identify the world in political terms, feminist in the case of care theory, Marxist in the case of standpoint theory, their point of departure is the determination that some groups have power over others. Their goals therefore are liberative, to free the oppressed voiceless groups from such domination. As Carol Gilligan herself emphasized in her introduction to *Carol Gilligan et l'éthique du "care"* (2010), a recent French study of her work, which followed the second French edition of *In a Different Voice* in 2008 (*Une voix différente*), care theory is rooted in radical feminism, "a movement

---

[6]Georg Lukács, *History and Class Consciousness: Studies in Marxist Dialectics*, trans. Rodney Livingstone (Cambridge, MA: MIT Press, 1971), pp. 166, 171, 172.

to liberate democracy from patriarchy."[7] Since before their voices were silenced by ideological indoctrination these "young women were speaking truth to power,... [expressing] resistance... to the norms and values of patriarchy" ["filles parlant vrai au pouvoir,... la résistance... aux normes et valeurs du patriarcat"] (33), Gilligan's feminist purpose was to retrieve and record these subversive voices, bringing them out of the silence of oblivion. When the oppressed are conceived as being morally significant, hearing their voices is an imperative step in the liberation process because it necessarily counters the ideological system that rules them insignificant, rendering them silent—that system being sexism in the case of women, speciesism in the case of animals.

Applying care/standpoint theory to animal ethics, as I have done,[8] means listening therefore to the "voice" of animals, hearing their standpoint vis-à-vis a system that oppresses them. As the silenced voice of women is inherently subversive of patriarchy, so is the silenced voice of animals necessarily subversive to the current speciesist regime of industrialized agriculture and abattoirs, as well as to other institutions abusive and exploitative of animals.

Like the proletariat, animals are subjects of a life, but they are even more commodified than human workers in the assembly-line meat production process in that their very bodies are turned into commodities—consumable objects—in the process. And, in the case of animals, it is clear that human advocates are required to articulate the standpoint of the animals—gleaned through interspecies communication in dialogue with them; to wit, that they do not wish to be slaughtered and treated in painful and exploitative ways. Human advocates are necessary as well to defend and organize against the practices that reify and commodify animal subjects.

To hear these silenced voices requires adopting the epistemological modes discussed in the Chapter 3—attentive love, the yielding praxis of Adorno's mimetic comportment. Such a shift in perspective turns away from ego- and anthropocentric ways of

---

[7]Carol Gilligan, "Une voix différente: un regard prospectif à partir du passé," in *Carol Gilligan et l'éthique du "care,"* ed. Vanessa Nurock (Paris: Presses Universitaires de France, 2010), p. 37. My translation from the French. Further references follow in the text.

[8]Josephine Donovan, "Feminism and the Treatment of Animals: From Care to Dialogue," *Signs* 31, no. 2 (2006):319–20.

seeing toward an animal- and eco-centric viewpoint. Since fiction by definition requires the author to imagine and articulate the point of view of her or his characters, the role of interpreting the animals' point of view in fiction falls to the author. It is a fact, however, that most authors—especially in the modern era—have failed in this endeavor. It is therefore up to animal-standpoint critics to call attention to this lapse.

Animal-standpoint criticism starts therefore from the premise that animals are seats of consciousness—subjects, not objects; that they are individuals with stories/biographies of their own, not undifferentiated masses; that they dislike pain, enjoy pleasure; that they want to live and thrive; that in short they have identifiable desires and needs, many of which we human animals share with them. It behooves us as ethical subjects to hear the "different voices" of these fellow creatures. Literature, as Horkheimer and Adorno stress, is uniquely capable of giving them a voice. That much of it has failed in this obligation is a central concern of animal-standpoint criticism.

Critics in this tradition have not been remiss in pointing out the manifest authorial and critical blindness that often accompanies animal representation, questioning the absences and elisions, the lapses and lacunae in texts where animals appear. As an example, David Perkins notes that although many novels of the past, as well as memoirs and travel books, include travel by horse-drawn coach, they "almost never" mention the horses' "suffering," which remains "invisible to most passengers or, perhaps, the novelist considered them irrelevant to the theme of the novel."[9] An animal-standpoint critic might ask why this suffering is ignored or repressed by the author, the likely answer being that speciesist assumptions condone such unmindfulness.

Animal-standpoint critics also take note of past critical impercipience to animals' existence and suffering in literary texts. Perkins, for example, provides a long list of Wordsworth scholars who have managed to write about Wordworth's poem "Hart-Leap Well" (in *Lyrical Ballads*, 1800) without acknowledging and responding to the suffering of the deer who is the focus of the poem.

---

[9]David Perkins, *Romanticism and Animal Rights* (Cambridge: Cambridge University Press, 2003), p. 105.

"Commentaries on this poem...show that if [it] seeks to instill compassion for animals, it was written in vain" (80). Had the poem been about an abject human, Perkins speculates, "interpreters [had been less likely to] reduce or ignore the creaturely desperation it describes" (81). Contrary to these earlier critics who ignored or minimized the deer's agony, critic Peter Mortensen (in a 2000 article, "Taking Animals Seriously") notes of the poem that "for Wordsworth the hart's suffering is a subject of ethical interest in itself, not merely a figure for other, more noteworthy forms of human suffering." Indeed, Mortensen insists that Wordsworth intended for the poem to point up "man's shockingly cruel treatment of animals," thus "inaugurat[ing] a new kind of Romantic nature poetry, which brings animals into the foreground and takes their suffering seriously."[10]

Similarly, Erica Fudge criticizes the anthropocentric bias in much eco-criticism for its "avoidance of and silence about the place of non-human animals."[11] For, as Fudge notes (109), a broadly conceived ecological approach in fact risks degenerating into what animal rights theorist Tom Regan has labeled "environmental fascism"[12]; that is, it focuses on abstract generalities such as species and ecosystems, ignoring the individual creature and discounting her suffering. Instead, Fudge proposes that the focus be on the individual rather than "general and abstract" conceptions. "The truly meaningful animal is often a very individualized being" (110). One might similarly critique the New Materialists for failing to ethically distinguish among the varieties of "vibrant matter" that constitute the universe (see my critique of Bennett in Chapter 1).

Several literary critics have objected to the pervasive figurative use of animals in literature, another procedure that deadens their subjectivity. John Simons, a pathbreaker in animal-standpoint criticism, notes, in *Animal Rights and the Politics of Literary Representation* (2002), "The symbol is, perhaps, the most common

---

[10]Peter Mortensen, "Taking Animals Serious: William Wordsworth and the Claims of Ecological Romanticism," *Orbis Litterarum* 55, no. 4 (2000):296.
[11]Erica Fudge, Introduction to "Reading Animals," *Worldviews* 4 (2000):109. Further references follow in the text.
[12]Regan, *Case for Animal Rights*, p. 362.

form of representation of animals,"[13] but, he protests, "animals are not symbols" (7). Let us seek, he advocates, texts in which animals are not "displaced metaphors for the human" (6). In *Romanticism and Animal Rights* (2003), Perkins likewise criticizes the use of animal as metaphor for human emotion. Shelley's "To a Skylark," he notes, has little to do with an actual bird, but rather "elevates the animal to bewail the human condition," a "device" he finds "dubious." "The animal is just a metaphor, with little character of its own" (147).

The fictional animal-standpoint critic Elizabeth Costello in J. M. Coetzee's recent work similarly critiques humans' chronic tropological use of animals in literature. "The life-cycle of the frog," she notes, "may sound allegorical, but to the frogs themselves it is no allegory, it is the thing itself, the only thing."[14] In a public lecture that lays out her animal-standpoint approach to literature, Costello rejects literature where "animals stand for human qualities; the lion for courage, the owl for wisdom, and so forth." In Rilke's poem "The Panther," for example, "the panther is there as a stand-in for something else." As an example of a poem where the poet does not use the animal figuratively but attempts to represent the animal's being directly, Costello points to Ted Hughes's "The Jaguar." In representing the jaguar, "Hughes," she says, "is feeling his way towards a different kind of being-in-the-world … [I]t is a matter … not of inhabiting another mind but of inhabiting another body" (94–96). Hughes, in other words, is paying serious attention to the jaguar *qua* jaguar and not as a metaphor for human speed, agility, or whatever. Scholmeijer expressed a similar sentiment. "Personally, I like beetles," she wrote, "not because they represent resurrection but because they are fascinating creatures with tiny wills and ways of being of their own" ("Animals and Spirituality" 379).

The kind of "attentive love" or "mimetic comportment" that is exercised in an aesthetics of care is manifest in the work of several nineteenth-century women writers, for example, Dorothy

---

[13]John Simons, *Animal Rights and the Politics of Literary Representation* (Houndsmills, Basingstoke, England: Palgrave, 2002), p. 115. Further references follow in the text.

[14]J. M. Coetzee, *Elizabeth Costello* (New York: Viking, 2003), p. 217. Further references follow in the text.

Wordsworth, sister of the celebrated Romantic poet William. In Dorothy's journals, one finds an attempt to capture the natural world as directly and literally as possible with little aesthetic reshaping of the material and with sympathetic attention to its inhabitants. Critic Margaret Homans sees her praxis as an example of the preference of many women writers for a "presymbolic or literal language, with its lack of gaps between signifier and referent,"[15] a practice of intense *mimesis* with little authorial intervention.

Unlike her brother, whose figurative language, according to Homans, often required the "death of nature" (49) it is representing, Dorothy "invents a mode of figuration…that does not demand the distance or absence of the referent…a nonsymbolic discourse" (53). Even for her brother, Dorothy's writing came to signify a mode where "images [are] not killed into meaning" (51). In other words, Dorothy managed to write "in a language that is as literal as possible and that literalizes" (39). Her brother, on the other hand, although desirous of retaining an unmediated connection with nature and the natural entities, whom he often treated sympathetically in his poetry, nevertheless in many cases ended by imposing his own autobiomythography upon them, transforming them into signs that are significant within that myth, but which thereby erase the literal referents, absenting them from his field of significance. Dorothy, on the other hand, in her journals "speaks for the literal nature that is often silent within his texts" (56).

Homans provides a comparative example of the way the two treat a common subject—an encounter with a river gorge on a journey taken by William through the Alps in 1790, treated in *The Prelude* (written c. 1805) and retraced in 1820; the latter trip is covered in Dorothy's *Journal of a Tour of the Continent*. Dorothy's description of a gorge is contrasted to William's as follows:

Dorothy: Skeletons of tall pine-trees beneath us in the dell, and above our heads—their stems and shattered branches as grey as the stream of the Vedro, or the crags strewn at their feet…We sate upon the summit of a huge precipice of stone to the left of the

[15]Margaret Homans, *Bearing the Word: Language and Female Experience in Nineteenth-Century Women's Writing* (Chicago: University of Chicago Press, 1986), p. 14. Further references follow in the text. Parts of the following discussion appeared in my article, "Ecofeminist Literary Criticism," pp. 164–69. See also Bohls, *Women Travelers*.

road—the river raging below after having tumbled in a tremendous cataract down the crags in front of our station. On entering the Gallery we cross a clear torrent pent up by crags. (Homans 61)

William: The immeasurable height
Of woods decaying, never to be decayed,
The stationary blasts of waterfalls,
And in the narrow rent at every turn
Winds thwarting winds, bewildered and forlorn,
The torrents shooting from the clear blue sky
The rocks that muttered close upon our ears,
Black drizzling crags that spake by the way-side
...

Were all like workings of one mind, the features
Of the same face, blossoms upon one tree;
Characters of the Apocalypse,
The types and symbols of Eternity,...
                (*Prelude* VI. 624–39, in Homans 48–49)

The contrast is evident. Dorothy is clearly concerned with transcribing the reality of the gorge as faithfully as possible, remaining in touch with the literal specifics of nature. William, on the other hand, first, hyperbolizes the scene with a melodramatic violence that is imposed by his own imagination. Second, he interprets the natural world symbolically; its significance lies not on the literal level but rather as a reference for Wordsworth's symbolizing theory, that of transcendental idealism, where natural elements become "types and symbols of Eternity."

Jonathan Bate in *The Song of the Earth* argues that William Wordsworth struggled with the problem of how to represent the spiritual side of nature without resorting to objectifying figures. In the end, Bate proposes that Wordsworth tried to avoid "carv[ing] the world into subject and object" (147), instead recognizing, as he states in "Lines: Composed a Few Miles above Tintern Abbey" (1798),

A presence ...
Of something far more deeply interfused,
Whose dwelling is the light of setting suns,

And the round ocean, and the living air,
And the blue sky, and in the mind of man,
A motion and a spirit, that impels
All thinking things, all objects of thought
And rolls through all things. (ll. 94–102)

Wordsworth thus perceives a vital force or spirit infusing "all things," uniting them in a common medium. Bate interprets then that for Wordsworth "a river or a plant" is both "the object of thought…[and] a thinking thing." For the poet "the distinction between subject and object is a murderous dissection" (147).

Dorothy Wordsworth seemed, however, better able than William to resist figuration of the literal, allowing it instead to speak for itself. Homans gives another pertinent example. It occurs in Dorothy's journal of 1802 where she follows for several days the fates of a pair of swallows who have built a nest by her window. Instead of turning their story into a metaphor for events in her own life (which would have been easy because the episode occurred in the period just prior to her brother's marriage, a traumatic event in Dorothy's life), she is concerned only with the swallows as swallows: "she convinces us by her long and minute observations of their behavior that the swallows have their own life quite apart from hers" (55).

In short, unlike her brother, Dorothy "sees before she reads" and in this way corrects his tendency (and indeed the tendency of much Western literature) "to obliterate the image in favor of meaning" (63)—to impose a symbolic order upon the literal, the natural, denying its "thouness," killing it in order to exploit it for the signifying purposes of the author. To be interested in the swallows as swallows suggests that the swallows have a being that is valuable and worthy of attention. Such attention indicates respect; it validates the ontological status of the swallow. It acknowledges the swallow as "thou."

In her *Spiritually-Engaged Knowledge*, Crawford offers a similar contrast between two poems, both dealing with a flower. The first is a much-cited passage by Alfred, Lord Tennyson.

Flower in the crannied wall,
I pluck you out of the crannies–
Hold you here, root and all, in my hand
Little flower—but if I could understand

What you are, root and all, all in all,
I should know what God and man is.

The other, a *haiku* by a seventeenth-century Japanese poet, Basho:

When I look carefully
I see the nazuna blooming
By the hedge!

(Crawford 80)

As Crawford notes, in the latter example, the flower "is not interrupted from persevering in its own being. The gaze is attentive and situated within the encounter... Basho's experience is direct, unmediated by ideas" (81). In Tennyson's handling, by contrast, the flower is not only destroyed but is manipulated and "twisted" (to reprise Cather's term) to make an anthropocentric ideological point, fitting it into a prescripted grid.

Further examples of an attempt at an unmediated, literal *mimesis* may be found in the writings of American writer Sarah Orne Jewett. Jewett came to express a kind of existentialist mysticism via the influence of Swedish theosophist Emmanuel Swedenborg and his American disciple, Sampson Reed.[16] Reed postulated a prelapsarian, preverbal world of "presymbolic language" (to use Homans's term), where "there is a language, not of words but of things": "[E]verything which is, whether animal or vegetable, is full of the expression of that use for which it is designed, as of its own existence. If we did but understand its language... [but] we are unwilling to hear... and drown the voice of nature." Instead, he urges, "[L]et [us] respect the smallest blade which grows and permit it to speak for itself. Then may there be poetry which may not be written perhaps, but which may be felt as part of our being."[17]

While Swedenborgians in general did not permit nature "to speak for itself," as Reed enjoins, but rather cast upon it heavy

---

[16]See Josephine Donovan, "Jewett and Swedenborg," *American Literature* 65, no. 4 (1993):731–50.

[17]As cited in Kenneth Walter Cameron, *Young Emerson's Transcendental Vision* (Hartford, CT: Transcendental Books, 1971), pp. 266–67.

allegorization, Jewett did seek a language and literary style—a mimetic comportment—that would remain faithful to the literal (she was, not surprisingly, an admirer of Dorothy Wordsworth). For Jewett figuration should not be imposed upon nature by the artist to explicate his or her own inner spirit (as William Wordsworth often did) nor is it a "pasteboard mask" (Herman Melville's term) which the poet strips away or deciphers in order to reveal a transcendent signified. Rather, the literal or the natural is itself significative; it speaks in its own language, which humans must seek to hear—not erase through their own symbolic code.

In a little-known essay "A Winter Drive" (1881), Jewett explains her animist theory in connection with trees. There is, she notes approvingly, "an old doctrine called Hylozoism...the theory of the soul of the world, of a life residing in nature, and that all matter lives; the doctrine that life and matter are inseparable." Thus, while "trees are to most people as inanimate and unconscious as rocks," she contends that, "it is impossible for one who has been a great deal among trees to resist the instinctive certainty that they have thought and purpose." But she rejects dryadic theories that the trees' thouness can be explained as human spirits encased within them, which she sees as distorting the trees' reality *as trees*, making them "too much like people." On the contrary, "the true nature and life of a tree [can] never be...personified."[18] Thus, Jewett espouses a theory of nature as a subject, a *thou*, which must not be distorted through personification, allegorization, or other exploitative figuration.

Martin Buber articulated a similar idea in *I and Thou*.

In a moving meditation on a tree Buber wrote:

I contemplate a tree.
I can accept it as a picture...
I can feel it as a movement...
I can assign it to a species...

But it can also happen, if grace and will are joined, that as I contemplate the tree I am drawn into a relation, and the tree ceases to be an It...Does the tree have consciousness, similar

---

[18]Sarah Orne Jewett, "A Winter Drive," in *Country By-Ways*, pp. 168–70.

to our own? I have no experience of that ... What I encounter is neither the soul of a tree nor a dryad, but the tree itself. (57–59)

Jewett's theory is reflected in her fiction. In her celebrated story "A White Heron," as we have seen, a tree and a bird are "persons" or *thou*s whose moral significance weighs as greatly as those of the human characters and who are therefore important players in the unfolding of the plot, which indeed hinges on the issue of whether the bird, the white heron, will be treated as an *it*, an object, to be used for scientific purposes as a specimen, or as a *thou* with rights of his own. The protagonist Sylvia, aided by an old pine-tree, comes to the determination to save the bird's life, to defy the ornithologist who has asked her to reveal the bird's whereabouts. Speaking of the tree, Jewett notes,

> it must truly have been amazed that morning through all its ponderous frame as it felt this determined spark of human spirit creeping and climbing from higher branch to branch. Who knows how steadily the least twigs held themselves to advantage this light, weak creature on her way! The old pine must have loved his new dependent. More than all the hawks, and bats, and moths, and even the sweet-voiced thrushes, was the brave, beating heart of the solitary gray-eyed child. And the tree stood still and held away the winds.[19]

Significantly, in her critical decision whether to disclose the bird's location to the ornithologist, Sylvia recalls the pinetree's presence: "The murmur of the pine's green branches is in her ears, she remembers how the white heron came flying through the golden air and how they watched the sea and the morning together, and Sylvia cannot speak; she cannot tell the heron's secret and give its life away" (171). Thus Sylvia, an illiterate rural child, resists the dominative intrusions of scientific discourse, which would colonize her natural environment, erasing it as a subject, objectifying it for exploitative purposes.

"[S]he must keep silence!" (170) because the language of scientific discourse cannot hear the "presymbolic language" she shares with

---

[19]Jewett, "A White Heron," p. 169. Further references follow in the text.

the tree, the bird, and other creatures of the wood. They and she are constituted as subjects in a "bioregional narrative" that the dominative discourses of modernity cannot hear.

In an early work, *Deephaven* (1877), Jewett suggested that uneducated country people, because they "are so instinctive and unreasoning...may have a more complete sympathy with Nature, and may hear voices when wiser ears are deaf."[20] Jewett does not intend the terms "instinctive" and "unreasoning" pejoratively but rather as alternatives to the hegemonic discourses of Western "Reason." The "voices" they hear are those of nature as a subject, a *thou*: "the more one lives out of doors the more personality there seems to be in what we call inanimate things. The strength of the hills and the voice of the waves are no longer only grand poetical sentences, but an expression of something real" (186–87).

Jewett's literary theory, which was expressed in informal advice she gave to younger writers over the years—including, as we have seen, Willa Cather—reflects her belief that the "inanimate" world of nature is indeed animate. When she enjoined writers, "Don't write a 'story'...just *tell the thing!*" she implied that the "thing" is itself animated with a spiritual presence; do not allow this *thou* to be silenced as an absent referent. In an early letter to a mentor Jewett said she needed "new words," which I interpret as a "presymbolic language," to express her sense of nature.[21] And in a late letter to a friend, she commented on how "it is those unwriteable things that [a] story holds in its heart...that makes the true soul of it."[22]

Animals and other natural entities do not symbolically *represent* transcendence or spirituality in Jewett's theory; they *are* themselves spiritual beings. For, as Scholtmeijer observes in "Animals and Spirituality," "the mystery that is the animating spark of life belongs as much to animals as to ourselves" (374). Recognizing and honoring the sacred in animal life has not, however, in the past necessarily translated into treating them humanely or respecting

---

[20]Sarah Orne Jewett, *Deephaven* (Boston: James R. Osgood, 1877), p. 186. Further references follow in the text.

[21]Sarah Orne Jewett, Letter to Theophilus Parsons, August 24, 1876. Special Collections, Miller Library, Colby College, Waterville, Maine. Quoted by permission of the library.

[22]*Letters of Sarah Orne Jewett*, ed. Annie Adams Fields (Boston: Houghton Mifflin, 1911), p. 112.

their right to life, Scholtmeijer notes, even though "in theory, since spirituality and the sacred should dictate a 'hands off' approach, animals...should be protected when they are viewed as spiritual beings" (374). However, the widespread use of animal sacrifice as a means of accessing the sacred in religious rites, which I discuss in Chapter 8, is evidence that such a "hands-off" reverence is not afforded in either traditional or new-age religious approaches. Instead, acknowledging animals' "spirituality requires knowing [them] in a different way from that which allows us to use them" (377)—in other words, knowing and representing them nondominatively and noninstrumentally. That different way is through an aesthetics of care.

In an article on the status of animals in various religious traditions, Kimberley C. Patton (2000) explores the idea of "animals as theological subjects." In Abrahamic traditions, as expressions of and in some sense embodiments of God's creation, each animal, she notes, may be seen to express a certain aspect of God. Thus, one theologian speaks of the "rabbithood of God," meaning that "there is an aspect of God's Self that at creation expressed itself as a rabbit, and that nothing can better reveal that particular aspect of the divine nature than a real, living rabbit." "Watch the animal," she further proposes (citing James Hillman), "and see the divine in self-display."[23] Even one who abjures religious approaches to the issue must sense that there is a sacred dimension to natural creatures, a unique living presence that evokes the traditional religious emotions of reverence and awe. It is a recognition of this dimension of animal being that animal-standpoint critics seek in literature and art.

One work of art that is exemplary of an aesthetics of care in this respect is Robert Bresson's film *Au Hasard Balthazar* (1966), which treats the donkey Balthazar as a subject worthy of "attentive love," a sacred being. In her analysis of the film in *Creaturely Poetics* (2011) Anat Pick proposes that it evinces a sympathetic wit(h)nessing of animal suffering, thereby revealing the sacrality of the living body. Pick follows Simone Weil in seeing the "oppression" of "vulnerable bodies" not as "a crime against humanity but a

---

[23]Kimberley C. Patton, "'He Who Sits in the Heavens Laughs': Recovering Animal Theology in Abrahamic Traditions," *Harvard Theological Review* 93, no. 4 (2000): 421, 427, 431.

violation of the sacred."[24] Pick sees the donkey in the Bresson film as exemplifying the existence of the sacred in the everyday because he is "the embodiment of creaturely suffering" (190) or "Weilian *affliction*" (191). As such, and because he communicates via a negative dialectics the existence of the sacred, Balthazar is a kind of saint, an "embodied revelation" (189) "of truth, a pure witness" (190). The animal's silence, thus, "in Bresson has an almost material quality which makes God's presence felt through and as the vacuum of his absence" (190).

In the film, however (to disagree slightly with Pick), Balthazar is not silent; he is more of a witness than a victim. He speaks with his ears, with his expressive eyes, with his brays; on occasion, he runs away, he rebels, and he attempts to escape. Bresson thus pays attention to the donkey's voice and registers it sympathetically. Balthazar is not a passive recipient of affliction, nor a silent martyr. Unlike most of the human characters in the film, who either practice evil or collaborate in it, Balthazar *witnesses* critically and in so doing represents an alternative to evil, namely, the sacred, the inviolate essence of goodness.

The suffering of Balthazar is therefore not gratuitous or exploitative—unlike the literary examples given in Chapter 1. As an active agent, Balthazar is a subject who resists suffering and thereby serves as a witness to something *other* than evil and affliction, inviting a compassionate recognition of his dignity and worth, a connection to his sacred heart.

Unfortunately, much literature and art which depicts animals does not rise to the level of compassionate comprehension seen in the Bresson film. Rather much of it remains locked in conventional I-it modes of perception, conceiving animals as objects usable for aesthetic purposes. The central underlying concern of animal-standpoint critics remains, therefore, the aesthetic exploitation of animal pain and the aestheticization of cruelty, which is undergirded by and justified in the aesthetics of modernity. A prominent example is, of course, the treatment of bulls in Hemingway's works (as noted in Chapter 1), where, as Scholtmeijer points out in *Animal Victims in Modern Fiction*, the bulls are reduced to inanimate objects in an aesthetic order, part of its "geometric interplay of abstract forces" (264).

---

[24]Pick, *Creaturely Poetics*, p. 48. Further references follow in the text.

Literature that operates according to an aesthetics of modernity, which denies, represses, and ignores animals' subjectivity, "tacitly encourage[s] aggression against real animals," Scholtmeijer observes, "by implying that nonhuman animals are devoid of experience worthy of human consideration." Such fiction "reflect[s] that deadening of sensibility which in life allows humans to victimize animals without scruple." Thus, "the obligation to heed the voice of compassion evaporates" (*Animal Victims* 260).

By contrast, an aesthetics of care recognizes the animals' subjectivity and engages with it through the various means outlined in Chapter 3—meditative attentiveness, "attentive love," "mimetic comportment," dialogue, a participatory epistemology, which enable a radical empiricism—getting to the "thing itself"—that skirts aside "mythic troping" and ideological constructions which screen us from the suffering at hand.

Literature, in short, is a human activity but insofar as it aspires to register the realities of and communications with other species it needs to expand its repertoire beyond conventional fictional devices. In literature conceived under an aesthetics of care, animals are seen as particular creatures of value in their own right as sacred subjects and not simply as aesthetic objects, vehicles of use to comment on human situations. Their viewpoint is not to be ignored as if it were nonexistent, but their realities and standpoint are detailed and included as part of the whole picture.

In *On God and Dogs* (1998) Stephen H. Webb pleads,

> Must the rhetoric we use to discuss animals always assimilate, like the meals we eat, animal otherness to human expectations? Does animal literature... necessarily serve up animals... on the plate of human interests and desires? Is there a kind of vegetarian discourse that permits the animal other to be really other?[25]

Such a reconception of the status of animals in literature—the adoption of a "vegetarian discourse" under an aesthetics of care—may lead to an ontological reconception of their place in the world, so that they will no longer be commodified, used, and abused for human purposes. That is the hope.

---

[25]Webb, *On God and Dogs*, p. 89.

5

Tolstoy's animals

In the work of that "greatest of all novelists," Leo Tolstoy (so characterized by Virginia Woolf),[1] we find model examples of sensitive, perceptive, and empathetic treatment of animals. His artistic credo and praxis embody an aesthetics of care.

Late in life, Tolstoy published a moral fable that encapsulates his approach. In this story, the standpoint of an ass is vividly recreated so as to promote ethical awareness of the animal's subjectivity on the part of the human protagonist. Understanding the animal's being empathetically forces the human to reexamine his own ethical priorities, making him realize that the animal has interests and wishes similar to his own. It thus disrupts "habitual ways of thinking" about animals, the speciesist assumption that they are for humans' use, and leads him to a realization that he and all living creatures are bound together in a common subjecthood, linked in a chord of sympathy.

"Esarhaddon, King of Assyria" (1903) concerns a king who is magically made to enter the consciousness of an enemy he had defeated and animals he had hunted. As he prepares to carry out the execution of his enemy, an old sage tells him he should not carry out his plan. When asked why not, the old man says, "[Y]ou are Lailie [the enemy]."[2] Puzzled, Esarhaddon asks the sage to explain.

---

[1]Virginia Woolf, "The Russian Point of View," in *Collected Essays*, vol. 1 (London: Chatto and Windus, 1966), p. 244. A shorter version of this chapter appeared as "Tolstoy's Animals," *Society & Animals* 17, no. 1 (2009):38–52.

[2]Leo Tolstoy, "Esarhaddon, King of Assyria," in *Collected Shorter Fiction*, vol. 2, trans. Louise Maude, Aylmer Maude, and Nigel J. Cooper (New York: Knopf, 2001), p. 742. Further references follow in the text.

The sage puts the king's head under water during which time he finds himself inside the consciousness of Lailie, as well as that of a hunted animal.

He was astonished that he was an animal, and astonished, also, at not having known this before. He was grazing in a valley, tearing the tender grass with his teeth, and brushing away flies with his long tail. Around him was frolicking a long-legged, dark-grey ass-colt, striped down its back. Kicking up its hind legs, the colt galloped full speed to Esarhaddon, and poking him under the stomach with its smooth little muzzle, searched for the teat, and, finding it, quieted down, swallowing regularly. Esarhaddon understood that he was a she-ass, the colt's mother, and this neither surprised nor grieved him, but rather gave him pleasure...

But suddenly something flew near with a whistling sound and hit him in the side, and with its sharp point entered his skin and flesh. Feeling a burning pain, Esarhaddon...tore the udder from the colt's teeth, and laying back its ears galloped to the herd...The colt kept up with him...when another arrow in full flight struck the colt's neck. It pierced the skin and quivered in its flesh. The colt sobbed piteously and fell upon its knees. Esarhaddon could not abandon it, and remained standing over it. The colt rose, tottered on its long, thin legs, and again fell. A fearful two-legged being—a man–ran up and cut its throat. (2:745–46)

When the sage releases Esarhaddon from the water, he points up the moral. "'Do you now understand,' continued the old man, 'that Lailie is you,...[and] the animals which you slew and at your feasts, were also you...Life is one in them all, and yours is but a portion of this same common life'" (2:746).

Even in his early work, that done before his celebrated conversion to pacifist Christianity—which included vegetarianism—in the early 1880s, Tolstoy depicted animals sensitively and with an empathetic eye to their feelings and sufferings. "Strider: The Story of a Horse" ("Khostomer," begun in 1861 but not published until 1886) is told almost entirely from the animals' point of view.

The horses were not at all frightened or offended at the horseman's sarcastic tone: they pretended that it was all the same to them and moved leisurely away from the gate; only one old brown mare, with a thick mane, laid back an ear and quickly turned her back on him...Of all the horses in the enclosure (there were about a hundred of them) a piebald gelding, standing by himself in a corner...and licking an oak post with half-closed eyes, displayed least impatience.[3]

The story centers upon this animal, an aged, battered horse who, Tolstoy stipulates, remains "majestic" despite his ugliness (1:589). A lengthy minute description of the animal—an example of Tolstoy's characteristic attention to detail (one of the reasons for his claim to fame as a novelist)—illustrates an author giving an animal serious moral attention.

The big bony head, with deep hollows over the eyes and a black hanging lip that had been torn at some time, hung low and heavily on his neck, which was so lean that it looked as though it were carved of wood. The pendant lip revealed a blackish, bitten tongue and yellow stumps of worn teeth. The ears, one of which was slit, hung low on either side, and only occasionally moved largely to drive away the pestering flies...The veins of his neck had grown knotty, and twitched and shuddered at every touch of a fly. The expression of his face was one of stern patience, thoughtfulness, and suffering...Yet in spite of the hideous old age of this horse one involuntarily paused to reflect when one saw him...Like a living ruin he stood alone in the midst of the dewy meadow, while not far from him could be heard the tramping, snorting and youthful neighing of the scattered herd. (1:589–90).

Strider tells his life story—which is one of being traded from master to master (not unlike Bresson's Balthazar), sometimes abused, sometimes treated well—in the first person to the assembled horses in the stables over a period of five nights. Tolstoy then switches the scene to the wealthy owner's house where humans discuss the relative merits of their equine property from a purely economic point of view. In thus ironically juxtaposing the subjective point

---

[3]Leo Tolstoy, "Strider: The Story of a Horse," in *Collected Shorter Fiction*, vol. 2, trans. L. Maude, A. Maude, and Cooper, p. 585. Further references follow in the text.

of view of the animals with the objective/commodifying view of
the human masters, Tolstoy appears to be borrowing a page from
Harriet Beecher Stowe's technique in *Uncle Tom's Cabin* (a novel
Tolstoy greatly admired) where scenes in the slave cabins, which
depict slave lives sympathetically from their point of view, are
juxtaposed against those in the big house where the masters discuss
slave-trading from a purely mercenary perspective, seeing the slaves
as but feeling-less commodities. Whether Tolstoy intended a slave/
animal analogy in "Strider" is not clear, but it is apparent that, like
Stowe, he deplores the commodification of living, feeling creatures
as but objects for sale.[4]

In the drawing room discussion, a former owner of Strider
(Strider's favorite former master), himself now old and defeated,
talks with pride about his favorite horse, the young Strider.
Ironically, earlier in the day this owner, Serpukhovskóy, had seen
Strider in the paddock but hadn't recognized him, whereas Strider
knew his former owner and neighed fondly.

The next day Strider develops an ailment and it is decided to
do away with him. This is done by taking him out in the fields
and cutting his throat until he bleeds to death—a process Tolstoy
describes in detail from the horse's point of view. Strider's body is
left to feed the wild animals, and therefore is at least put to some
use, Tolstoy implies, unlike the body of his former master who is
buried in full dress uniform in a leaden casket, which the author
characterizes as a vain and presumptuous human ritual. The story's
main point is that immersed in a smug and false sense of superiority
humans fail to appreciate the dignity and nobility of animals.

The description of Strider's death may derive from an actual
visit Tolstoy paid to a slaughterhouse at about this time. As he was
finishing this story (and perhaps a motivation for doing so) in the
mid to late 1880s, Tolstoy read Howard Williams' *Ethics of Diet*
(1883), a treatise on vegetarianism to which Tolstoy wrote a preface
for the Russian edition published in 1892. In this preface, published
in English as "The First Step," Tolstoy describes his observations in
the slaughterhouse, delineating in novelesque detail the deaths of

---

[4]On the slave-animal analogy see Marjorie Spiegel, *The Dreaded Comparison:
Human and Animal Slavery* (Philadelphia: New Society, 1988).

several individual animals—possibly the most vivid and horrifying descriptions of animal slaughter ever written.

[A] large sleek ox was brought in...Two men were dragging him...[After being hit "above his neck" with a "pole-axe" it was] as if his four legs had been suddenly mown from under him, the ox fell heavily on his belly to the floor...and began to move his legs and his back convulsively...[After his throat is cut]...from out of the gaping wound the black-red blood came spurting...Then another butcher...broke the leg and cut if off. And the belly and the remaining three legs continued to quiver convulsively.[5]

Strider's death is similarly described. Unaware of what is happening, the horse

began to drowse to the sharpening of the knife. Only his swollen, aching, outstretched leg kept jerking. Suddenly he felt himself being taken by the lower jaw and his head lifted. He opened his eyes. There were two dogs in front of him...The gelding looked at them and began to rub his jaw against the arm that was holding him. (1:623)

Trustingly, Strider considers the slaughterers are about to help him. Then he

felt that something had been done to his throat. It hurt, and he shuddered and gave a kick with one leg...Then he felt something liquid streaming down his neck and chest. He heaved a profound sigh....He closed his eyes and began to droop his head. Then his legs quivered and his whole body swayed...The knacker waited till the convulsions had ceased. (1:623–24)

As the reader has come to know Strider as a subject, his death necessarily evokes feelings of sadness, compassion, and sympathy, as well as anger at human indifference to the fate of this remarkable and admirable animal.

---

[5] Leo Tolstoy, "The First Step," *The New Review* (1892):37. Further references follow in the text.

In "The First Step," Tolstoy describes another animal, this one a bull "of real beauty with white spots and white feet" who fights against the butchers but is finally subdued: "The noble animal, which but a moment before was full of exuberant life, fell down in a heap, convulsively moving its feet... Five minutes later the black head had become red and skinless, and the eyes that had shone with such brilliancy and color were glassy and fixed" (38). Contrast Tolstoy's treatment of the bull's death to the aestheticization of animal torment seen in the bullfighting scenes criticized by Scholtmeijer and others.

Tolstoy's personal sensitivity to and respect for animals is described by his fellow novelist Ivan Turgenev, who noted the trait on a late-nineteenth-century visit to Tolstoy's estate Yasnaya Polyana. Turgenev reported he

was amazed at Tolstoy's... profound understanding of animals. There was more than a familiarity between them—something like an organic intimacy. He stood by a bony, mangy old nag, stroking its back and whispering gently into its ear, while the horse listened with evident interest. Then he translated the animal's feelings to those around him. "I could have listened forever," Turgenev later said, "He had got inside the very soul of the poor beast and taken me with him. I could not refrain from remarking, 'I say, Leo Nikolayevich, beyond any doubt, you must have been a horse once yourself.'"[6]

Throughout his work, even minor references to animals include acknowledgment that what is involved is a living, feeling creature. In the early story, "Snow Storm" (1856), for example, which does not centrally concern animals but rather depicts an arduous trek several men make through a winter blizzard, animals are nevertheless treated neither as background furniture nor to point up human traits or issues, but rather as separate active living creatures worthy of attention in their own right.

The large piebald horse, stretching its neck and straining its back, went evenly along the completely snow-hidden road,

---

[6]As cited in Henri Troyat, *Tolstoy* (Garden City, NY: Doubleday, 1967), p. 388.

monotonously shaking its shaggy head under the whitened harness-blow, and pricking one snow-covered ear when we overtook it.[7] The shaft-horse, a good, big, shaggy animal, stumbled more than once, though immediately, as if frightened, it jerked forward again and tossed its shaggy head almost as high as the bell hanging from the bow above it. The right off-horse... noticeably let its traces slacken and required the whip, but from habit as a good and even mettlesome horse seemed vexed at its own weakness, and angrily lowered and tossed its head at the reins. (1:250)

At the end of this arduous journey "the off-horse... kept running in the same way, only the sunken, heaving belly and drooping ears showing how exhausted she was" (1:257). Finally, after being lost for some time, the travelers come upon a fresh trail of "a three-horsed sledge, and here and there pink spots of blood, probably from a horse that had overreached itself" (1:257) When they reach town and safe haven, "near the inn stood a tróyka of grey horses, their coats curly from sweat, their legs outstretched and their heads drooping wearily" (1:257).

During the course of the journey, the narrator has a dream about a drowning incident that happened in his youth. Even in this dream, which centers upon the death of a peasant, a rescuer's dog is given pronounced attention. Seeing his master enter the water, "Tresórka, perplexed by the quickness of his master's movements, has stopped near the crowd and with a smack of his lips eats a few blades of grass near the bank, then looks at his master intently and with a joyful yelp suddenly plunges with him into the water" (1:245). While the master swims toward the drowned man, "Tresórka, having swallowed some water, returns hurriedly, shakes himself near the throng, and rubs his back on the grass" (1:246).

While not developed in this story, the exuberant liveliness of the dog in the face of death foreshadows a theme Tolstoy was to pick up in what is perhaps his greatest story (and in my opinion, one of the greatest stories of all time), "Three Deaths" (1859), the conclusion of which describes the exuberant thriving of vegetation,

---

[7]Leo Tolstoy, "Snow Storm," in *Collected Shorter Fiction*, vol. 1, p. 235. Further references follow in the text.

signifying the eternal resurrection of life, in the aftermath of the deaths the story depicts.

The three deaths in question are of an invalid woman, who is traveling to Italy against medical advice seeking to regain her health; a poor homeless man whose last weeks are spent lying atop an oven in a coach house; and a tree that is cut down for a cross to mark the poor man's grave. Human indifference to the suffering and dying of the two humans is presented critically by Tolstoy. The dying woman resentfully reflects, "None of them has any thought for me,"[8] as they bustle about her in vigorous health. Sergey, a nephew of Theodore, the poor man, thoughtlessly asks him for his new boots, pointing out that as he is dying, he will have no further use for them. And a cook wishes Theodore would hurry up and die since he's taking up too much space. Theodore gives Sergey his boots in exchange for a promise that he will set up a marker over his uncle's grave.

Sometime after Theodore's death, Sergey cuts down an ash tree in the forest to make a cross for the grave. As he does so, the point of view becomes that of the surrounding natural world whose voice Tolstoy thus attends to and records—an example of a writer's giving voice to nature in the manner advocated by Horkheimer and Adorno.

> Suddenly a strange sound, foreign to Nature, resounded and died away…A tree-top began to tremble in an unwonted manner, its juicy leaves whispered something, and the robin who had been sitting in one of its branches fluttered twice from place to place with a whistle, and jerking its tail sat down on another tree…
>
> The tree, shuddering in its whole body, bent down and quickly rose again, vibrating with fear on its roots…
>
> The sounds of the axe and of the footsteps were silenced. The robin whistled and flitted higher. A twig which it brushed with its wings shook a little and then with all its foliage grew still like the rest. The trees flaunted the beauty of their motionless branches still more joyously in the newly cleared space.
>
> The first sunbeams, piercing the translucent cloud, shone out and spread over earth and sky (1:580–81).

---

[8]Leo Tolstoy, "Three Deaths," in *Collected Shorter Fiction*, vol. 1, p. 569. Further references follow in the text.

Earlier, at the woman's wake, a psalter had intoned the words of the psalm: "Thou renewest the face of the earth" (Psalm 104:30) (579), sounding the resurrectory theme. Although dead, the woman "seemed all attention. But had she now understood those solemn words?" (579). The humans' earlier apparent indifference— their robust bustle which the woman resented—now can be seen as connecting to and reflecting the robustness of nature in its resurrectory cycle. Though the ash tree dies, the other growth in the forest exuberantly fills its place.

> The birds stirred in the thicket and, as though bewildered, twittered joyfully about something; the sappy leaves whispered gladly and peacefully on the tree-tops, and the branches of those that were living began to rustle slowly and majestically over the dead and prostrate tree. (581)

"Master and Man" (1895), another acknowledged masterpiece, picks up on many of the themes developed in earlier stories. As in "Snow Storm," the ostensible issue is the survival of travelers in a terrible winter storm, but as in "Strider" and "Three Deaths," a larger theme is developed in the implicit contrast drawn between the natural world, including animals and the vain falsities of the human world; in this story, one is governed by capitalist entrepreneurialism. And as in other stories, full attention is paid to the horse who struggles for survival along with his peasant driver, Nikíta, and his owner, the capitalist Vasíli Andréevich.

> Picking his way out of the dung-strewn stable, Mukhórty frisked, and making play with his hind leg pretended that he meant to kick Nikíta…After a drink of the cold water the horse sighed, moving his strong wet lips, from the hairs of which transparent drops fell into the trough; then standing still as if in thought, he suddenly gave a loud snort.[9]

Of another horse they pass on their way:

> Their shaggy, big-bellied horse, all covered with snow breathed heavily under the low shaft-bow and, evidently using the last

---

[9]Leo Tolstoy, "Master and Man," in *Collected Shorter Fiction*, vol. 2, p. 546. Further references follow in the text.

of its strength, vainly endeavoured to escape from the switch, hobbling with its short legs through the deep snow … Its muzzle, young-looking, with the nether lip drawn up like that of a fish, nostrils distended and ears pressed back from fear, kept up for a few seconds … [Nikíta thinks:] "They've tired that little horse to death. What pagans!" (2:558–59)

Having become completely lost in the raging storm, Vasili and Nikíta decide to give Mukhórty the reins, hoping he can lead them to safety. "'The one thing he can't do is talk' Nikíta kept saying. '[J]ust see what he's doing with his ears! He doesn't need any telegraph. He can scent a mile off'" (2:560). The horse does succeed in bringing them to a village and Mukhórty is briefly stabled, a scene Tolstoy describes with detailed attention to the other animals present.

The hens and the cock had already settled to roost … and clucked peevishly, clinging to the beam with their claws. The disturbed sheep shied and rushed aside trampling the frozen manure with their hoofs. The dog yelped desperately with fright and anger and then burst out barking like a puppy at the stranger. Nikíta talked to them all, excused himself to the fowls and assured them that he would not disturb them again, rebuked the sheep for being frightened without knowing why, and kept soothing the dog, while he tied up the horse … [T]urning to the dog [he said] "Be quiet, stupid! Be quiet. You are only troubling yourself for nothing. We're not thieves, we're friends …" (2:562)

After a few hours of rest, the master insists on setting out again. He is determined to continue on through the storm, despite warnings and the misgivings of both horse and driver, because he hopes to make a killing in a business deal—"the purchase of the Goryáchkin grove" (2:576) and time is of the utmost. He will make a profit of 10,000 rubles, thereby furthering his dream of becoming a millionaire (2:576).

Once again, they lose their way and must spend the night without shelter in the raging storm. The master and the horse freeze to death; only the peasant Nikíta manages to survive. "Mukhórty, buried up to his belly in snow … stood all white, his dead head pressed against his frozen throat; icicles hung down from his nostrils, his eyes were covered with hoar-frost as though filled with tears, and he had grown so thin in that one night that he was nothing but skin and bone" (2:594).

Tolstoy's sensitivity to animals as subjects—as characters in their own rights—is manifest in his great novel *Anna Karenina* (1873–76). While rarely noticed by critics or readers, the animals in this novel are treated as separate characters who have points of view into which the narrative enters. As in Tolstoy's other works, it seems to be taken for granted by the author that one would include their perspectives as part of the story.

Detailed attention, for example, is paid to the subjective reactions and reflections of Konstantin Levin's dog Laska, an elderly female setter. Greeting Levin on his return to his country estate from a trip, she rushes out excitedly and jumps up, "longing but not daring to put her forepaws on his chest."[10] As Levin settles into his study and as she knows he is upset,

> Laska kept poking her head under his hand. He stroked her, and she promptly curled up at his feet, laying her head on a hind-paw. And in token of all now being well and satisfactory, she opened her mouth a little, smacked her lips, and settling her sticky lips more comfortably around her old teeth, she sank into blissful repose. Levin watched all her movements intensely. (115)

Always eager to go on a hunting expedition, Laska manifests impatience while waiting for the hunters to get their gear in order.

> Laska, aware since early morning that they were going shooting, after much whining and darting to and fro, had set herself down in the wagonette beside the coachman, and, disapproving of the delay, was excitedly watching the door from which the sportsmen still did not come out ... [When one finally appears,] Laska flew up to him ... and jumping up, asked him in her own way whether the others were coming, but getting no answer from him she returned to her post of observation and sank into repose again, her head on one side, and one ear pricked up to listen (686–87).

---

[10]Leo Tolstoy, *Anna Karenina*, trans. Constance Garnett (New York: Random House, 1939), p. 111. Further references follow in the text.

On various hunting expeditions, Laska shows a mind of her own, often expressing a different (and more accurate) opinion than Levin. Focused as she is on retrieving birds, she becomes manifestly annoyed when he becomes otherwise occupied, losing sight of the objective. At one point as Levin becomes engrossed in a conversation with another hunter, Laska looks "reproachfully at them. 'They have chosen a time to talk,' she was thinking. 'It's on the wing...Here it is, yes, it is. They'll miss it' thought Laska" (198).

On another occasion, When Levin, "in feverish haste...got more and more out of temper and ended by shooting almost without a hope of hitting. Laska...seemed to understand this. She began looking more and more languidly, and gazed back at the sportsmen...with perplexity or reproach in her eyes" (696). Laska comes to believe Levin isn't serious and when he shoots another bird and orders her to fetch it, she "did not believe he had shot it, and when he sent her to find it, she pretended to hunt for it, but did not really" (698).

In one lengthy episode, Tolstoy details how the dog's mind is working, and how she disagrees with Levin about how to flush some grouse birds from the bush. Tolstoy seems to be able to enter into her mind, noting how smells guide her thinking.

> Running into the marsh among the familiar scents of roots, marsh plants, and slime, and the extraneous smell of horse dung, Laska detected at once a smell that pervaded the whole marsh, the scent of that strong-smelling bird that always excited her more than any other. (708)

Following the scent, trying to determine where it intensified, she realizes she has to go downwind but since the scent is elusive she has to be ready to turn on a dime. Once she has located the birds' likely location, she begins to circle around them; however, to her annoyance just then Levin calls her, pointing in a different direction. She knows he is wrong: "he is pointing to a spot covered with water, where there could not be anything" (708). Nevertheless, "she obeyed him, pretending she was looking, so as to please him, went round it, and went back to her former position...Now that he was not hindering her, she knew what to do" (708).

Having found the birds by scent,

she stood still, feeling more and more conscious of it, and enjoying it in anticipation. Her tail was stretched straight and tense, and only wagging at the extreme end. Her mouth was slightly open, her eyes raised. One ear had been turned wrong side out as she ran up, and she breathed heavily but warily, and still more warily looked round... to her master. (709)

This further example of Tolstoy's remarkably detailed descriptions of animal being and behavior reflects the author's attitude of "attentive love" toward them, exemplifying thus his aesthetics of care. Levin, too, like the author (whom he is believed to roughly represent) shows attentive love toward not just Laska, whose "movements," we noted, he "watched... attentively" (118), he also knows the other animals on his estate "so intimately to the minutes detail of their condition" (184). Most of them he seems to know by name.

When his cow Pava calves, he shows caring concern, and the animals' feelings and points of view are duly noted by him and the author.

Walking across the yard, passing a snowdrift by the lilac tree, [Levin] went into the cowhouse. There was a warm, steamy smell of dung when the frozen door was opened, and the cows, astonished at the unfamiliar light of the lantern, stirred on the fresh straw. He caught a glimpse of the broad, smooth, black and piebald back of Hollandka. Berkoot, the bull, was lying down with his ring in his lip, and seemed about the get up, but thought better of it, and only gave two snorts as they passed by him. Pava, a perfect beauty, huge as a hippopotamus, with her back turned to them, prevented their seeing the calf, as she sniffed her all over.

Levin went into the pen, looked Pava over, and lifted the red and spotted calf onto her long, tottering legs. Pava, uneasy, began lowing, but when Levin put the calf close to her she was soothed, and, sighing heavily, began licking her with her rough tongue. The calf, fumbling, poked her nose under her mother's udder, and stiffened her tail out straight. (112)

"[I]sn't she splendid?" Levin exclaims to the farmhand accompanying him.

Near the end of the novel as Levin is pulling out of a nearly suicidal depression and experiencing a kind of epiphany about the value and meaning of life, he idly helps a beetle who is struggling on a blade of grass near him:

> Looking intently at the untrampled grass before him, and following the movements of a green beetle, advancing along a blade of couch-grass and lifting up in its progress a leaf of goat-weed. "What have I discovered?" he asked himself, bending aside the leaf of goat-weed out of the beetle's way and twisting another blade of grass above for the beetle to cross over onto it. (944)

His redemptive discovery is that a materialist explanation of the world is not sufficient. Ironically, as he is meditating, the beetle in effect proves his point, showing that she has a mind of her own.

> Of old I used to say that in my body, that in the body of this grass and of this beetle (there, she didn't care for the grass, she's opened her wings and flown away), there was going on a transformation of matter in accordance with physical, chemical, and physiological laws. (944)

But such a theory—what philosopher Thomas Nagel calls "reductive materialism"[11]—is not sufficient, Levin realizes, for it lacks the subjective spiritual dimension—soul—that inheres in himself and in all living creatures.

Shortly thereafter, a further example of Levin's attentive sensitivity to other living creatures occurs in his visit to his bee house. As he approaches "one bee hummed angrily, caught in his beard, but he carefully extricated it" (952). After putting on "his veil,"

> he went into the fence-in bee-garden, where there stood...all the hives he knew so well, the old stocks, each with its own history...In front of the openings of the hives, it made his eyes giddy to watch the bees and drones whirling round and round...while...the working bees flew in and out...always in the same direction into the wood to the flowering lime-trees and back to the hives.

---

[11]Thomas Nagel, *Mind and Cosmos: Why the Materialist Neo-Darwinist Conception of Nature is Almost Certainly False* (New York: Oxford University Press, 2012), p. 4.

His ears were filled with the incessant hum in various notes,
how the busy hum of the working bee flying quickly off, then the
blaring of the lazy drones, and the excited buzz of the bees on
guard. (953)

In his treatise on literary theory, *What Is Art?* (1896), Tolstoy
gives as an example of the kind of art he favors a hunting scene
by the Russian painter Vasnetsov, which was drawn to accompany
Turgenev's story "The Quail," "in which it is told how, in his son's
presence, a father killed a quail and felt pity for it."[12] Another
example (not unlike his own story "Esarhaddon") Tolstoy draws
from a play he read about that had been created by a primitive
tribe, the Voguls. In it two characters represent a reindeer-doe and
her fawn, another represents a hunter, and a fourth, a bird who
"warns the reindeer of their danger." The deer and fawn escape
momentarily but in the end "the arrow strikes the young deer.
Unable to run, the little one presses against its mother. The mother
licks its wound. The hunter draws another arrow. The audience, as
the eyewitness describes them, are paralyzed with suspense; deep
groans and even weeping is heard among them. And, from the mere
description, I felt that this was a true work of art" (138).

The gist of Tolstoy's theory in *What Is Art?* is that literature and
art should communicate powerful feelings honestly and sincerely,
feelings that bring people together, creating a sense of community
among all life-forms. The Vogul play exemplifies "that sense of
infection with another's feeling, compelling us to joy in another's
gladness, to sorrow at another's grief, and to mingle souls with one
another—which is the very essence of art" (138).

In this treatise, Tolstoy rails against "counterfeit art," or "art for
art's sake," as well as the similarly specious "science for science's
sake" which he sees as corrupting modern science (182). Too often,
he argues, science and modern engineering have not been "for the
benefit of the workmen, but to enrich capitalists who produce
articles of luxury or weapons of man-destroying war" (184). Instead,
he argues, science should have moral purposes: "how to use the land,
how to cultivate it oneself without oppressing other people,...how

---

[12]Leo Tolstoy, *What Is Art?* trans. Aylmer Maude (Indianapolis: Bobbs-Merrill,
1960), p. 136. Further references follow in the text.

to treat animals" (185). "[T]he business of real science" should be "to demonstrate the irrationality, unprofitableness, and immorality of war and executions... [and] the absurdity, harmfulness, and immorality of... eating animals" [186]. "Art," similarly, "should cause violence to be set aside... evok[ing instead] reverence for the dignity of every [person] and for the life of every animal" (190). Tolstoy thus invokes a "vegetarian discourse," endorsing an aesthetics of care.

Great writers, Iris Murdoch contends, are those who are able to break through ideological and mythic preconceptions to *see* the individual in his or her unique particularity. Of Tolstoy, Murdoch noted that, like Shakespeare, he exhibited what Keats termed "negative capability," a capacity to enter into the being of another—a process of yielding (as characterized by Adorno)— and to render it faithfully without imposing upon it self-serving personal or ideological design[13]—an ability which Jonathan Bate characterized as "wise female passivity and responsiveness to nature... prototypically ecofeminist" (108). "The camelion Poet," Keats wrote, "has no Identity—he is continually in... some other Body—the Sun, the Moon, the Sea."[14] In the case of animals, Tolstoy is able to render them as they are without imposing upon them anthropocentric and speciesist perspectives. The inclusion of animals as part of the picture, the recognition of their otherness and independence provide for a holistic realism that necessarily challenges such humanist assumptions.

An aesthetics of care embraces literature of this type, in which animals are taken seriously, not ignored or silenced, but with their realities empathetically entered into; speciesist ideology—which holds that animals are but objects for human use—is broken through and discarded, in favor of a view that recognizes and respects their subjectivity, their souls.[15] In much of his work, Tolstoy exemplifies this view.

---

[13]Iris Murdoch, "Negative Capability," *Adam International Review* 284–86 (1960):172, 173.

[14]*Letters of John Keats*, ed. Frederick Page (London: Oxford University Press, 1965), p. 172. The term *negative capability* is in a letter of December 21, 1817, p. 53.

[15]On the question of animal souls see Gary Kowalsky, *The Souls of Animals* (Walpole, NH: Stillpoint, 1991) and Randy Malamud, "Poetic Animals and Animal Souls," *Society & Animals* 6, no. 3 (1998):263–77.

6

Local-color animals

The world Tolstoy treated in his short stories was largely a premodern provincial one, sited before industrialization, before the ideas of Enlightenment modernity and capitalist commodification and development had taken hold. It was thus an era of personalist relation between the species before the land and animals were quantified and objectified as property, inert objects lacking personalist, subjective character, and where space and time were identified less by quantitative measurement than by the processes of nature, personal emotional connection, and by local knowledges or *mētis*. Historically, the premodern era in Western provincial locales was before the late nineteenth and early twentieth century when institutionalized agriculture and mass production ("factory farms") came to prevail.

Another access to that world is provided in the works of the "local-color" writers of the nineteenth century who focused on rural life in "Pre-Railroad Times,"[1] as labeled by Harriet Beecher Stowe, one of the founders of the local-color school in the United States. Literally, hundreds of stories and novels were produced in this "local-color" tradition, to which my studies *European Local-Color Literature* and *New England Local Color Literature* provide introduction.[2] The movement flourished in the early 1800s in Europe and later—until

---

[1]Harriet Beecher Stowe, *The Minister's Wooing* (1859) (Ridgewood, NJ: Gregg, 1968), chap. 1. An earlier version of this chapter appeared as "Provincial Life with Animals," *Society & Animals* 21, no. 1 (2013):17–33.

[2]Josephine Donovan, *European Local-Color Literature: National Tales, Dorfgeschichten, Romans Champêtres* (New York: Bloomsbury Continuum, 2010) and *New England Local Color Literature* (New York: Continuum Ungar, 1983).

around 1900—in the United States. Its works give us a window into the realities of premodern peasant and village life, a world that has largely been lost in the West through industrialization and mass transportation and communication systems.

Because domestic animals were such an important part of that world, this literature shows us how rural people related to animals in the premodern, preindustrial era, providing us with alternative models of the human-animal relationship to that described and prescribed in the ideologies of modernity. For, while, as E. P. Thompson notes in his study of bygone rural life in England, "we shall not ever return to a pre-capitalist human nature, yet a reminder of its alternative needs, expectations and codes may renew our sense of our nature's range of possibilities."[3]

We find in this world, for example, that boundaries between the species commonly accepted now were then blurred, less restrictive, or in many cases simply nonexistent. There was little distinction, for example, drawn among "pets," farm animals, and even in some instances wild animals. One finds intense love for and devotion to work animals, such as horses, shepherd dogs, or oxen, who are considered companions. Animals are often seen as part of one's family, as "folks," recognized as subjects. And despite centuries of theology to the contrary, many of these uneducated villagers and peasants persist in thinking that animals have souls. Because of their recognition of animals as like beings, many characters express empathy for them and advocate humane treatment, a few even vegetarianism and "rights" for "dumb animals."[4] Knowing the animals thus familiarly fostered in many cases an ethic and aesthetics of care where the animal is known as a particular individual, as a subject understood sympathetically, as part of the same web of relationships as contingent humans, rooted in the same environment. "[D]omestic beasts...were frequently spoken to, for their owners unlike Cartesian intellectuals, never thought them incapable of understanding," remarks Keith Thomas in his magisterial *Man and the Natural World*.[5]

---

[3]E. P. Thompson, *Customs in Common* (New York: New Press, 1991), p. 15.

[4]Harriet Beecher Stowe, "Rights of Dumb Animals," *Hearth and Home* 1 (January 2, 1869):24.

[5]Keith Thomas, *Man and the Natural World: A History of the Modern Sensibility* (New York: Pantheon, 1983), p. 96.

While the humane movement was by the early nineteenth century in full swing—numerous treatises had been published advocating humane treatment of animals, it doesn't appear that the characters in these works—most of whom were barely literate, if that—were consciously aware of "animal rights" theory or were modeling their behavior on it. Rather it appears that "farmers and poor people" were following age-old tradition in making "very little distinction between themselves and their beasts," as noted by one seventeenth-century commentator, Celia Fiennes.[6] Many characters indeed register a manifest resistance to ideas imported from and imposed upon them by metropolitan authorities and intellectuals, who are resented and seen as having little understanding of rural life, operating instead in terms of rationalist schemes derived from Enlightenment theory and capitalist economics, such as Adam Smith's *Wealth of Nations* (1776), which treats their particularized animate life-worlds in abstract and alien terms, as commodities. (See especially Smith's recommended agricultural "improvements" involving consolidation, greater productivity, and enhanced profitability).[7] One can indeed postulate the existence of two distinct cultures operating according to separate ethics or "moral economies"[8]: on the one hand, a peasant culture with its personalist ethic that accords animals' equal ontological status; on the other, an elite intellectual culture under the influence of Enlightenment rationalism and capitalism that endorse a "speciesist" ethic where humans are ontologically superior and animals reduced to commodities or indeed (as in Cartesian theory) to feelingless machines. The imposition of the latter ethic on the former was, I have argued elsewhere, a form of ideological colonization that the local-color authors (and their characters) were resisting.[9]

A Black Forest village mayor, Buchmaier, for example, in a story by German author Berthold Auerbach, "Der Lauterbacher" (1843)

[6]As cited in ibid., p. 98.

[7]Adam Smith, *The Wealth of Nations* (New York: Bantam Dell, 2003), pp. 298–309.

[8]A term used by E. P. Thompson, *Customs in Common*, (New York: New Press, 1991) pp. 259–351, to distinguish the economic worldview of the lower classes, as against that of a capitalist market economy to which it was often drawn in resistance. See also James C. Scott, *Weapons of the Weak: Everyday Forms of Peasant Resistance* (New Haven, CT: Yale University Press, 1985).

[9]Donovan, *European Local-Color Literature*, chap. 1.

(included in his collection *Schwarzwälder Dorfgeschichten*), rails against animal welfare regulations being issued by metropolitan authorities, claiming such rules are unnecessary. These urban bureaucrats, he protests, don't understand farm animals and farmers' relationships with them. "I have seen that people cry more when an ox of theirs passes on than when one of their children dies" ["ich hab' schon gesehen, dass die Leut' mehr heulen, wenn ihnen ein Rind draufgeht, als wenn ihnen ein Kind stirbt."][10]

A Scottish village preacher, Micah Balwhidder in John Galt's *Annals of the Parish* (1821), rejects the Enlightenment reliance on reason as a guide for capitalist rural development schemes—then proliferating in the Western world, which commodified animals and land (one of the worst of which was the so-called Highland Clearances in Scotland at the end of the eighteenth century and into the early nineteenth, which introduced large-scale industrialized sheep-farming). Balwhidder observes that the "birds and beasts" are "governed by a kindly instinct in attendance on their young," which suggests "that love and charity, far more than reason or justice, formed the tie that holds the world…together"[11]—thus rejecting Enlightenment intellectualism in favor of what he sees humans as having in common with animals, their emotional capacity for sympathy, seen as a cosmic interspecies bond.

"Phil Purcel: The Pig Driver," a story by Irish writer William Carleton, in his collection *Traits and Stories of the Irish Peasantry* (1843), concerns a clever scam Phil developed with his pet pig wherein he manages to sell the same pig over and over to twenty-four different, unwitting English buyers. The pig seems to understand the game and escapes from his new buyer each time to rejoin Phil for the next go-round.

The narrator observes, "Nothing could present a finer display of true friendship found upon a sense of equality, mutual interest, and good-will, than the Irishman and his pig…He and his family, and

---

[10]Berthold Auerbach, "Der Lauterbacher," in *Samtliche Schwarzwälder Dorfgeschichten*, vol. 2 (Stuttgart, Germany: F. E. Cotta'chen, 1884), p. 68. My translation from the German.

[11]John Galt, *Annals of the Parish: Or the Chronicle of Dalmailing during the Ministry of the Rev. Micah Balwhidder Written by Himself* (London: Oxford University Press, 1967), p. 157.

his pig...all slept in the same bed."[12] Phil is especially attuned to his pigs, having had "from his infancy...an uncommon attachment [to them], and by a mind naturally shrewd and observing, made himself intimately acquainted with their habits and instincts" (1:413). (A lengthy footnote gives an "authentic account" of a horse *"Whisperer"* who had a similar way with horses) (1:413 n.)

With its serious and respectful treatment of the pig-human relationship, Carleton's story must be seen as a repudiation of the by-then common English stereotype of the Irish as animals, indeed pigs. By Carleton's day "the British colonial imaginary" obsessed with "the simianized monster of Fenian rebellion [focused on] the pig [as] a dominant representation of the Irish as animal."[13]

Like many other local-color authors Carleton is critical of Enlightenment improvement and capitalist development schemes and claims people and animals were better off in the unregulated, "unimproved," and premodern era in which Phil lived.

In Phil's time [he sarcastically notes]...pig-driving...had [not]...made such rapid advances as in modern times. It was then...unaccompanied by the improvements of poverty, sickness, and famine. Political economy had not then taught the people how to be poor upon the most scientific principles. Free trade had not shown the nation the most approved plan of reducing itself to the lowest possible state of distress. (1:408)

The pigs too were better off in the old days—leaner, longer-legged, able even to outrun a greyhound. But now, only a "few specimens" of this hardy breed remain "except in the mountainous parts of the country, whither these lovers of liberty...have retired to avoid the encroachments of civilization, and exhibit their Irish antipathy" to being marketed in England (1:409).

Peasants' relationships with work animals appear to have been especially intense. These animals were daily companions, helpers in

---

[12]William Carleton, "Phil Purcel: The Pig Driver," in *Traits and Stories of the Irish Peasantry*, vol. 1 (Savage, MD: Barnes and Noble, 1990), p. 410. Further references follow in the text.
[13]Maureen O'Connor, *The Female and the Species: The Animal in Irish Women's Writing* (Bern, Switzerland: Peter Lang, 2010), p. 13.

difficult labor—for which their human owners were often deeply grateful—sometimes becoming the primary relationship in their lives. James Hogg (1770–1835), a Scottish provincial writer—known as "The Ettick Shepherd"—wrote movingly about the shepherd's relationship with his dog. In an autobiographical sketch "Further Anecdotes of the Shepherd's Dog" (1818), Hogg speaks to the collie's "sagacity."[14] "Some" shepherd dogs, he says, "excel...in a kind of social intercourse. They understand all that is said to them, or of them, in the family; and often a good deal that is said of sheep, and of other dogs, their comrades" (622). He gives several examples of these dogs' amazing ability to find lost sheep, sometimes traveling miles to do so.

Of his own dog, Sirrah, he writes, "My dog was always my companion. I conversed with him the whole day—I shared every meal with him, and my plaid in the time of a shower" (623). Hogg remarks his intelligence:

> I can never forget with what anxiety and eagerness he learned his different evolutions...and when once I made him to understand a direction, he never forgot or mistook it again. Well as I knew him, he very often astonished me; for, when hard pressed in accomplishing the task he was put to, he had the expedients of the moment that bespoke a great share of the reasoning faculty. (623)

He gives examples of his dog's intelligence, but remarks, "an Edinburgh man" (i.e., an urban intellectual influenced by Scottish Enlightenment ideas) would not be able "thoroughly to understand" them (624).

When Sirrah is too old for heavy work, Hogg has to sell him, but the dog refuses to work for anyone else, instead returning to watch his old master every day from a distance. Hogg comes to regret his decision (though Sirrah ends up in a comfortable "foster" home where he doesn't have to work), considering that the dog's loyal behavior had "a kind of heroism and sublimity" to it (626). "The parting with old Sirrah, after all that he had done for me, had such an effect on my heart" (626) that he resolves never to sell another dog.

---

[14]James Hogg, "Further Anecdotes of the Shepherd's Dog," *Blackwood's Edinburgh Magazine* 2 (March 1818):621. Further references follow in the text.

Two of the stories collected in Hogg's collection *Winter Evening Tales* (1820) deal centrally with men's relationships with their "colleys." Highlander Duncan Campbell (in a story of that title) (1811) is deeply bonded to his "colley" Oscar but has to leave the dog behind when he goes to Edinburgh for his education. Unhappy in the city, Duncan runs away from the school and heads back to the Highlands. He soon encounters a "drove of Highland cattle" with whom he identifies and sympathizes. "They were all in the hands of Englishmen;–poor exiles like himself;–going far away to be killed and eaten, and...never [to] see the Highlands again."[15] Suddenly, among them he sees Oscar, "hungry and lame" (81), having been beaten and abused by the drovers. Duncan rescues Oscar and they travel about as vagabonds the next few years, finally settling down with Oscar dying peacefully of old age at sixteen. "The sagacity which this animal possesses is almost incredible...[he had] undaunted spirit and generosity" (87).

Another story, "The Shepherd's Calendar" (1817), recounts in vividly realistic detail the heroic attempts by a shepherd and his "colley" Sparkie to save scores of sheep during a fierce winter storm.[16] Other local-color stories depict intense bonding between solitary human figures and their dogs. Two stories, for example, in S. C. Hall's *Sketches of Irish Character* (1829) concern such characters: "Jack the Shrimp," an eccentric shrimp gatherer with his dog Crab and Grey Lambert, a hermit who lives with his dog Bang in an abandoned castle in "The Barrow Postman."[17]

As one might expect, horses are another work animal to whom owners become deeply attached. That relationship is strikingly portrayed in one of the peasant novels of French writer George Sand, *Le Meunier d'Angibault* (*The Miller of Angibault*) (1845). Here the bond is between miller Grand-Louis and his horse Sophie. Like Hogg, he doubts the urbanites' capacity to understand the depth of peasants' attachments to their animals.

---

[15]James Hogg, "Duncan Campbell," in *Winter Evening Tales: Collected among the Cottagers in the South of Scotland* (Edinburgh: Edinburgh University Press, 2002), p. 81. Further references follow in the text.

[16]James Hogg, "The Shepherd's Calendar," in *Winter Evening Tales*, pp. 372–92.

[17]S. C. Hall, "Jack the Shrimp" and "The Barrow Postman," in *Sketches of Irish Character*, 3nd edn (London: Chatto and Windus, 1854), pp. 88–109 and 166–74.

We relate to animals as to people [he explains] and we miss an old horse as an old friend. You wouldn't understand that, you city people, but we peasants live with animals from whom we differ little [On s'attache aux animaux comme aux gens, et on regrette un vieux cheval comme un vieux ami. Vous ne comprendriez pas ça, vous autres gens de la ville; mais nous, gens de paysans nous vivons avec les bêtes, dont nous ne différons guère].[18]

Here again we sense a strong distinction being made between peasant culture in which animals are valued like beings and urban educated elite culture which misprizes these human-animal bonds. When Sophie is missing for a period and Grand-Louis fears she's been stolen, he is distraught. But it's not a matter of economic loss.

I scorn the paltry amount the old beast would bring...! Do you think I would care so much for 100 francs? Oh no! What I miss is her, and not her price... She was so courageous, so intelligent, she knew me so well [Je me moque bien du peu d'argent que la vieille bête pouvait valoir...! Croyez-vous que pour une centaine de francs j'aurais tant de souci? Oh! non pas: ce que je regrette, c'est elle, et non son prix... Elle était si courageuse, si intelligente, elle me connaissait si bien] (255).

Grand-Louis is here upholding a personalist kin-based ethic as against a capitalist exchange-value ethic. Sophie is valued for who she is as a living being, not for her monetary worth. (Happily, Sophie eventually turns up unharmed.)

In another of Sand's peasant novels *La Mare au diable* (*The Devil's Lake*) (1846) the main character Germain, a plowman, sings to his oxen, calling them by name, as they plow the fields. Such singing is an ancient custom, the narrator explains, designed to "uphold the courage of these animals, to pacify their discontent, and to alleviate the tedium of their lengthy toil" ["entretenir le courage de ces animaux, d'apaiser leurs mécontentements et de charmer l'ennui de leur longe besogne"].[19]

---

[18]George Sand, *Le Meunier d'Angibault* (Paris: Calmann Lévy, 1888), p. 253. My translation from the French.
[19]George Sand, *La Mare au diable* (Paris: Nelson/Calmann Lévy, 1931), pp. 31–32. My translation from the French. Further references follow in the text.

Oxen, we learn, often form strong bonds with one another, especially with their comrade under the yoke ["son camarade d'attelage"] (27). When one dies, the other will refuse to work or eat and will die of grief.

> The poor gaunt weakened animal [can be found] deep in his stall...panting with fear and disdain over his food, his eyes always turned toward the door, scratching his foot at the empty place by his side, sniffing the yoke and chains his companions wore, and calling him endlessly with deplorable bellows [au fond de de l'étable un pauvre animal maigre, exténué...soufflant avec effroi et dédain sur la nourriture qu'on lui présente, les yeux toujours tournés vers la porte, en grattant du pied la place vide à ses côtés, flairant les jougs et les chaînes que son compagnon a portés, et l'appelant sans cesse avec de déplorables mugissements.] (27)

Such an animal, lamentably, has to be sent to market, Sand notes. Otherwise, he will starve himself to death.

A similar bonding is seen in the novel between two horses, a mare and her mother, one named "la jeune Grise" [the young Grey], the other, "la vieille Grise" [the old Grey]. As with the oxen, Germain is very sensitive to the animals' moods; indeed the young la Grise becomes a central player in the novel. When Germain leaves on an excursion with her, she whinneyed a good-bye to her mother, who tried to follow her daughter, then "whinneyed in reply and remained pensive, uneasy, her nose to the wind, her mouth full of grass that she no longer thought to eat" ["elle hennit à son tour, et resta pensive, inquiète, le nez au vent, la bouche pleine d'herbes qu'elle ne songeait plus à manger"] (69–70). The animals themselves are thus seen as having emotional relationships with one another, which the human characters respect and include as a significant factor in their own decision-making.

A German regionalist Adalbert Stifter (1805–68), who wrote about Bohemia, then a part of the Austrian Empire, describes the intense relationship that developed between a rural doctor and his horse. In *Die Mappe meines Urgrossvaters* (*My Great-Grandfather's Papers*) (1841), the doctor exclaims at one point: "O, these good, these true, these willing animals—in the end they are the only ones on earth who love me so truly from the ground up" ["Ach diese guten, diese treuen, diese willigen Tieren—sie sind am Ende doch das einzige auf dieser Erde, was mich so recht vom Grunde aus liebt"].[20] The doctor develops an acute sensitivity to the languages of other non-humans, as well. "The voice of the cricket…throbs in my heart—likewise…the neglected animal beats in my heart, as if he were speaking to me in clear human words" [die Stimme der Grille…klopfte…an mein Herz–gleichsam…klopfte das misachtete Tier an mein Herz, als sagte er mir deutliche menschliche Worte"] (1:469). As noted in Chapter 3, in her essay "River Driftwood" (1881) American local-colorist Sarah Orne Jewett spoke similarly of the "languages" of nonhumans and urged that humans should learn their tongues, an idea rearticulated more recently by Patrick Murphy.[21]

Conversing with animal companions is seen in other local-color works. Manuel, the protagonist of Max Buchon's regional French novel *Le Matachin* (1854), for example, converses nonverbally with his ox, Dsaillet, with whom he relates as to a close friend. When Manuel begins courting a young woman, Dsaillet chastises him: "Giving him a sly look, he seemed to say, 'Take us as an example, my dear. Resign yourself to the life you are assigned'" ["Dsaillet le regardait…d'un air narquois qui semblait lui dire:…'Prends example sur nous, mon cher. Resigne-toi à la vie qui t'est faite'"].[22]

At Manuel's wedding celebration, which Dsaillet attends, "he opens his eyes completely surprised at seeing so many people. Manuel, who notices, imagines that he is confused at having so poorly prophesied in his famous advice" ["Dsaillet ouvre ses yeux tout surpris en voyant tant de monde. Manuel qui s'en aperçoit s'imagine qu'il est tout confus d'avoir si mal prophétisé dans son fameux discours"] (157).

---

[20]Adalbert Stifter, "Die Mappe meines Urgrossvaters," in *Gesammelte Werke*, vol. 1, *Studien* (Wiesbaden, Germany: Insel-Verlag, 1959), p. 646. My translation from the German. Further references follow in the text.

[21]See Chapter 3, p. 85. For more on learning animal languages, see Josephine Donovan, "Interspecies Dialogue and Animal Ethics: The Feminist Care Perspective," in *The Oxford Handbook of Animal Studies*, ed. Linda Kalof (New York: Oxford University Press, 2015).

[22]Max Buchon, *Le Matachin, in En Province: Scènes Franc-Comtoises* (Paris: Michel Lévy, 1858), p. 84. My translation from the French. Further references follow in the text.

Manuel finally, reluctantly, has to sell Dsaillet in order to buy back a cow, La Bouquette, to whom his mother is deeply attached. (The cow had also been in attendance at the wedding, another indication of the fluid boundary in this premodern culture between human and animal space [viz. the Irish sleeping with their pigs, dogs in church, etc.].) Dsaillet ends up being butchered and Fifine, Manuel's new wife, realizes she may have inadvertently put his meat in a soup she has prepared. She warns Manuel, saying it would be heartless to eat his old companion. He proceeds to eat the soup, however, he immediately throws it up. Fifine laughs: "Ha! Ha! Poor Dsaillet...thus are you avenged" ["Pauvre Dsaillet...te voilà vengé"] (171). The novel includes a lengthy disquisition on what admirable beings oxen are and how people should treat them more humanely (87–90).

One of the most intense relationships depicted in this local-color literature is between a peasant Érembert and his goat Scripant in Ferdinand Fabre's novel *Le Chevrier* (*The Goatherd*) (1867). Érembert considers Scripant his "best friend" ["meilleur ami"].[23] "I kissed my goat...Heavens! Had I any other friend on earth" ["j'embrassai mon bouc...Hélas! Avais-je d'autre ami sur la terre"] (57). "Touched" by his response, "I scratched [my hands] against the grain of his hair, as goats like to be caressed" [Emu, j'allongeai les mains...et je les grattai à travers poils, comme chèvres aiment être caressées"] (57).

Érembert sings Scripant's praises. He was

the most handsome, the strongest, the most valiant of nature's creatures that had ever been known in the Hautes Cévennes [mountains]. Scripant had intelligence and knowledge to more than match the schoolmaster [le plus beau, le plus fort, le plus vaillant aux entreprises de nature qu'on eût jamais connu aux Cévennes-Hautes. Scripant avait de l'esprit et de la connaissance à en revendre au maître de l'école (70)].

Based on Scripant, Érembert concludes that "animals love better, regret more, take greater offense than we do, because, when they love, it's forever" ["bêtes aiment mieux, regrettent

---

[23]Ferdinand Fabre, *Le Chevrier* (Paris: Bibliothèque-Charpentier, 1913), p. 257. My translation from the French. Further references follow in the text.

mieux, s'estomaquent mieux que nous tous, car, aimant, c'est pour toujours"] (111). Indeed, he considers that humans may in fact be fallen animals, reversing the myth of the fall. "It often occurred to me that before being hard, querulous, wicked men, we were perhaps gentle, affectionate, peaceful animals" ["Il m'est souvent fois venu l'idée qu'avant d'être hommes durs, querelleurs, méchants, avions-nous été peut-être animaux doux, affectueux, paisibles"] (16).

For many of these characters, animals are simply part of the family; human space—the home—and animal space are not held as ontologically distinct. Érembert's mother, for example, who also loves animals, has chickens, hens, rabbits, turkeys, and a pig running through her house (149), all sharing the same home territory. Aunt Carleton, the town herbalist in Mary Leadbeater's *Annals of Ballitore* (ca. 1824), a nonfictional account of an Irish village, has several animals living in her house, including a clever pig who can open door latches and pet hens who lay eggs on a cushion under her chair.[24]

Jenny Wrayn in American local-colorist Mary E. Wilkins [Freeman]'s story "Christmas Jenny" (1891) has turned her house into a kind of unofficial veterinary rehab hospital.

> It had a curious sylvan air; there were heaps of evergreens here and there, and some small green trees leaned in one corner. All around the room...were little rough cages and hutches, from which twittering and chirping sounded. They contained forlorn little birds and rabbits and field mice.[25]

A neighbor explains that Jenny

> picks [the animals] up in the woods when they're starvin' and freezin' an' half dead, an' she brings "em in here an" takes care of em' an' feeds em' till they gets well, an' then she lets 'em go again...You see that rabbit there? Well, he's been in a trap.

[24]Mary Leadbeater, "Annals of Ballitore," in *The Leadbeater Papers*, vol. 1 (London: Routledge/Thoemmes, 1998), p. 70.

[25]Mary E. Wilkins, "Christmas Jenny," in *A New England Nun and Other Stories* (New York: Harper, 1891), p. 170. Further references follow in the text.

Somebody wanted to kill the poor little creature. You see that robin? Somebody fired a gun at him an' broke his wing (172).

A similar character operating as a local veterinarian out of her house may be found in Annie Trumbull Slosson's story "Anna Malann."[26] Another New England local-colorist, Rose Terry Cooke (1827–92), depicts two memorable women characters whose primary relationships are with their animals in "Miss Lucinda" (1861) and "Dely's Cow" (1865), both collected in *Somebody's Neighbors* (1881). Lucinda keeps a cat and three kittens, "an old blind crow, a yellow dog," a rooster, and three hens in her house with her.[27] "In her life her pets were the great item: Her cat had its own chair in the parlor and kitchen; her dog, a rug and a basket...; her old crow, its special nest of flannel and cotton, where it feebly croaked as soon as Miss Lucinda began to spread the little table for her meals" (156). Lucinda "cared more for her garden" and her animals "than for all the humanity of Dalton [her town] put together" (157).

She eventually adopts a pet pig to whom "she took an astonishing fancy. Very few people know how intelligent an animal a pig is" (161). He "wiggled his curly tail as expressively as a dog's and 'all but speakin'...He was always glad to see Miss Lucinda, and established a firm friendship with her dog" (162). Lucinda lavishes care on her animals (which the author/narrator disapproves of); she believes that "animals have feelings that are easily wounded, and are capable of 'like passions' with [humans], only incapable of expression" (162). Indeed, she "believed creatures had souls" (163), thus elevating animals to equal ontological status.

This story is unusual among local-color works in that the author takes a critical view of the character's relationship with her animals, considering it silly and juvenile. Thus, eventually Lucinda is made to conform to adult norms, of subordinating animals to human use, including having the pig sold for butchering.[28]

---

[26]Annie Trumbull Slosson, "Anna Malann," in *Dumb Foxglove and Other Stories* (New York: Harper, 1898).

[27]Rose Terry Cooke, "Miss Lucinda," in *How Celia Changed Her Mind and Other Stories* (New Brunswick, NJ: Rutgers University Press, 1986), p. 155. Further references follow in the text.

[28]I present a detailed critique of this story in "Breaking the Sentence" (1993).

A more sympathetic account by Cooke is "Dely's Cow," which similarly depicts a woman who loves her three cats, dog, horse, and a lame robin. "For all these dumb things she had a really intense affection."[29] Dely develops an especial attachment to her cow Biddy, who "was really Dely's friend" (189), and she is distressed at Biddy's "cries of appeal and grief" (189) when her heifer is sold to the butcher. As with the other rural folk we have considered, Dely saw her cow

as a real sentient being, capable of love and sympathy. Many a time did the lonely little woman lay her head on Biddy's neck, and talk to her about George [her husband, who is off at the Civil War] with sobs and silences interspersed; and many a piece of dry bread steeped in warm water, or golden carrot, or mess of stewed turnips and bran, flavored the dry hay that was the staple of the cow's diet. (189)

Further examples where animals are accorded kin status include *The Wild Irish Girl* (1806) by Lady Morgan (Sydney Owenson) in which a starving Irish peasant says that seeing the suffering of his equally starving cow is as hard to bear as that of his family. "One can better suffer themselves a thousand times over than see one's poor dumb baste want: it is, next…to feeling one's child in want. God help him who has witnessed both!"[30]

Some characters adopt as domestic pets animals we would consider wild. Terence Oge O'Leary, an eccentric rustic philosopher in another of Lady Morgan's novels, *Florence Macarthy* (1818), has a pet eagle.[31] A similar character in George Sand's *Mauprat* (1837), named Patience, has a pet owl.[32]

---

[29]Rose Terry Cooke, "Dely's Cow," in *How Celia*, p. 183. Further references follow in the text.

[30]Lady Morgan, *The Wild Irish Girl* (London: Pandora, 1986), p. 13.

[31]Lady Morgan, *Florence Macarthy: An Irish Tale*, vol. 1 (New York: Garland, 1979), p. 299.

[32]George Sand, *Mauprat* (Paris: Calmann Lévy, 1930), p. 48. Whether these adoptions involved coercive control or harm to the birds or whether the birds "hung around" because of the ready food and shelter is unclear. My point, however, is not to condone such practice but to illustrate how the borderline between wild and domestic was less rigid in premodern times than today.

Perhaps because of their close association with animals, many characters exhibit strong empathy with them and react viscerally against any cruelty they encounter. The title character in *The Life of Mansie Wauch* by D. M. Moir (1828), a Scottish regional novel, is appalled at the cruel treatment of an exhausted mare, who is driven to her death in a horserace. "I turned round my back, not able to stand it."[33]

Natzi, an illiterate German peasant boy in an Auerbach novella, is intensely sensitive to the farm animals he tends, lamenting that they exist only to be slaughtered. "That is why the sow cries and screams so when she is slaughtered," he says ["dessenthalben auch so eine Sau am ärgsten schreit und heult, wenn man's metzget"].[34] He has a shepherd dog who is "smarter than ten doctors" ["gescheiter war als zehn Doktor"] (1:125) and could read his "innermost thoughts" ["verborgesten Gedanken"] (1:125). He teaches his friend Ivo to love these animals and "encouraged him in this care for the defenseless enslaved creatures" ["Zu dieser Sorgfalt für die wehrlos Angejochten hielt ihn Natzi…an"] (1:137).

King Corny, a rustic authority in Maria Edgeworth's Irish novel *Ormond* (1817), similarly advocates humane treatment of farm animals, rejecting the use of a cruel farming practice: "That is against humanity to brute *bastes*, which…I practice."[35]

Guillaume Inot, an abandoned wild child in Léon Cladel's *Le Bouscassié* (The Woodcutter) (1867), set in Languedoc, France, grows up in even closer proximity to animals than most. Nursed by a dog ["une chienne allaitait"],[36] he early learns to model his behavior on the animals around him.

Paddling in the pond with the ducks and geese, crawling under the pensive oxen before the manger, hanging around the dog who nursed him, sometimes walking on all fours like his wetnurse, and sometimes on two in the manner of poultry, he conducted

[33]D. S. Moir, *The Life of Mansie Waugh, Tailor in Dalkeith, Written by Himself* (Edinburgh: William Blackwood, 1828), p. 88.

[34]Berthold Auerbach, "Ivo der Hajrle," *Samtliche Schwarzwälder Dorfgeschichten*, 1: 126. Further references follow in the text.

[35]Maria Edgeworth, *Ormond* (New York: Penguin, 2000), p. 51.

[36]Leon Cladel, *Le Bouscassié* (Paris: Alphonse Lemerre, 1869), p. 10. My translation from the French. Further references follow in the text.

himself in imitation of his companions whom he had taken for
models. [Barbotant dans la mare avec les canards et les oies,
rampant sous les boeufs pensifs devant la crèche, fréquentant la
chienne qui l'avait allaité, tantôt marchant à quatre pas comme
sa mère la nourrice, et tantôt sur deux avec des allures de volaille,
il se dirigeait à l'instar de ses compagnons qu'il avail pris pour
modèles]. (12)

He understands animal language and empathizes with animals'
emotions, protesting when other humans ignore their cries.

Initiated from his earliest years into their commerce and speaking
their language, he undoubtedly understood amazingly what the
animals said ... "Deaf as you are," he said one day to some diggers
who asked him why he was sad and groaning, "don't you hear
over there ... that ewe who is crying and calling back her lamb
whom they have taken or killed?" [Initié, dès son plus bas âge, à
leur commerce et parlant à leur langage, il comprenait sans doute
à merveille ce que disaient les animaux ... "Sourds que vous êtes,"
dit-il un jour à des terrassiers qui lui demandaient pourquoi il était
chagrin et gémissait, "n'entendez-vous pas là-bas ... cette brebis
qui bêle et réclame son agneau qu'on lui a pris ou tué"?]. (26)

There are several other instances where Guillaume shows
compassion for and/or saves animals from harm. In a lengthy scene,
he cares for a dying mule and insists on giving the animal a decent
burial when the owner wants to dismember the body to sell the skin
(27–34). Later, at some risk to himself, he intervenes in a cruel sport
where rats are being set on fire (133–35). And while consulting a
fortune-teller/witch about how to avoid the military draft, he refuses
to permit as part of the procedure a ritual decapitation of a bird (256).

Characters in other works show similar compassion. The title
character in *La Petite Fadette* (1850) by George Sand, for example,
expresses empathy for a caterpillar.

Me, I am not like those who say: Look, there's a caterpillar, an
ugly creature; oh, how ugly! We must kill it! Me, I don't crush
God's poor creature and if the caterpillar falls in the water I
extend her a leaf so she can save herself [Moi, je ne suis pas
comme ceux qui disent: Voilà une chenille une vilaine bête; ah!

qu'elle est laide! il faut la tuer! Moi, je n'écrase pas la pauvre créature du bon Dieu, et si la chenille tombe dans l'eau, je lui tends une feuille pour qu'elle se sauve].[37]

Mara, a character in Harriet Beecher Stowe's New England local-color novel *The Pearl of Orr's Island* (1862), protects some eagle's eggs from destruction, showing empathy for the mother eagle.[38] In Galt's Scottish *Annals of the Parish*, the local schoolmistress, Sabrina Hookie, saves a duck by performing a caesarian operation on her when she eats too many uncooked beans.[39]

Some characters articulate a coherent "animal rights" theory, advocating in some cases vegetarianism. Again, this doesn't seem to have derived from any theory they read in books but rather from a direct emotional response to animals' suffering. Grandmother Badger, for example, a central character in Harriet Beecher Stowe's *Oldtown Folks* (1869), laments the practice of separating a cow from her calf a day before the latter is to be slaughtered, exclaiming that "calf-killing [is] an abominable cruelty, and the parting of calf and cow for a day beforehand an aggravation."[40]

I say it's a shame... and I always shall. Hear that cow low! She feels as bad as I should... If I had things *my* way, folks should n't eat creatures at all... I know an old cow's feelings, and I would n't torment her to save myself a little trouble. (170)

Sam Lawson, another character in the same novel, goes so far as to claim that fishes have rights, noting how they suffer when caught on a hook.

He was a soft-hearted old body, and the wrigglings and contortions of [the fish] used to disturb his repose so... he [would] kill the fish by breaking their necks when he took them from the hook ..."

[37]George Sand, *La Petite Fadette* (Paris: Livre de Poche, 1973), p. 10. My translation from the French. Further references follow in the text.

[38]Harriet Beecher Stowe, *The Pearl of Orr's Island: A Story of the Coast of Maine* (Boston: Houghton Mifflin, 1896), pp. 175–79.

[39]Galt, *Annals*, p. 66.

[40]Harriet Beecher Stowe, *Oldtown Folks* (Boston: Houghton Mifflin, 1894), p. 169. Further references follow in the text.

I can't bear to see no kind o' critter in torment. These "ere pouts ain't to blame for bein" fish, and ye ought to put "em out of their misery. Fish has their rights as well as any on us." (29)

Patience, the eccentric hermit in George Sand's novel *Mauprat*, has a similarly empathetic response to animal suffering and adopts a vegetarian diet as a result, becoming a follower of the "Pythagorean doctrine" (vegetarianism). "Inclined toward Pythagorean ideas, he was horrified by bloodshed. The death of a doe brought him to tears" ["Enclin aux idées pythagoriciennes, il avait horreur du sang répandu. La morte d'une biche lui arrachait des larmes"].[41] After becoming a vegetarian, "he felt...a secret joy...in no longer having occasion to see death delivered...to innocent animals" ["il éprouvait...une secrète joie...de n'avoir plus occasion de voir donner la mort...à des animaux innocents"] (42).

The world depicted in these local-color works is premodern, preindustrial, and largely precapitalist. This doesn't mean that animals are not sent to market and slaughtered or sold for other reasons—though, as noted, numerous characters are wrenched by the process. As a farmer notes on selling a horse in Karl Immerman's *Münchhausen* (1838), "It always saddens one when one sells a creature one has raised, but what can one do?" ["Es tut einem immer leid, wenn man eine Kreatur, die man aufzog, losschlägt, aber wer kann wider?"].[42] The horse looks back wistfully ["als wolte sie klagen"] (3:141) and a young boy observes that a cow companion too is mournful at the departure ["Das Vieh grümt sich"] (3:141). The farmer replies, "why shouldn't she?...we're all mourning" ["Warum sollte es nicht...grämen wir uns doch auch"] (3:141).

But the personal relationship with the animals meant that they had a subject status—they were persons—in the eyes of their owners— something no longer possible under industrialized agriculture where animals are but mass objects, commodities for sale, slaughter, and consumption; or under Cartesian science but object matter for vivisection and other experimentation. Nor does this personal

---

[41]Sand, *Mauprat*, p. 146. Further references follow in the text.
[42]Karl Immermann, "*Münchhausen*," in *Werke*, ed. Benno von Wiese, vol. 3 (Frankfurt am Main, Germany: Athenäum, 1972), p. 141. My translation from the German. Further references follow in the text.

knowledge of animals guarantee that they were never treated cruelly in preindustrial eras and regions. Undoubtedly, instances occurred then as now; however, in this local-color literature, cruelty is generally deplored and humane treatment seems to have been the norm, a humane treatment rooted in intimate knowledge of animals as fellow beings who experience similar emotions, who suffer similarly as we, and who therefore deserve to be treated with respect and compassion.

These characters therefore point to an animal ethic that is not based on rights or utilitarian theory—Enlightenment offshoots— but rather on personal, emotional, and dialogical knowledge rooted in interspecies communication—in short, an ethic of care. Nor is the aesthetic entailed in these works framed in terms of the Kantian aesthetics of modernity. Rather it reflects an aesthetics of care, wherein animals are treated not as objects framed for aesthetic manipulation or to comment upon human situations but rather seen as independent subjects with different voices of their own that merit and receive ethical attention from the characters and from the author. "Don't you hear over there...that ewe who is crying?"

7
Coetzee's animals

The most prominent writer in our day to take up the issue of human exploitation and abuse of animals is South African author J. M. Coetzee, the recipient of the Nobel Prize in Literature, the Booker Prize twice, and of widespread and deserved critical acclaim. Concern about human treatment of animals is central in his hotly discussed novel *Disgrace* and in the dramatic essay *The Lives of Animals*, both published in 1999, but it is apparent in his earliest work and is manifest as well in his autobiography, *Boyhood* (1997).[1] That certain protagonists equate human mistreatment of animals with the Holocaust suggests the severity of his moral opprobrium.

Nevertheless, while Coetzee's sensitivity to animal ethical issues is undeniable, aspects particularly of his novel *Disgrace* are troublingly problematic from the point of view of an ecofeminist aesthetics of care. For, as I explore in Chapters 8 and 9, the animal sacrifice upon which the novel ends harks back to age-old masculinist rituals, on the one hand (implicating the character David Lurie) and replicates an aesthetic of the "transgressive sublime," on the other (implicating the author): both aspects decidedly disturbing and reprovable from an ecofeminist aesthetic and ethical perspective. In this chapter, however, I focus on aspects of Coetzee's oeuvre that reflect to a great extent an aesthetics of care.

---

[1] The opening incident in Coetzee's *Boyhood: Scenes from a Provincial Life* (New York: Viking, 1997), p. 2, recounts his revulsion at a grisly operation his mother performs on some hens: "The hens shriek and struggle, their eyes bulging...[The boy] shudders and turns away." The memoir details several similar episodes. A shorter version of this chapter appears as "'Miracles of Creation': Animals in the Work of J. M. Coetzee," *Michigan Quarterly Review* 43, no. 1 (Winter 2004):78–93.

Most of Coetzee's fiction is set in South Africa with its colonialist history as backdrop; they thus bring to the fore the imperialist aspects of modernity—the drive to, as Zola put it in *The Experimental Novel*, "dominate and control," (31) "to penetrate to the wherefore of things, to become superior to these things, and to reduce them to a condition of subservient machinery" (25). That "these things" include indigenous peoples and their habitat, as well as animals and the earth itself, is inherent in the imperialist ideology of domination.

This mentality is the subject of Coetzee's first published writing, "The Narrative of Jacobus Coetzee," a novella that appeared in *Dusklands* (1974). The novella deals centrally with the eighteenth-century European colonization of the South African bush, through the figure of Jacobus Coetzee, an ancestor of the current writer, who purports to be the translator of Jacobus's 1760 narrative about his exploratory journeys into the interior regions of southern Africa.

Jacobus fashions himself pridefully as "a tamer of the wild."[2] "Destroyer of the wilderness, I move through the land cutting a devouring path from horizon to horizon" (79). Reflecting a Cartesian I-it epistemology, Jacobus perceives his relation to his environment as one of self versus other. That relationship is mediated through his gun, which enables the self-other distinction.

> The tidings of the gun: such and such is outside, have no fear. The gun saves us from the fear that all life is within us...I move through the wilderness with my gun...and slay elephants, hippopotami, rhinoceres, buffalo, lions, leopards, dogs, giraffes, antelope and buck of all descriptions, fowl..., hares, snakes; I leave behind me a mountain of skin, bones, inedible gristle and excrement. (79)

Killing living creatures—rendering them dead—establishes them as *other* than the living self, thereby enabling the ego to assert and be confident of its own separate identity.

> The death of the hare is the logic of salvation...the death of the hare is my metaphysical meat, just as the flesh of the hare is the

---

[2]J. M. Coetzee, "The Narrative of Jacobus Coetzee," in *Dusklands* (New York: Penguin, 1996), p. 77. Further references follow in the text.

meat of my dogs. The hare dies to keep my soul from merging
with the world. (79–80)

Thus, as "metaphysical meat," the killed animal serves the
psychological purpose of ensuring Jacobus's separate identity. By
casting the animal as dead *other*, he establishes himself as a distinct
entity that is *not that*, engaging in an "inside-outside," subject-
object Cartesian epistemology, which enables him to disconnect
from other living creatures ("the gun saves us from the fear that all
life is within" [79]). By casting them as out-there and alien, he thus
renders them vulnerable to subjugation by the conquering ego: "I
am all that I see" (79).

Part of the colonization process is the transformation of
qualitatively valued entities into quantifiable commodities. As "a
domesticator of the wilderness," Jacobus notes, "I am...a hero
of enumeration" (80). For, "the essence of" domesticated land
and animals—the agricultural industry—"is number," and "our
commerce with the wild is a tireless enterprise of turning it into
orchard and farm" (80). By contrast, objectifying quantification
does not exist in the yet undomesticated territories: "we cannot
count the wild" (80); and the language of the native Bushmen "does
not include a procedure for counting" (80). Jacobus's imperialist
project then is seen to connect to capitalism, transforming living
entities into exchange-value commodities; it also shows forth the
Cartesian quantifying epistemology that underlies the enterprise.

In constradistinction to Jacobus Coetzee, many protagonists in
J. M. Coetzee's later works evince a nonviolent, nondominative,
"yielding" attitude toward the natural world and animals, one
that evinces an ethic and aesthetics of care. In the *Life and Times
of Michael K* (1983), for example, the protagonist, who is often
likened to innumerable animals from earthworms and moles to
elephants,[3] develops a benign, respectful relationship to the natural
world in which he

become[s] one with the earth...Rather than transforming
the...landscape, the perceiving subject is one with it and leaves it

---

[3] J. M. Coetzee, *The Life and Times of Michael K*. (New York: Viking, 1983), pp. 182,
155. Further references follow in the text.

open and intact, exactly as it was before it was observed. Instead of imposing a metaphysical sense on the terrain, K is at one with its real sense, its *Dasein*: its "being there" rather than its "being something."[4]

Michael K is a hapless, homeless man, an off-again-on-again gardener who gets inadvertently caught up in various military sweeps during an unspecified South African war that is going on around him. Michael relates to the world in an immediate, nonconceptual way and is himself "above and beneath classification, a soul blessedly untouched by doctrine, untouched by history" (151).

Michael resists or is unable to bend the world into aesthetic or ideological shapes; he rather accepts things as they are. "He did not seem to have a belief... Perhaps I am the stony ground, he thought" (48). "There were long periods when he sat staring at his hands, his mind blank" (33). He seems, in short, to operate in terms of epistemological *ascesis* (as characterized by Simone Weil).

After a stretch when he lives in an abandoned rural home raising a garden, he seems to merge with his environment, not unlike Crazy Ivar in Cather's novel *O Pioneers!*.

He breathed into his lungs the clear sweet smell of water brought up from inside the earth. It intoxicated him, he could not have enough of it. *Though he knew no names* he could tell one bush from another by the smell of their leaves. He could smell rain-weather in the air. (115, emphasis added)

Not only does he know no names—and thus does not transcribe the matter of his environment into a chain of human signifiers, he "did not know what to do with... numbers" (110), thus remaining unschooled in the mathematizing perspective of Cartesian imperial science and incapable of operating within an exchange-commodity commerce.

His purportedly unmediated perspective reflects a nondominative aesthetics of care. As he lies "with his eyes open" staring at the makeshift iron-corrugated ceiling roof of his hut, with its "tracings of rust, his mind would not wander, he would see nothing but the iron,

[4]Michael Marais, "The Hermeneutics of Empire: Coetzee's Post-colonial Metafiction," in *Critical Perspectives on J. M. Coetzee*, ed. Graham Huggan and Stephen Watson (New York: St. Martin's Press, 1996), p. 77.

the lines would not transform themselves into pattern or fantasy; he was himself, lying in his own house, *the rust was merely rust*" (115, emphasis added). He thus declines or refuses to compose what he sees into an aesthetic composition, assenting instead to let it be. Michael develops a caring attachment to his garden. "[A] cord of tenderness...stretched from him to the patch of earth" where his pumpkins grew. "It seemed to him that one could cut a cord like that only so many times before it would not grow again" (66). He thinks of the pumpkins as "his children...beginning their struggle upward through the dark earth toward the sun" (101). Unfortunately, Michael doesn't seem, however, to extend his caring attitude toward animals, whom he occasionally kills and eats.

Coetzee poses Michael's lifestyle and epistemology as an alternative to the mentality of imperial domination that expresses itself in a perennial state of war. Michael himself dimly realizes that he is not one of the warriors but that his destiny lies in being their opposite, a gardener.

> Men had gone off to war saying the time for gardening was when the war was over; whereas there must be men to stay behind and keep gardening alive, or at least the idea of gardening; because once that cord was broken, the earth would grow hard and forget her children. (109)

Michael intuits, like Alexandra in *O Pioneers!*, that there is an invisible cord or bond "of tenderness" between humans and the earth—a bond of ecosympathy—that must be kept alive by "gardening," for when once broken—by war, by violence, by forgetfulness, and by lack of attention—it may not grow again. Gardening is thus seen to represent a mentality of nurturing and caring, a practice of peace that ties one to the earth in nondestructive ways.

The themes adumbrated in *Dusklands* and *Michael K* are amplified to much greater effect in what is perhaps Coetzee's greatest novel, *Waiting for the Barbarians* (1980), where the issue of abusive animal treatment becomes a central concern.

In many ways a brilliant work, *Waiting for the Barbarians*, is a sort of allegorical fable in the tradition of Kafka,[5] about Western

---

[5]See Patricia Merivale, "Audible Palimpsests: Coetzee's Kafka," in *Critical Perspectives*, ed. Huggan and Watson, pp. 152–67.

imperialism. It takes place in an outpost of an unspecified empire and concerns the imperial officials' attempts to "deal with" a tribe of "barbarians" whom they deem a threat to the empire; they use torture and ineffectual military excursions in their attempt to annihilate the barbarians. Caught in the middle is the narrator, the "Magistrate," an "homme moyen sensuel," who like many Coetzee figures has lived a life of moral apathy and lazy indifference before the campaign against the barbarians begins. The Magistrate is a passive, nonjudgmental figure not unlike Michael K, though better connected; he is content to let things drift until forced, by the evidence of imperial torture, to confront the problem of evil. He has a visceral, nonrational reaction against the use of torture, and indeed nearly all of his reactions are visceral ones that he is unable to explain.

The sort of unmediated and otherwise inexplicable empathy he feels toward a young barbarian woman (referred to throughout as the "barbarian girl"), whom he tends after she's been tortured, is also seen in his sensitivity to the subjectivity of animals. Perhaps the most dramatic instance of this occurs in a hunting episode where the Magistrate finds he cannot kill a waterbuck he has in his gun sight: "My pulse does not quicken: evidently it is not important to me that the ram die."[6] He wonders "what it is that has robbed the hunt of its savour." While he hesitates, "the buck wheels off and with a whisk of its tail and a brief splash of hooves disappears into the tall reeds" (40). The moment seems to signify that a gradual process or "feminization" is occurring within the protagonist, effecting his transformation from one of the victimizers to one of the victims. In a later scene, once he's been accused of siding with the barbarians, part of the Magistrate's own torture entails a public shaming dressed in women's clothes, a final sign that he is now one of the scorned and despised, no longer an agent of the dominant caste. As with David Lurie in *Disgrace* (discussed below), the Magistrate's social fall into outcast status occasions a kind of moral awakening.

The torturers are, unlike the Magistrate, successful hunters. Colonel Joll, the leading imperial "interrogator" (read torturer),

---

[6]J. M. Coetzee, *Waiting for the Barbarians* (1980; New York: Penguin, 1982), p. 39. Further references follow in the text.

boastingly describes in the manner of Jacobus Coetzee a "great drive he rode in, when thousands of deer, pigs, bears were slain, so many that a mountain of carcases [sic] had to be left to rot" (1). His chief interrogation assistant is "a hunter who has shot pigs up and down the river all his life" (22). In fact, overhunting and the expanding imperial settlement have depleted the area of animals: "A generation ago there were antelope and hares in such numbers," the Magistrate laments. Trapping is similarly described by him in pejorative terms. "By mid-morning they are back with huge catches: birds with their necks twisted, slung from poles... by their feet, or crammed alive into wooded cages, screaming with outrage" (57).

The Magistrate's sensitivity to animals may also be seen in his adoption of an orphaned fox cub, whom he plans to rehabilitate and release. He jokingly tells the barbarian girl, whom he has also taken in, "People will say I keep two wild animals in my rooms, a fox and a girl" (34). In fact, like the Magistrate (and like sympathetic characters in *Disgrace*, where sensitivity to animal suffering becomes almost a sign of grace), the barbarian girl has a special talent in relating to animals. In a windstorm during the Magistrate's arduous trek to barbarian territory to return the girl home, she calms frightened horses by means of her special touch. She "stands with her arms stretched like wings over the necks of two horses. She seems to be talking to them: through their eyeballs glare, they are still" (67).

On the same journey, one of the horses collapses and has to be killed. As he approaches the animal, the Magistrate "swear[s] the beast knows what is to happen. At the sight of the knife its eyes roll" (62). Later, when another horse collapses and as they are short of food, the Magistrate allows his men to slaughter the horse and eat it. He notes, "I give my permission but do not join in" (75).

When he returns from this journey and is (wrongly) accused of having betrayed the outpost to the barbarians, he is imprisoned and tortured. Under this treatment, he describes himself as an animal. "I guzzle my food like a dog. A bestial life is turning me into a beast" (80). "Like a wounded snail I begin to creep along the wall" (42). "Scuttling from hole to hole like a mouse I forfeit even the appearance of ignorance" (101). After a beating, "I trot around the room holding my face, whining like a dog" (108). His cheek wound has a "crust like a fat caterpillar" (115) on it; similar imagery is used to describe the torture scars on the eyelid of the barbarian girl.

"There is no way of dying allowed me, it seems, except like a dog in a corner" (117).

Other subjugated peoples are similarly appropriated to animals. The "fisher folk," an innocuous group who live outside the outpost and are rounded up and incarcerated during the obsessive search for barbarians, are treated "as if they were indeed animals" (20). A group of barbarian prisoners are marched into town "meek as lambs" (103) because of a hideous system of interlinking them with wires run through their cheeks.

After the Magistrate's torture and public humiliation, he is released but treated as an animal pariah by the inhabitants of the outpost.

> I, the old clown who lost his last vestige of authority the day he spent hanging from a tree in a woman's underclothes shouting for help, the filthy creature who for a week licked his food off the flagstones like a dog... I live like a starved beast at the back door, kept alive perhaps only as evidence of the animal that skulks within every barbarian-lover. (124)

The latter comment indicates that in this novel Coetzee subtends an underlying pattern of domination: on one side are those victimized as "barbarian" by members of the "Empire." These include all who are deemed uncivilized from the perspective of patriarchal imperial authority: feminized men, alien tribes, and animals. The Magistrate's drama is that he goes from being a member of the imperial order to one of its outcasts. The reasons for his transition lie in his innate sensitivity[7] to barbarians and animals—a feminine attribute. Such empathy leads him in a sense

---

[7]He, indeed, like Coetzee, believes there is an inborn sense of justice: "all creatures come into the world bringing with them the memory of justice" (139). In an interview, Coetzee commented that *Waiting for the Barbarians* "asks the question: Why does one choose the side of justice when it is not in one's material interest to do so? The Magistrate gives the rather Platonic answer: because we are born with the idea of justice." Similarly, he notes, one may ask why seek the truth when it may not be in one's interest to do so? "I continue to give a Platonic answer: because we are born with the idea of the truth." In *Doubling the Point: Essays and Interviews*, ed. David Attwell (Cambridge: Harvard University Press, 1992), p. 395.

to join the ranks of these "others," which entails acknowledging the barbarian-woman-animal within himself ("the animal that skulks within every barbarian-lover"). It also leads to his being branded a barbarian-woman-animal by the imperial authorities, which legitimizes in their eyes his contemptuous treatment. The Magistrate's moment of truth comes when he has a visceral reaction against the torture of the barbarians. An unpremeditated "No!" wells up from within him. "Look," he shouts, "We [humans] are the great miracle of creation!" (107). He is then beaten and cannot remember what he was trying to say. "I pursue the thought but it eludes me like a wisp of smoke. It occurs to me that we crush insects beneath our feet, miracles of creation too, beetles, worms, cockroaches, ants, in their various ways" (107). Thus, his moment of revolt involves a recognition of the commonality of all life forms which provokes his protest not just of the cruel treatment of other humans but implicitly of humanity's ruthless treatment of animals, also "miracles of creation." Both subjugations are legitimized by the same imperial mentality.

In one of his few analytical statements, the Magistrate blames this imperial mentality for the fallen state of the outpost (i.e., of humanity).

What has made it impossible for us to live in time like fish in water, like birds in air, like children? It is the fault of Empire! Empire has created the time of history. Empire has located its existence not in the smooth recurrent spinning time of the cycle of the seasons but in the jagged time of rise and fall, of beginning and end, of catastrophe...One thought alone preoccupies the submerged mind of Empire: how not to end, how not to die, how to prolong its era. (133)

Like Michael K, the Magistrate longs to escape from the linear "progressive" narrative of history, because it entails an inauthentic rejection of mortality, which is (as seen in the events of the novel) projected onto an *other*—be it barbarian, animal, or woman— whom the imperial authorities (the beneficiaries of history thus conceived) must destroy in order to secure their own claims to immortal transcendence through historical triumph. So, while Coetzee seems to be advocating through the Magistrate an escape into "being" from "becoming" (as one critic has proposed Coetzee protagonists habitually do)[8]and thus apolitical evasion—I suggest that, instead, he is offering a critique of the inauthentic uses to which history and politics may be put. Coetzee likely has in mind here not just Western imperialism, to which the novel clearly refers allegorically, but also Nazism and Communism, which similarly offered ideologies of historical redemption.

The novel ends somewhat inconclusively with the imperial guard in strategic retreat, leaving the outpost to "wait for the barbarians" on its own. One of the last gestures of the withdrawing forces is to confiscate local livestock animals, in one case, "a cock and hen, the cock a magnificent black and gold creature. Their legs are bound, [the soldier] grips them by the wings, their fierce bird-eyes glare... [H]e stuffs them into the oven" (141)—an echo which anticipates the Holocaust allusion Coetzee develops in later works.

Like the Magistrate, the protagonist of *Disgrace*, David Lurie, falls from a more or less secure insider position of authority within the establishment to that of pariah; from victimizer to victim; from predator to prey. Unlike the Magistrate, however, he doesn't seem to have an inborn sense of empathy for animals and other oppressed creatures; rather, that sensitivity awakens in part because of his own loss of status. That awakening sensitivity seems to connote a kind of conversion—a *metanoia* in Iris Murdoch's sense—to a heightened state of moral awareness.

The reason for Lurie's fall into social disgrace (but paradoxically into a kind of spiritual grace) is an improper affair he initiates with a student (he is a 52-year-old adjunct professor of communications at a technical college in Cape Town, South Africa). The affair entails coercive sex, which parallels the gang rape of his daughter Lucy that occurs later in the novel. Of a sexual encounter with the student, Melanie Isaacs, Lurie thinks, "Not rape, not quite that but undesired nevertheless, undesired to the core. As though she had decided to go slack, die within herself for the duration, *like a rabbit when the jaws of the fox close in on its neck*" (emphasis added).[9]

---

[8]Stephen Watson, "Colonialism and the Novels of J. M. Coetzee," in *Critical Perspectives*, ed. Huggan and Watson, notes how Coetzee protagonists are "drawn towards placing a higher value on the notion of 'being' rather than 'becoming'" (30).
[9]J. M. Coetzee, *Disgrace* (New York: Viking, 1999), p. 25. Further references follow in the text.

From victimizer Lurie soon finds himself victimized, as news of the affair becomes public, and he is dismissed from his position. Media representatives "circle around him *like hunters who have cornered a strange beast* and do not know how to finish it off" (56, emphasis added). To escape from Cape Town, he arranges to visit his grown daughter Lucy, who runs a farm and a kennel in a remote rural area. Lucy is an "animal lover" and introduces him to Bev Shaw, who runs the local animal shelter where David comes to work as a volunteer. Initially, he is indifferent to the plight of animals; the most he can say is that "he has nothing against... animal lovers" (72), and at times he finds their "do-good" attitude annoying, complaining facetiously that they're so "cheerful and well-intentioned... after a while you itch to go off and do some raping and pillaging. Or kick a cat" (73). Even in the early stages of his exposure to animal caring, however, he exhibits an awareness of animal subjectivity, wondering, for example, if the kennel dogs are bored (62).

He has several discussions about animals with Lucy and Bev but remains generally skeptical of their contentions. Lucy, for example, believes in "shar[ing] some of our human privilege with the beasts. I don't want," she says, "to come back in another existence as a dog or pig and have to live as dogs or pigs live under us." David feels she has lost "perspective" on the issue. She laments how humans treat dogs as "part of the furniture... They do us the honour of treating us like gods and we respond by treating them like things" (78).

The two discuss the question of whether animals have souls, with David reminding Lucy of the centuries-long debate on the subject by the Church Fathers, who "decided they don't have proper souls... Their souls are tied to their bodies and die with them" (78). Lucy says she doesn't believe in souls period: "I wouldn't know a soul if I saw one" (79). He replies emphatically in one of his few declarative statements, "You are a soul... We are souls before we are born." Thus, like the Magistrate (and like Coetzee—see n. 7), David adheres to a Platonic ontology. By the end of the novel, he has decided that animals do have souls: "The business of dog-killing is over for the day, the black bags are piled at the door, each with a body and a soul inside" (161).

After this discussion and in reference to an abandoned bulldog, Katy, whom Lucy has decided to adopt, "a shadow of grief falls over

[David], for Katy, alone in her cage, for himself, for everyone" (79)—
the first sign perhaps of his changing sensitivity. At this moment,
he decides to volunteer at the animal shelter. Initially, he remains
skeptical of Bev's attribution of sensitivity and intelligence to animals.
She tells him while holding the animals he should "think comforting
thoughts...[because] they can smell what you're thinking," an idea
he rejects as "nonsense" (81). Shortly thereafter he has to check
himself from feeling that a dog has "an intelligent look"; "it is
probably nothing of the kind" (85) he remonstrates himself.

What precipitates David's conversion is his own experience of
being victimized by a gang of assailants who set him on fire and
rape his daughter. As Bev treats his injuries, he compares himself
to a miserable goat he had helped Bev with earlier. "He recalls the
goat...and wonders whether, submitting to her hands, it felt the
same peacefulness" (106). It is the recognition of his own suffering
body seen as a shared condition with the goat that leads to David's
awakening and change of heart.

In an interview conducted in the early 1990s, Coetzee
acknowledged that the suffering body is a kind of epistemological
touchstone in his worldview, a point of authenticity that is immune
in a sense to skepticism, to doubt. "The body with its pain," he
states, "becomes a counter to the endless trials of doubt...Not
grace, then, but at least the body." He amplifies, "[I]t is not that
one *grants* the authority of the suffering body: the suffering body
takes this authority: that is its power. To use other words: its power
is undeniable." Coetzee adds parenthetically, "I as a person...am
overwhelmed...by the fact of suffering in the world, and not only
human suffering."[10] Thus Coetzee accords the suffering body an
authenticity and authority that supersede rational knowledge. He
comes close to revising the Cartesian formula to read, "I feel pain,
therefore I exist."[11]

It is in his unquestioned acknowledgment that animals can suffer,
feel pain, and experience humiliation that Coetzee parts company

---

[10]Interview in *Doubling the Point*, p. 248.
[11]Coetzee claims not to "assert the ethical superiority of pain over pleasure"
(*Doubling*, p. 248), but I agree with Brian May that his fiction belies this claim
("J. M. Coetzee and the Question of the Body," *Modern Fiction Studies* 47, no. 2
[Summer 2001]:404).

from most other authors who include animals centrally in their fiction. Although some modern writers—as documented by Marian Scholtmeijer and Margot Norris—succeed in granting subjectivity to the animals who figure in their work, few—if any—of their human characters exhibit the intense empathetic identification with animal suffering and loss of dignity as do Coetzee's.

In the wake of his own suffering, David Lurie therefore undergoes a kind of *metanoia*, the first sign of which is evident in the concern he registers shortly after his own victimization about some sheep who are tethered in Lucy's yard in preparation for their slaughter. He untethers them to allow them to eat and drink more comfortably, reflecting how they were surely

> destined since birth for the butcher's knife. Well, nothing remarkable in that ... Sheep do not own themselves, do not own their own lives. They exist to be used, every last ounce of them, their flesh to be eaten, their bones to be crushed and fed to poultry. (123)

Despite this knowledge,

> a bond seems to have come into existence between himself and the two Persians, he does not know how. Nevertheless, *suddenly and without reason*, their lot has become important to him ... He remembers Bev Shaw nuzzling the old billy-goat ... stroking him, comforting him, entering into his life. How does she get it right, this communion with animals? ... One has to be a certain kind of person, perhaps ... Do I have to change ...? Do I have to become like Bev Shaw? (126, emphasis added).

Thus, like the Magistrate, David Lurie, once awakened to the reality of suffering bodies, has a kind of epiphany in which he perceives the reality of animal suffering and recognizes human communion with this pain in a community of suffering beings. He doesn't, however, take the next step—the one Coetzee's political critics would like—namely, to commit himself to changing the system that causes the pain. Despite, therefore, their manifest and striking ethical awareness of animal suffering, Coetzee's characters seldom go beyond passive awareness. Coetzee seems—and this is why politically minded critics have challenged him—to stop short of Albert Camus' famous political emendation of Descartes: *Je me révolte, donc nous sommes*[12] ("I rebel, therefore we exist"), meaning "I rebel against the fact that suffering and injustice continue, therefore we as a community exist." In the end, Coetzee does not adopt Camus' vision of solidarity, of an awakened community engaged in political action. (Nadine Gordimer, like Coetzee a Nobel-prize-winning South African writer but perhaps his most trenchant critic, laments that Coetzee "denies the energy of the will to resist evil.")[13] Instead, he concludes the novel on a note that is more reminiscent of the absurdist fatalism of Samuel Beckett, another conspicuous influence, reflecting perhaps the author's cynicism about the ability of the average man (whom Lurie represents)—the non-saint—to make that level of commitment (rather than that he, the author, abjures such commitment). David, in fact, as I explore in Chapter 8, remains blocked from meaningful ethical action—despite his heightened level of ethical awareness, because he is constricted by the ritual scripts of male narcissism.

Through David's job at the animal shelter, which is to comfort animals who are being euthanized and to dispose of their bodies, he comes to realize that most people bring their animals to the shelter as a convenient way of getting rid of them.

They do not say straight out, "I have brought you this dog to kill," but that is what is expected: that they will dispose of it, make it disappear, dispatch it to oblivion. What is being asked for is, in fact, *Lösung*. (142)

Lösung is the German word for solution—as in *Endlösung*, the Nazi term for the "final solution" —which draws an implicit association between human treatment of animals and the Holocaust.

---

[12]Albert Camus, *L'Homme Révolté* (Paris: Gallimard, 1951), p. 36. The complete passage is:
> Le mal qui éprouvait un seul homme devient peste collective. Dans l'épreuve quotidienne qui est la nôtre, la révolte joue le même rôle que le "cogito" dans l'ordre de la pensée: elle est la première évidence. Mais cette évidence tire l'individu de sa solitude. Elle est un lieu commun qui fonde sur tous les hommes la première valeur. Je me révolte, donc nous sommes.

[13]Nadine Gordimer, "The Idea of Gardening," *New York Review of Books* (February 2, 1984):6.

So on Saturday afternoons ... he helps Bev Shaw *lösen* the week's superfluous canines ... To each, in what will be its last minutes, Bev gives her fullest attention, stroking it, talking to it, easing its passage. If more often than not, the dog fails to be charmed, it is because of his presence: he gives off the wrong smell (*they can smell your thoughts*), the smell of shame. (142)

David's shame is for the real disgrace the novel's title refers to, namely, the atrocious suffering inflicted upon animals by humans. Like Bev, who is a kind of secular saint (she is compared to a saint at one point), exhibiting, as seen in the above passage, Simone Weil's "attentive love" toward the animals she cares for, David commits himself to his task with no thought of ultimate redemption—either for himself, for humanity, or for the animals. In this, like certain of Camus' protagonists, notably Rieux in *La Peste* (*The Plague*), he approaches the status of absurd saint, carrying out a sense of obligation to relieve affliction, while not believing in any higher justification for such acts. A particularly absurd gesture is his determination to make sure the dogs' bodies are treated honorably in the cremation process. When workers bash at the dogs' stiffened limbs with shovels to make them fit more neatly on the oven's feeder trolley, he intervenes, feeling that such battering deprives them of dignity, and taking it upon himself to handle each body individually, reverentially. Why is he doing this? "For his idea of the world, a world in which men do not use shovels to beat corpses into a more convenient shape for processing" (146). He realizes this commitment to the dead animals has marked him as "a dog-man ... a *harijan*" (146), an outcast, a pariah.

The novel ends with a gesture of resignation. David yields up a dog with whom he has developed a relationship to the euthanasia needle. "[T]he dog would die for him, he knows" (215), but "it cannot be evaded" (219). He holds the dog "like a lamb" (220) in his final moments. The phrase "like a lamb" has Christian overtones; however, in the interview noted above, Coetzee claims not to believe in sanctifying grace or any supernatural intervention, only in the efficacy of human "charity." "As for grace, no regrettably no: I am not a Christian, or not yet."[14] Rather, it appears that David's

---

[14]Interview in *Doubling the Point*, p. 250.

resigned attitude reflects the author's despair over humans' lack of charity, as seen in their callous treatment of animals, and pessimism about the likelihood that things will soon change. But perhaps another cause for despond is the character's evident inability to slip the coils of male narcissism—as proposed in Chapter 8.

In *The Lives of Animals*, a thinly fictionalized philosophical dialogue presented in 1997–98 as the Tanner Lectures at Princeton, Coetzee extends Lurie's "animal rights" reflections into a full-fledged, hard-hitting, and unambiguous condemnation of human treatment of animals. He does so, however, through the vehicle of a problematic voice, that of Elizabeth Costello, an elderly, vaguely dotty, professor, who is invited to give a distinguished lecture, plus a seminar, at a small college. One senses that the position articulated in these presentations, which are on the subject of animal abuse, is probably that of the author—if only from the fact that Coetzee supplements the essay with twenty-three scholarly footnotes, all but three of which support Costello's views (also, of course, the character's name is similar to Coetzee). Yet, because he chooses as his mouthpiece so unauthoritative a voice suggests perhaps a realization of how marginalized and subversive her position is. Like the Magistrate and David Luring, Costello is a social outcast.

The most incendiary point Costello develops in her first lecture is the one hinted at in Coetzee's use of *Lösung* in *Disgrace*, that the human treatment of animals is comparable to the Holocaust, and that the willful ignorance people display toward animal slaughter and suffering is similar to that shown toward the fate of the Jews by the Germans. Of the latter she notes, "they lost their humanity in our eyes because of a certain willed ignorance."[15] Similarly, she argues, Americans today live in willed ignorance of "drug-testing laboratories... factory farms... abattoirs... [which] are here... They

---

[15]J. M. Coetzee et al., *The Lives of Animals*, ed. Amy Gutmann (Princeton, NJ: Princeton University Press, 1999), p. 20. Further references follow in the text. At the end of the essay, Costello acknowledges that the "willed ignorance" of acquaintances has come to obsess her:

It's as if I were to visit friends, and to make some polite remark about the lamp in their living room, and they were to say, "Yes it's nice, isn't it? Polish-Jewish skin it's made of, we find that's best, the skin of Polish-Jewish origins." And then I go to the bathroom and the soap-wrapper says, "Treblinka–100% human stearate" (69).

are all around us" (21): "Each day a fresh holocaust" (35). "Let me say it openly: we are surrounded by an enterprise of degradation, cruelty, and killing which rivals anything that the Third Reich was capable of, indeed dwarfs it" (21).

Costello further claims, "the crime of the Third Reich...was to treat people like animals": "'They went like sheep to the slaughter,' 'They died like animals.' 'The Nazi butchers killed them.' Denunciation of the camps reverberates...with the language of the stockyard and slaughterhouse" (20). Indeed, "it was from the Chicago Stockyards that the Nazis learned to process bodies" (53).

Costello theorizes the attitude the Magistrate and David Lurie inarticulately exhibit, namely, that moral awareness depends upon a kind of visceral empathy. Dismissing "cool" rationalistic philosophical arguments pro and con animal rights and expressing instead an ethic of care, she claims, "reason is simply a tautology" (25). What is needed is the understanding that "an animal...is an embodied soul" (33). "To thinking, cogitation, I oppose fullness, embodiedness, the sensation of being...alive to the world" (33)— attributes humans share with animals. "The horror" of the death camps, she concludes,

> is that the killers refused to think themselves into the place of their victims...In other words, they closed their hearts. The heart is the seat of a faculty, *sympathy*, that allows us to share at times the being of another. (34)

Costello thus proposes in effect an ethic of care.[16]

After her lecture Costello receives various criticisms, not least of which is an objection to the Holocaust analogy. These objections somewhat problematize her position in a way that raise once again the question of why Coetzee seems to feel compelled to destabilize coherent political assertion.

In her second presentation, a seminar entitled "The Poets and the Animals," Costello articulates what is in effect an aesthetics of care, extending her discussion of sympathy to include literary treatment of animals (she herself is the author of a celebrated feminist novel).

---

[16]I have argued a similar point in "Attention to Suffering" in *Feminist Care Tradition*, ed. Donovan and Adams, pp. 174–97.

Fiction-writing, she claims, is preeminently an exercise of the "sympathetic imagination" (35). Rejecting the metaphoric use of animal imagery, she urges that writers get inside the body of the animal, understanding the creature as a subject, not aestheticizing her as an object. As noted in Chapter 4, Costello posits Ted Hughes' jaguar poems as exemplary, because of the way the poet "is feeling his way toward a different kind of being-in-the-world...The poems ask us to imagine our way into [the jaguar's] way of moving, to imagine that body" (51). She praises writers who like Hughes "return the living electric being to language" (65).

By expanding peoples' sympathetic imagination into the realities of animal lives, she hopes that thereby they might be awakened to an ethical awareness that will lead them to modify their treatment of animals. She is not sanguine about prospects for success; however, instead she concludes each lecture with an ominous prediction: the first ends with her venturing that humans will continue to allow the "daily holocaust" to continue and like the Germans "we will get away with it" (35); the second, with the observation that by "slaughtering and enslaving a race of divine or else divinely created beings," humans have brought a "curse" upon themselves (58).

Coetzee's treatment of the animal issue throughout his work suggests that although he is not an overtly political writer, he is acutely aware of the realities of creatural suffering and addresses attendant ethical issues forthrightly. To the extent, however, that Coetzee's protagonists represent humanity, their inability to move beyond absurd, ineffectual gestures or, in the case of David Lurie, beyond male narcissism—despite their awakened ethical awareness—offers a very bleak vision indeed. Humans' inability or unwillingness to change, Coetzee seems to be saying, is the ultimate disgrace.

8

Metaphysical meat: "Becoming men" and animal sacrifice

Central episodes in two prominent contemporary novels concern animal sacrifice, that of a baby water buffalo in Tim O'Brien's *The Things They Carried* (1990) and of a young crippled dog in J. M. Coetzee's *Disgrace* (1999). Both episodes enact what Griselda Pollock termed "a mythic troping of gender and death" ("Dying" 220). The rite of animal sacrifice may be seen as encompassed in the developmental process of "becoming men." Intimately connected to or derived from male bonding rituals, animal sacrifice enables a distancing from the feminized abjection the victim represents. Such slaughter of an objectified, feminized animal helps thereby to establish the masculine subject. "The death of the hare," Jacobus Coetzee realized, "is the logic of salvation ... The death of the hare is my *metaphysical meat* ... The hare dies to keep my soul from merging with the world" (79–80, emphasis added). The deaths of the respective animals in the O'Brien and Coetzee novels similarly serve the male protagonists their "metaphysical meat."

The episode in the Tim O'Brien novel, which is set during the Vietnam War, occurs when a beloved buddy of an American G.I. is killed by an explosive device. The distraught G.I., Rat Kiley, takes out his grief on a baby water buffalo who happens by. He begins methodically and ritualistically shooting the animal—one shot at a time to different parts of the body, in effect torturing the animal to death. "He stepped back and shot it through the right front knee ... [H]e took careful aim and shot off an ear. He shot it in the hindquarters and in the little hump at its back. He shot it twice in the flanks. It wasn't to kill; it was to hurt."[1] The other G.I.s in his unit stand around watching, apparently in disbelief, but no one attempts to stop him (as they presumably would if the victim were a human), nor is any sympathy expressed for the victim. "Nobody said much. The whole platoon stood there watching...there wasn't a great deal of pity for the baby water buffalo" (79). The agony of the animal is not described; indeed, the creature could well be an inanimate object for all the reaction she or he displays. "The animal did not make a sound. It went down hard, then got up again" (78). After several more shots, "again the animal fell hard and tried to get up, but his time it couldn't quite make it. It wobbled and went down sideways" (79). As it is highly improbable that any living creature would react impassively to such treatment and as this purports to be a realistic novel, the failure to describe realistically the animal's reaction would seem to be a flaw in the narrative. However, it is often the case in contemporary fictional treatment of animals that the point of view or subjectivity of victimized animals is elided. In this novel, as in much literature (as noted in Chapter 1), cruelty toward animals serves as a literary device used to reveal something about or to reflect on the human protagonist(s). Here the episode is used to reveal the depths of the G.I.'s anguish over losing his friend and to illustrate the novel's underlying theme—that war brings out the worse in everyone and that it is a setting where atrocity becomes so routine that participants become resigned to it.

O'Brien does not elaborate on the scene and offers little interpretive guidance; except in a metafictional comment which follows, the author/narrator scornfully puts down sympathy for the animal, insisting that the episode is about the G.I.'s grief. Noting how

---

[1]Tim O'Brien, *The Things They Carried* (New York: Broadway, 1990), pp. 78–79. Further references follow in the text. A preliminary version of this chapter was presented in a seminar organized by Rebecca Saunders at the American Comparative Literature Association annual meeting, Brown University, March 31, 2012. My thanks to the members of that seminar for stimulating my thinking on the topic. An earlier version of this chapter appeared in *Creatural Fictions: Human-Animal Relationships in 20th- and 21st-Century Literature*, ed. David Herman (Houndsmills, Basingstoke, England: Palgrave Macmillan, 2016). Interestingly, Phil Klay opens *Redeployment* (New York: Penguin, 2014), his much-heralded Iraq-era war story collection as follows: "We shot dogs...We did it on purpose" (1). Klay's ostensible point is similar to O'Brien's—that war is horrible, but it also provides further evidence of how deeply embedded the mythic trope of animal sacrifice is in the American cultural imagination.

when he tells this story to audiences, "usually ... an older woman of kindly temperament and humane politics" will say, "the poor baby buffalo, it made her sad" (84), the narrator, "pictur[ing] Rat Kiley's face, his grief," thinks, "*You dumb cooze ...* It *wasn't* a war story. It was a *love* story" (84), thus disdainfully dismissing a "feminine" response to the animal's suffering for deflecting attention from the animal to the G.I. It's *his* grief that is the point of the story, the author/narrator insists. The animal is irrelevant.

Despite this authorial assertion, the episode invites further analysis as to its meaning. It is clear that as in traditional animal sacrifice, the baby water buffalo here is operating as a scapegoat—an object upon whom are being enacted the feelings of the human protagonist. One can hypothesize that those feelings are a mixture of grief and anguish over his buddy's death, anger at the forces that caused it, impotence and guilt at not being able to restore his friend or to have prevented his death, and fear rooted in a shocking realization of his own vulnerability. That these feelings are projected onto the victim and thus disposed of recapitulates the traditional operation and function of a scapegoat in ritual animal sacrifice. By doing to the buffalo what had been done to his buddy (and indirectly to him), the G.I. rehearses ritualistically a mimetic cycle of violence.

The feelings the G.I. thereby expunges—grief, impotence, fear, and vulnerability—are traditionally held to be feminine. In her study of the roots of organized male violence (war), *Blood Rites* (1997), Barbara Ehrenreich theorizes that in its origins, ritual violence served the purpose of signifying human males' transition from prey to predator.[2] In the earliest human societies all humans, "male and female [were] prey to larger, stronger animals" (114); before "the age of man-the-hunter, there [was] ... man-the-hunted" (40). The transition to the former from the latter is the underlying story in the rise of patriarchal civilization, she contends. In the process, emotions connected to prey status had to be rejected, projected, and/or otherwise repressed. "Grief, depression, helplessness—these are the experiences of *prey*." To deal with them men had to assume "the stance of the predator: Turn grief to rage, go from listless mourning ... [to] offensive attack" (139).

---

[2]Barbara Ehrenreich, *Blood Rites: Origins and History of the Passions of War* (New York: Metropolitan, 1997), p. 22. Further references follow in the text.

In another important study, *Women and Sacrifice: Male Narcissism and the Psychology of Religion* (1992), a psychoanalytic approach, William Beers proposes that in the male maturation process, feminine aspects of the self are split off as "not-me," projected onto another and sacrificed. "The sacrificial victim is a marginal being on which is focused the [feminine] 'not-me' parts, which are then destroyed or violently cut off from the group's culture."[3] In her study of hunting rites, Marti Kheel similarly notes, "hunting and killing animals is a standard rite of passage out of the world of women and nature into the masculine realm."[4]

Maurice Bloch emphasizes the "femininity of the sacrificial animal" (67) in his seminal study of ritual sacrifice, *Prey into Hunter: The Politics of Religious Experience* (1992)—on which Ehrenreich relied in constructing her theory. Bloch links animal sacrifice to the sacrifice of the woman in exogamous kinship systems.[5] Both enabled a revitalization of the group and the elevation of male practitioners to the status of dominator/conqueror, "the transformation of initiates from prey to hunters" (8). In traditional animal sacrifice, the victim is always a domesticated—i.e., feminized—animal and in traditional male hunting rituals, it is nearly always a herbivore or non-raptor bird, such as a dove or duck (the exception being modern trophy hunting). It also appears important, though theorists fail to comment on this aspect, that the victim be perceived as innocent, like prey. Perhaps this is why non-carnivores are the preferred sacrificial victims.

---

[3]William Beers, *Women and Sacrifice: Male Narcissism and the Psychology of Religion* (Detroit: Wayne State University Press, 1992), pp. 143, 145. Further references follow in the text.

[4]Marti Kheel, "License to Kill: An Ecofeminist Critique of Hunters' Discourse," in *Animals and Women: Feminist Theoretical Explorations*, ed. Carol J. Adams and Josephine Donovan (Durham, NC: Duke University Press, 1995), p. 106.

[5]Maurice Bloch, *Prey into Hunter: The Politics of Religious Experience* (Cambridge: Cambridge University Press, 1992), p. 69. Further references follow in the text. In *Brutal: Manhood and the Exploitation of Animals* (Urbana: University of Illinois Press, 2007), p. 115, Brian Luke theorizes that animal sacrifice originally served the purpose of establishing men's power in this way: by using the sacrificed animal as proxy for a human child, the male sacrificer established a kind of protection racket whereby he implicitly warned other, weaker humans that this would be their fate unless they submitted to his power.

While the gender is unclear, as a baby the water buffalo in the O'Brien novel is clearly a feminized entity, and as the prey-predator issue is starkly present in the wartime setting, the theories of Ehrenreich et al seem apropos. Moreover, initially the G.I. tried to feed the animal—a "feminine" gesture of kindness; it is only when rebuffed by the animal that he begins shooting (78), an expression of narcissistic rage, I explain below. It seems therefore that by destroying the animal, the soldier is rejecting his own prey-like, feminine feelings in an attempt to resume his dominator status as male predator.

The leading current theory, according to Douglas Hedley (2011), about the function of ritual scapegoat sacrifice in human society is that developed by René Girard, namely that it enables the human group—whether clan or nation—to cohere peacefully. A society threatened by intra-group rivalry or conflict "can unite itself by concentrating its ire upon a scapegoat."[6] Animal sacrifice thus effects a unification of the community: "A chaotic ensemble of particular conflicts" is replaced by "the simplicity of a single conflict: the entire community on one side and, on the other, the victim."[7] The victim is made "responsible for the disorder and catastrophe" and "is killed as the one responsible for crimes that are synonymous with the disintegration of the community" (38).

The sacrifice of the buffalo in *The Things They Carried* fulfills this purpose. The emotional and social "disorder and chaos" created by the death of one of their group is projected onto the victim and thus expelled and dispelled. A human (and male) bonding ensues. Indeed, the little sympathy that is expressed during the episode by the other soldiers in the unit is offered to the distraught G.I. ("Rat Kiley had lost his best friend in the world…it was a question of pain" [79])—not to the tortured animal, thus effecting a reunification of the human community.

The ritual wren hunt in England exemplifies how the linkage between human communal solidarity and animal sacrifice continued into the modern era. "The wren hunt," Elizabeth Laurence notes,

---

[6]Douglas Hedley, *Sacrifice Imagined: Violence, Atonement and the Sacred* (New York: Continuum, 2011), p. 85.

[7]René Girard, *Things Hidden Since the Foundation of the World*, trans. Stephen Ban and Michael Metter (Stanford, CA: Stanford University Press, 1987), p. 24. Further references follow in the text.

"is comparable to other rites...involving the chasing, killing, and carrying in procession of an animal who takes the role of scapegoat, atoning for the sins and anxieties of the community."[8] Indeed, modern holidays throughout the global human community still revolve around the death of an animal whose body forms the communal feast through which participants celebrate their bonding.

In ancient Greece and other early societies (and continuing in patriarchal institutions to this day), women were excluded from the practice of animal sacrifice. "A male monopoly" existed "in matters of blood sacrifice and everything connected with meat-eating."[9] One might hypothesize that the association of women with blood because of menstruation and childbirth led metonymically to their being associated with the blood-letting in sacrifice and thereby with the victim in animal sacrifice. Aristotle, for example, compares the first menstrual period to the blood of "an animal that has just been stabbed" (*Historia Animalium* 7.1.581a 31-b2, as cited in Detienne and Vernant 147). Blood, wounding, and bleeding are inherently associated with prey and with abjection and thus are feminized.[10]

William Beers ties "the obsession with blood" seen in ritual sacrifice back to exogenous patrilineal kinship power relations; it "has...to do with controlling consanguinous women" who are themselves sacrificial entities in the "exchange of women"

---

[8]Elizabeth Laurence, "Hunting the Wren: A Sacred Bird in Ritual," in *A Communion of Subjects: Animals in Religion, Science, and Ethics*, ed. Paul Waldau and Kimberley Patton (New York: Columbia University Press, 2006), p. 409.

[9]Marcel Detienne and Jean-Pierre Vernant, *The Cuisine of Sacrifice*, trans. Paula Wissing (Chicago: University of Chicago Press, 1989), p. 133. Further references follow in the text.

[10]The term *abjection* commonly means a low, demeaned condition, rooted in the Latin *ab-jacere*—"to throw away"—thus implying that which is thrown away or devalued as trash. Julia Kristeva in *Powers of Horror: An Essay on Abjection*, trans. Leon S. Roudiez (New York: Columbia University Press, 1982) has revalorized the term linking it to what is expelled from or rejected by the civilized self. "The abject confronts us, on the one hand, with those fragile states where man strays on the territories of the animal...[and] on the other hand...with our earliest attempts to release the hold of *maternal* entity...what, having been the mother, will turn into an abject" (12–13). Kristeva thus links abjection with both animality and with the rejection/expulsion of the preoedipal mother entailed in the (male) maturation process, a point similar to that made by Beers.

that defines patriarchal society (37, 62).[11] According to Girard, objects subject to "mimetic rivalry" (among males), such as family women, are rendered taboo and are "assimilated to the surrogate victim... The foundations of human culture, particularly the modes of matrimonial exchange... are built on the ritual of sacrifice" (77). Kimberley Patton notes how in ancient Greece "the trappings of marriage and those of sacrifice... were virtually the same"[12] Iphegenia, for example, who thought she was approaching an altar to be married, was "adorned in festive splendor like an animal walking to the sacrificial altar" (394). The chorus of women in Euripides' *Iphegenia at Aulis*, warns, however,

> You will be brought down from the hill caves
> Like a heifer, white, unblemished,
> And like a bloody victim
> They will slash your throat
>
> (1076–84, as cited in Patton 394)

The association if women and femininity with the sacrificed, scapegoated animal would seem to be thus well established. William Beers summarizes that "the complex ritual violence performed by men is an ancient way for men to identify with each other as men, and to separate from women" (144–45). Anthropologist Nancy Jay proposed that traditional blood sacrifice—which is only seen in patrilineal societies—enables men to "expiate, get rid of the consequences of having been born of woman," thereby "establishing bonds... between men that transcend their absolute dependence on childbearing women."[13]

Indeed, psychotherapist Carl Jung proposed a "matricidal theory of sacrifice" wherein the male in the maturation process must kill off

---

[11]On the exchange of women, see Gayle Rubin, "The Traffic in Women: Notes on the 'Political Economy' of Sex," in *Towards an Anthropology of Women*, ed. Rayna R. Reiter (New York: Monthly Review, 1975), pp. 157–210, and Juliet Mitchell, *Psychoanalysis and Feminism: Freud, Reich, Lang and Women* (New York: Vintage, 1975).

[12]Kimberley Patton, "Animal Sacrifice: Metaphysics of a Sublimated Victim," in *Communion*, ed. Waldau and Patton, p. 294. Further references follow in the text.

[13]Nancy Jay, *Throughout Your Generations Forever: Sacrifice, Religion, and Paternity* (Chicago: University of Chicago Press, 1992), pp. 40, 147.

his maternal/feminine connections and feelings in order to accede to manhood. He does this by projecting them onto a sacrificed victim. As a kind of self-evisceration, the process necessarily involves "narcissistic injury" (Beers 144) and mourning (185–86). But as the latter is not socially condoned for men (presumably because it signifies prey status), it is repressed, often erupting, however, as "narcissistic rage" and aggression, which is acted out against a feminized sacrificial victim (144). All of this brings us back to the G.I. in O'Brien's Vietnam novel. Himself wounded emotionally by the loss of his buddy—a feeling that connects to and re-evokes his own maturational "narcissistic injury," his break from the maternal/feminine; unable to mourn both losses; and rejected in his attempt to channel his feminine side, the G.I. lashes out in "narcissistic rage" at the hapless buffalo, who becomes a repository of his shameful womanly emotions, which are thereby killed off, expelled, and reburied.

Unlike O'Brien, who simply describes the water buffalo scene without comment or figurative language, J. M. Coetzee presents the death of the dog at the end of his novel *Disgrace* in terms that emphasize the sacrificial nature of the event. "Bearing [the dog] in his arms like a lamb," David Lurie, the protagonist, offers his dog up for euthanasia (220). As in the O'Brien novel, however, the character's motivations are obscure. Lurie's explanation—which is essentially that as the dog will have to die eventually, might as well kill him now—frankly makes little sense. "He can save the young dog … for another week. But a time must come, it cannot be evaded, when he will have to bring him" to the vet for euthanasia (219). By this logic, one would kill all living creatures forthwith, since they are destined to die anyway. Even if Lurie's point is that as an unwanted dog, the animal's destiny in an animal shelter is to be euthanized, the fact is that other alternatives are available. The dog could be adopted. Indeed, there is no reason Lurie himself couldn't adopt him. Nor is there much effort made at this particular shelter to adopt animals out; instead it is largely a rather mechanistic euthanasia clinic. Moreover, an alternative is present in the example of Lurie's daughter Lucy who also runs a kennel, but doesn't "put animals down" (79).

We are left then with the question of Lurie's motivation (and Coetzee's intention, which I treat below). While, unlike the situation with the G.I. in the O'Brien novel, there is no precipitating event that causes Lurie to sacrifice the dog, nor is it obvious that Lurie is discharging emotions and/or projecting onto the animal victim; he nevertheless resembles the O'Brien G.I. in important ways, such that the episode fits well within the parameters of ritual animal sacrifice outlined above.

For Lurie's trajectory in the course of the novel, as we have seen, is from predator to prey. His status as prey is reenforced when a gang of intruders rape his daughter Lucy with whom he is staying and set her on fire, while he is locked (by them) in a bathroom and thus rendered impotently unable to help her. After the gang's attack, in which he is injured, and as he is being treated by the veterinarian Bev Shaw, he recalls her kindly treatment of a badly injured goat and identifies with the suffering goat. His identification and empathy with animals soon extend to other animals such as the tethered Persian sheep. One might propose that Lurie is "becoming animal" to use French theorists Gilles Deleuze and Félix Guattari's evocative phrase, except that in their construction "animal" seems to represent the wild or feral side of the human psyche—the Dionysiac, seen as a means of escape from technocratic capitalist civilization. As Alice Kuzniar notes, Deleuze and Guattari's "'becoming animal' fetishiz[es] the wild indecipherable creature that would represent the opposite of tame social norms and thus promise liberation from them."[14] Indeed, Deleuze and Guattari's contempt for domestic companion animals in favor of raptor predators[15] suggests that their conception is really a reenactment of the perennial masculine flight from the feminine into the "masculine wilderness"[16]—seen in masculinist notions of the sublime, discussed in Chapter 9.

Unlike Deleuze's and Guattari's, Lurie's "becoming animal" involves a sympathetic identification with and/or attention to domestic or domesticated animals. In an episode with the sheep, for example, he notices that a fly is bothering one of the sheep. Lurie moves to help but the sheep moves away from him, a rejection not

[14]Alice Kuzniar, *Melancholia's Dog* (Chicago: University of Chicago Press, 2006), p. 4. Further references follow in the text

[15]Gilles Deleuze and Félix Guattari, "Becoming-Animal," trans. Brian Massumi, in *Animal Philosophy*, ed. Matthew Calarco and Peter Atterton (New York: Continuum, 2004), pp. 90–91.

[16]Carolyn Heilbrun, "The Masculine Wilderness of the American Novel," *Saturday Review* (January 29, 1972):41–44.

unlike that Rat Kiley received from the buffalo. Lurie interprets as meaning he lacks the ability to communicate with and comfort animals. Contrasting himself to the shelter caretaker,

> he remembers Bev Shaw nuzzling the old billy-goat...stroking him, comforting him, entering into his life. How does she get it right, this communion with animals? Some trick he does not have. (126)

Reflecting on a sudden impulse he has to buy the goats and save them from their fates, he once again feels impotent. What good would it do? He reasons in a logic that anticipates his decision to euthanize the dog at the end; they would soon be replaced by other sheep who would likewise be doomed. "And what will he do with the sheep anyway, once he has brought them out of slavery? Set them free on the public road? Pen them up in the dog-cages and feed them hay?" (126).

As noted, Nadine Gordimer has criticized Coetzee for his characters' failure to "resist evil" (Gordimer 6); certainly, Lurie, while awakened to and aggrieved by the suffering and evil he sees about him, does seem trapped in an envelope of impotence and abject resignation. Beyond this, however, he seems trapped within the confines of a narcissistic male identity. In this also, therefore, he resembles O'Brien's G.I. in *The Things They Carried*, and it helps to explain the—to many— baffling ending of *Disgrace*. While Lurie is able to and in some sense forced to "become animal" in that he perceives himself as reduced to their level and tries to enter into their world; he is unable to "become woman" or "become feminine," a process that might point to ways out of, ways to deal positively with abjection—possibilities suggested (albeit problematically) by Lurie's daughter Lucy.

Lurie, like O'Brien's G.I., is hamstrung by an inability to mourn. While he does feel grief and shows it (unlike the G.I.), he seems unable to process the feeling constructively. In an early episode that anticipates the scene with the sheep, Lurie attempts to comfort the abandoned bulldog Katy, who like the sheep fails to respond to him. Lucy explains that the dog is apathetic because "she's in mourning. No one wants her, and she knows it" (78). When they leave her cage, she "slumps down, closes her eyes" (78). Lurie in reaction feels a moment of grief, but it is largely narcissistic ("for himself") and abstract ("for everyone") (79).

After working with Bev Shaw in the animal shelter—where he mainly assists with an endless process of euthanizing unwanted pets, Lurie finds himself inexplicably moved and disturbed by the process. After one session, "tears flow down his face that he cannot stop; his hands shake. He does not understand what is happening to him. Until now he has been more or less indifferent to animals," but now he fears that unlike others who work in places of animal killing, such as slaughterhouses, he does not seem to be able to harden himself against feelings of anguish and remorse. He reproaches himself that "he does not seem to have the gift of hardness...He is not, he hopes, a sentimentalist" (143). He fears, in other words, becoming feminine.

He even develops a kind of mourning ritual, albeit an absurd and ineffectual one—as he acknowledges—in which he intervenes when workers at an incinerator plant bash the stiffened animal corpses with shovels so as to make them better fit on the feed trolley to the crematorium. Lurie tries to arrange the body bags so that the corpses are spared this indignity. Why does he do this? Because it better accords with his ideal of a world where "men do not use shovels to bend corpses into a more convenient shape for processing" (146). In other words, for a world in which animals are treated with dignity.

When he temporarily returns to the city abandoning his work at the shelter, he feels guilty, for "the dogs...will be tossed into the fire, unmarked, unmourned. For that betrayal, will he ever be forgiven?" (178). Lurie feels guilty and deserving of punishment for a number of other sins as well. Earlier he had asked Lucy forgiveness for being an inadequate parent (79). And eventually he apologizes for his treatment of Melanie—not, ironically, to the girl herself, but to her father (a fact that underscores the patriarchal context of the novel). The decision to sacrifice the dog at the end can thus be seen in terms of the function of the ritual scapegoat, who takes on the sins of the sacrificer in atonement for them. In this sense, Lurie's final act reaffirms the "metaphorical distance the scapegoat establishes between the human and the animal,"[17] thereby confirming Lurie's status as a human, a dominator, not one of the abject.

---

[17]Chris Danta, "'Like a dog...like a lamb': Becoming Sacrificial Animal in Kafka and Coetzee," *New Literary History* 38 (2007):723.

But Lurie's final decision must be seen as well to confirm and establish or reestablish not just his human status but also his manhood. Here, as in the O'Brien novel, animal sacrifice may be seen as a required part of the process of "becoming man," wherein things feminine must be rejected, cast off. Lurie struggles with the issue throughout the novel. His attitude toward women throughout is largely narcissistic. At one point, he tells Lucy, "Every woman I have been close to has taught me something about myself. To that extent they have made me a better person" (70). His daughter jokingly asks if the reverse were true but he doesn't answer. Later he thinks gratefully of all the women he's been involved with, remarking how they have *"enriched"* his life (192). In a grotesque image, he imagines women as having the function of removing toxins from men. "That is what [women] were for: to suck the complex proteins out of his blood like snake-venom, leaving him clear-headed and dry" (185). Indeed, a final scene with a drug-besotted prostitute, which occurs shortly before the terminal sacrifice of the dog, is described in starkly mechanistic, utilitarian terms. "She does her work on him...He feels drowsy, contented... *So this is all it takes!*, he thinks. *How could I ever have forgotten it!"* (194). This is all it takes to restore his sense of well-being. The episode occurs, significantly, immediately after Lurie has been humiliated by a new boyfriend of Melanie's, who tells him, "Melanie will spit in your eye if she sees you" (194). *"Spit in your eye,"* Lurie reflects shortly thereafter, "he had not expected that" (194). Whereupon he picks up the prostitute to reassert himself, for vindication. The animal sacrifice follows consequentially.

We noted above Lurie's fear of becoming feminine when he found himself weeping after a euthanasia session at the animal shelter. In lamenting his inability to relate to animals as Bev Shaw does, he thinks, "One has to be a certain kind of person, perhaps" (126). It is a moment of revelation: "The sun beats on his face in all its springtime radiance. Do I have to change, he thinks? Do I have to become like Bev Shaw?" (126). Do I have to become woman?

He tries at times, unsuccessfully, to do so—to imagine himself in a woman's shoes. He tries to imagine what the gang rape of Lucy was like.

Lucy was frightened, frightened near to death. Her voice choked, she could not breathe, her limbs went numb. *This is not happening*, she said to herself as the men forced her down, *it is just a dream, a nightmare.* (160)

The words are a haunting echo of those used to describe the feelings he imagined passing through Melanie's mind when he forced himself upon her: "as though she had decided to go slack, lie within herself for the duration" (25).

But both Bev Shaw and Lucy tell him he doesn't really understand what it was like for Lucy. The exchange with Bev is especially revealing

"Poor Lucy," [Bev] whispers, "she has been through such a lot?"
"I know what Lucy has been through. I was there."
"But you weren't there, David. She told me. You weren't."

You weren't there. You don't know what happened. He is baffled. Where, according to Bev Shaw, according to Lucy, was he not?...Do they think he does not know what rape is? Do they think he has not suffered with his daughter...Or do they think that, where rape is concerned, no man can be where the woman is? Whatever the answer, he is outraged, outraged at being treated like an outsider. (140–41)

This is one of the few moments in the novel where Lurie expresses extreme emotion; it is narcissistic rage in the terms described by Beers above, triggered by being cut off from, excluded from the feminine—a recapitulation of the original wounding inherent, according to Beers and others, in the male maturation process. As O'Brien's G.I.'s atrocious treatment of the buffalo may be seen to reflect narcissistic rage resulting when his attempts at "becoming feminine," so does Lurie's subsequent sacrifice of the dog reflect in part his own narcissistic rage at being rebuffed in his vain attempt to accede to feminine status and knowledge.

As Bev and Lucy accuse him of not understanding, he comes to realize that he understands all too well the point of view of the predator rapist: "he does understand; he can, if he concentrates, if he loses himself, be there, be the men, inhabit them...*The question is, does he have it in him to be the woman?*" (160, my emphasis). This seems to be the crucial question of the novel and perhaps of the day: do men have the capacity to abjure their predator status and through the experience of becoming prey/becoming animal/ becoming feminine arrive at a new and different way of being in the world? If David Lurie is representative, the answer appears to be no.

Lucy makes the explicit connection between rape/violence against women and animal sacrifice. In speaking of her rape, she says,

> When it comes to men and sex, David, nothing surprises me any more. Maybe, for men, hating the woman makes sex more exciting. You are a man, you ought to know. When you have sex with someone strange—when you trap her, hold her down, get her under you, put all your weight on her—isn't it a bit like killing? Pushing the knife in; exiting afterwards, leaving the body behind covered in blood—doesn't it feel like murder? (158)

Lurie's inability to "become woman"—to enter into the feminine experience and ethic and be changed thereby—must therefore be factored into his decision in the end to sacrifice the dog, seen as a resigned relapse into the traditional process of "becoming man." Similarly, the G.I. in the O'Brien novel goes on his violent rampage after his brief attempt at "becoming woman" by feeding the animal fails.

Lucy provides an alternative, though not entirely satisfactory, model of how to deal with abjection. Herself raped, as noted, she does not resolve her abjection through blood sacrifice or killing. She decides to carry to term the fetus generated by the rape and raise the child. We have already noted her life-affirmative attitude in her "no-kill" policy in her kennel. More problematic is her decision to capitulate to the "protection racket" enforced on her by the rising patriarchal overseer, Petrus, to in effect marry him (he already has two wives), and cede to him title to her land. Lurie protests to her that such capitulation is "humiliating." She replies:

> "Yes, I agree it is humiliating. But perhaps this is a good point to start from. Perhaps that is what I must learn to accept. To start at ground level. With nothing … No cards, no property, no rights, no dignity."

> "Like a dog."
> "Yes, like a dog." (205)

Thus, from her experience of "becoming animal" (reconceptualized from the Deleuze/Guattari construction) and its accompanying abjection, Lucy is set for rebirth. And indeed her final scene is one of her flourishing in her garden. Coetzee clearly conceives Lucy as a symbol of renewal; he even borrows a term from Goethe's *Faust*—"*das ewige Weibliche*" (the eternal resurrectory feminine principle) (218) to characterize her. And unlike Lurie's sacrificed dog, Katy, the abandoned bulldog, has been adopted by Lucy and is also thriving. In short, it is "a season of blooming" (216). The contrast between Lurie's death-orientation—seen in the animal sacrifice episode, which immediately follows this vision of Lucy blooming in her garden—and her life-affirmation couldn't be starker. It is clear that Coetzee set these up as contrasting responses to abjection—the male and the female.

The problem with the apotheosis of Lucy as a resurrectory symbol is that her psychology is never fully developed. Indeed, one can question how realistic a character she is. The fact that she seems to abandon her lesbian identity with nary a second thought seems improbable, and it is highly unlikely that a woman could undergo the appalling degradation she experienced and within a matter of weeks turn around and embrace life with enthusiasm. Nor can her capitulation to patriarchal authority be seen as a positive outcome; indeed it seems likely only to exacerbate her oppression and subjugation, perpetuating her abject condition. So while perceived by the author as redemptive, Lucy's blooming cannot be seen realistically as any sort of resurrectory triumph. Indeed, her reduction in the end to a symbol must be seen as a flaw in the novel or a limitation on Coetzee's vision. Lurie's sacrifice of the dog may finally be similarly faulted, I explain in Chapter 9, as a construction that trades upon and exploits the emotionally intense character of sacrifice for aesthetic purposes.

That Coetzee titled his novel "Dis-grace" suggests that he intended the animal sacrifice to be construed ironically. It effects no noticeable transformation in the practitioner, no touch of the divine, and certainly no state of grace—rather, the opposite. All of Lurie's attempts at transformation—at becoming animal, becoming woman—are aborted, not carried to term. This final pointless— indeed heartless—sacrifice of the dog merely recapitulates his failures and his capitulation to the inevitability of *Endlösen*.

In an earlier episode, Lurie refers to the shame he feels in participating in such a system (142). Alice Kuzniar notes that "blurring the distinctions between human and beast"—as happens in this novel–"is to enter the territory of shame." But out of this experience a positive transformation may occur: one may come to feel "empathetic shame," a "vicarious feeling for another's mortification. It is here," Kuzniar proposes, "that the roots of compassion lie" (9). Unfortunately, David Lurie doesn't follow this *via feminina*. Instead he resorts to the age-old masculine way— projection and sacrificial killing (though now perceived by the author as an empty, desacralized, and disgraceful gesture).

My conclusion therefore is that the episodes of animal sacrifice we have analyzed in the novels of O'Brien and Coetzee not only repeat a prescribed masculine maturation trajectory—that of becoming men through the vehicle of animal sacrifice, but these literary enactments of sacrifice may themselves be seen as a repetition of male expiatory rituals, abnegating the possibility of redemptive "wit(h)nessing" that might occur were the episodes otherwise construed. That most, if not all, modernist literature reenacts through its narrative trajectories—its mythic troping of ritual sacrifice—this pseudo-liberatory, masculine/humanist process, that the aesthetics of modernity embodied therein is rooted in the masculine developmental epistemology, distancing and dominating an objectified, feminized *other*, are further points to consider. It seems that not only the characters but also the authors remain "caught within the structure of [masculine] humanism"[18] unable to, as Jacques Derrida put it, "*sacrifice sacrifice.*"[19]

[18]Philip Armstrong, *What Animals Mean in the Fiction of Modernity* (Abinton, Oxon, England: Routledge, 2008), p. 186.

[19]Jacques Derrida, "'Eating Well,' or the Calculation of the Subject," in *Points ... : Interviews 1974–1994*, trans. Peter Conor and Avital Ronell (Stanford, CA: Stanford University Press, 1995), p. 279.

9

The transgressive sublime, *katharsis*, and animal sacrifice

A central purpose of ritual sacrifice, most theorists agree, is to provide access to the sacred. The Latin root of the word *sacrifice*—*sacrificium* from *sacer facere* (to make sacred)—implies as much. Walter Burkert, for example, saw "sacrificial killing [as] the basic experience of the sacred."[1] William Robertson Smith considered sacrifice as an "act of communion with the divine."[2] Henri Hubert and Marcel Mauss in their authoritative work on the subject maintain that sacrifice always involves "consecration." "The thing sacrificed serves as an intermediary between the sacrificer ... and the divinity."[3] Through the sacrifice the sacrificer or participant "has acquired a religious character which he did not have before, or has rid himself of an unfavourable character ...; he has raised himself from a state of sin ... he has been religiously transformed" (9–10). "[E]ither he has eradicated the evil to which he was prey or ... has regained a state of grace, or ... has acquired a divine power" (62).

Why it is the case that blood sacrifice is felt to provide access to the sacred is not clear. It may be that the connection of blood to life, on the one hand, and through its shedding, to death, on the other, makes of sacrifice a liminal experience between the profane and the sacred. Or it may be that by projecting one's profane (mortal) aspects—one's abjection—onto the sacrificial victim, the sacrificer

---

[1] As cited in Douglas Hedley, *Sacrifice Imagined*, p. 66.
[2] Ibid., p. 5.
[3] Henri Hubert and Marcel Mauss, *Sacrifice: Its Nature and Function* (1898), trans. W.D. Halls (Chicago: University of Chicago Press, 1964), p. 11. Further references follow in the text.

thereby perceives himself to have acceded to the sacred. Blood sacrifice would then effect and signify a celebratory resurrection for the practitioner, who proves through the act that he is predator, not prey; he is the one who lives on in triumph.

In modern, secular societies access to the sacred through religious rites has been discredited for many, if not most, people, displaced by other forms of rituals. In traditional patrilineal societies, as we have seen, access to the sacred is achieved through the sacrifice of an abject creature, a feminized animal, upon whom are ascribed aspects of otherness that threaten the practioners' survival or identity. Such practices, many contend, persist in the modern era in secular formations.

Patrick Wright proposes that in the era of modernity the sacred has been "subjugated" by the "logos," but that a "modern restructuring of the sacred," banished under Enlightenment rationalism, may be found in secular rituals of sacrifice that provide the limit experience of the sublime.[4] (The term *sublime* in fact derives from the Latin *sub-limen*, "at or up to the limit.") "The sublime is sacrificial...transferring the abjection onto an object, allowing the self's self-mastery to triumph" (87).

Literature in the modern era is one of the forms by which the sacred may be accessed through the experience of the sublime that comes through sacrifice of an abject scapegoat. Julia Kristeva has proposed indeed that in today's world, through its engagement with abjection, purification, and sacrality, literature has become a "secular religion."[5] "Writing," she claims, "implies an ability to imagine the abject, that is, to see oneself in its place and to thrust it aside only by means of the displacements of verbal play" (16). In other words, literature has come to perform the traditional functions of ritual sacrifice—projecting and dispelling the abject.

"Abjection," Kristeva continues, "accompanies all religious structurings and reappears, to be worked out in a new guise, at the time of their collapse" (17).

---

[4]Patrick Wright, "A Timeless Sublime? Reading the Feminine Sublime in the Discourse of the Sacred," *Angelaki* 15, no. 2 (August 2010):87, 91. Further references follow in the text.

[5]Kristeva, *Powers of Horror*, p. 17. Further references follow in the text.

The various means of *purifying* the abject—the various catharses—make up the history of religions, and end up with *that catharsis par excellence called art*...Seen from that standpoint, the artistic experience, which is rooted in the abject it utters and by the same token purifies, appears as the essential component of religiosity. That is perhaps why it is destined to survive the collapse of the historical forms of religions. (17, emphasis added)

The novels *Disgrace* and *The Things They Carried*—as perhaps most modern literature—may be seen, I propose, as ritual enactments that engage readers as participants through the mimetic slaughter of abject innocents. The act of reading such texts may be seen as a mimetic sacrificial ritual whereby the reader-participant accesses a desanctified sacred through the rejection of the abject animal, affirming human ascendancy as the sacrificer, the one who lives on, whose own mortality has been expelled and buried in the text itself—projected into the sacrificial victim. Through the vehicle of animal sacrifice the reader is thereby provided with the aesthetic experience of the transgressive sublime—an intensification of being, the thrill of entering into or glimpsing a powerful forbidden ontologically intense realm—transcending the here-and-now, transcending mortality. Aesthetic closure, as conceived in modern literature—the mythic troping of ritual sacrifice—requires a distancing, a deadening of the emotions, an affective cutoff, a polishing up and rounding off that precludes the messy, interactive, unresolved process of compassionate sympathetic engagement—which some have labeled the "feminine sublime"—entailed in an aesthetics of care.

Theodor Adorno argues against tying things up aesthetically thus in an essay on the poet Hölderlin whom he vaunts for resisting what Adorno terms "synthesis"; instead Hölderlin opted for a paratactic submission to the material being treated, operating in the mode of artistic "passivity,"[6] the "mimetic comportment" which, as we have noted, Adorno advocates elsewhere (see Chapter 3). For "synthesis," Adorno claims, "is equivalent to the domination

---

[6]Theodor W. Adorno, "Parataxis," *Notes to Literature* 2:142. Further references follow in the text.

of nature" (140). That is because it organizes material according to prescripted categories, shepherding it into pens—to reprise Virginia Woolf's image—rather than simply following the material responsively where it leads, as it speaks for itself. Instead, art must, in Adorno's view, "speak for what is suppressed by domination of any kind" (155).

As witness to mimetic ritual sacrifice of the kind seen in *Disgrace* and *The Things They Carried*, the reader-participant engages vicariously in the sacrificial process and experiences thus the transgressive thrill of violation and the transcendence that expurgation of the abject affords. As the reader remains personally disengaged from the process, his experience of the ritual slaughter remains the aesthetic one of the transgressive sublime.

Authors like O'Brien and Coetzee appear to have been aware of, but also perhaps attracted to, the aesthetic subliminal potential of violence and evil, as suggested in the following passages:

In "How to Tell a War Story," a section in *The Things They Carried*, O'Brien admits:

> For all its horror, you can't help but gape at the awful majesty of combat. You stare out at tracer rounds unwinding through the dark like brilliant red ribbons... You admire the fluid symmetries of troops on the move, the harmonies of sound and shape and proportion, the great sheets of metal-fire streaming down... the white phosphorus, the purply orange glow of napalm... [An] artillery barrage has the aesthetic purity of absolute moral indifference—a powerful implacable beauty. (81)

O'Brien is here describing what Samina Najmi calls the "military sublime,"[7] a peak experience of "shock and awe" before explosive violence. Kant, one of the originators of the concept of the sublime, indeed, famously noted that "war itself... has something sublime about it."[8] Such a viewpoint, needless to say, ignores the violent consequences—the suffering bodies—that result from such "great sheets of metal-fire." They are aestheticized.

---

[7]Samina Najmi, "Naomi Shihab Nye's Aesthetic Smallness and the Military Sublime," *MELUS* 35, no. 2 (Summer 2010):151–71.
[8]Immanuel Kant, "Analytic of the Sublime," in *The Critical Tradition*, ed. David H. Richter (New York: St. Martin's Press, 1989), p. 267.

Coetzee, through his character Elizabeth Costello, appears to be aware of the danger that aesthetic exploitation of evil and suffering can become pornographic. In a chapter entitled "The Problem of Evil" in *Elizabeth Costello*, the protagonist criticizes a luridly detailed book by Paul West on the execution of Hitler's plotters, *The Very Rich Hours of Count Von Stauffenberg*.

[P]age after page, leaving nothing out; and that is what she read, sick with the spectacle, sick with herself, sick with a world in which such things took place, until at last she pushed the book away and sat with her head in her hands. *Obscene!* She wanted to say... Obscene because such things ought not to take place, and then obscene again because having taken place they ought not to be brought into the light... Obscene: not just the deeds of Hitler's executioners... but the pages of Paul West's book too. (158–59)

While Costello doesn't develop the point, the implication is that aesthetic exploitation of evil is itself evil, a form of pornography—an instance of the "aesthetics of evil" decried by Anat Pick.

As noted in Chapter 1, Marian Scholtmeijer makes a similar point in her critique of Jerzy Kozinsky's novel *The Painted Bird*. Especially objectionable, she says, is "Kozinski's pornographic interest in the events [of human and animal cruelty] he describes" (*Animal Victims* 229). In short, there is a fine line between ethical, on the one hand, and purely aesthetic depictions of evil, on the other. That the authors under consideration here—Coetzee and O'Brien—have exploited ethically damnable episodes for aesthetic purposes is my contention.

In her exploration of the issue, Scholtmeijer proposes that "what should be inexplicable—violence against animals—becomes all too intelligible when one looks at artistic motivation" (261).

Animals are present in all works of fiction... primarily to illuminate the human condition... Animals... are... scarcely animals at all but schematic elements in an aesthetic or psychological design... Because human subjectivity is... bound to formalities of narrative, the obligation *to heed the voice of compassion* evaporates. (259–60, emphasis added)

Heeding the voice of compassion—operating through an aesthetics of care—would have made for a very different handling of the episodes of animal sacrifice in the Coetzee and O'Brien novels. I noted above how Lurie's dog could easily have been adopted, but such an ending would probably have been deemed too sentimental and therefore less effective aesthetically. Similarly, the torture of the water buffalo could have been averted or framed with compassion and empathy, but such a treatment would have undercut and contravened the narrative thematic.

Both episodes border on sadism, which leads one to consider that the authors likely appreciated their shock or titillation value and used them to make their texts more aesthetically interesting. For, as Susan Sontag noted, "shock has become a leading stimulus of consumption and source of value…How else to get attention for one's product or one's art?"[9]

The episodes of animal sacrifice in both O'Brien's and Coetzee's novels are certainly shocking, an effect intensified by the pathos and innocence of the victim and the indignity of the death agony. "The baby buffalo was silent, or almost silent, just a light bubbling sound where the nose had been. It lay very still. Nothing moved except the eyes, which were enormous, the pupils shiny black and dumb" (79). When Lurie opens the dog's cage to fetch him for his death, "the dog wags its crippled rear, sniffs his face, licks his cheeks, his face, his ears" (220), then as the euthanasia drug takes effect, "bewilderingly, his legs buckle" (219)—or so Lurie imagines. Visualizing the deaths in these terms, aesthetically, with these details, violates the animals' privacy, their dignity, expressing a lack of respect for their agency. With their subjectivity erased, they are reduced to abject victimhood, innocence betrayed. Death is perhaps the ultimate indignity, but an ethical response requires that one must labor to preserve a dying creature's dignity, as she was in life, not reduced to a victim-object—while we the living remain pridefully other, watching her aesthetically interesting performance. Otherwise, such voyeurism, as it separates actant from victim, predator from prey, invites a sadistic sexual response—titillation at the cruelty and death of an other, the transgressive sublime.

What is lacking in the depictions here under consideration is what Griselda Pollock, in her critique of modern, fascist aesthetics, terms "wit(h)nessing," where the artistic encounter "enjoin[s] a

---

[9]Sontag, *Regarding the Pain*, p. 23.

co-subjectivity...so that...something of the other is processed by the viewer [reader]—not as a repeating trauma, but as a working through, as Freud conceived...the work of mourning" (235). Wit(h)nessing requires that the sacrificial victim be seen as a *subject* who has feelings and with whom one respectfully engages, not simply cast off and distanced as an aesthetically entertaining *object*, over whom one has sublime mastery, as seen, for example, in the pornographic photos of the Abu Ghraib victims discussed in Chapter 1.

In his study, *The Aesthetics of Murder* (1991), Joel Black contends that aestheticization of violence requires that the victim's point of view be excluded. Instead we readers or viewers see the scene as distanced onlookers whose "focus is shifted" by the narrative trajectory "from the point of view of the victim to that of the murderer," rendering the episode thus "aesthetically interesting,"[10] which it would not be were the victim's brutal experience replicated or entered into empathetically in the fashion of Pollock's "wit(h)nessing." Aesthetics thus follows "the Kantian principle that scenes of imminent destruction *cannot be presented from the perspective of the subject as victim*" (69). Rather, Black notes, Kant "established aesthetic contemplation as a purely disinterested activity on the part of the beholder" (79). The victim and the violence inflicted upon him are thus aestheticized.

"The victims are turned into works of art," Adorno laments in a similar observation, a critique of Arnold Schönberg's *A Survivor of Warsaw* (1947); they are

> tossed out to be gobbled up by the world that did them in. The so-called artistic rendering of the naked physical pain of those who were beaten down with rifle butts contains...the possibility that pleasure can be squeezed from it. The morality that forbids art to forget this for a second slides off into the abyss of its opposite.[11]

Like Black, Laura E. Tanner in *Intimate Violence: Reading Rape and Torture in Twentieth-Century Fiction* (1994) argues that

---

[10]Joel Black, *The Aesthetics of Murder: A Study in Romantic Literature and Contemporary Culture* (Baltimore: Johns Hopkins University Press, 1991), p. 60. Further references follow in the text.

[11]Theodore W. Adorno, "Commitment," *Notes to Literature* 1:88.

traditional formalist aesthetics inherently entails a distancing from the object of pain or violation whose point of view is absented and the consequences of the pain thus elided, as O'Brien does in his rapturous description of combat explosions.

> The distance and detachment of a reader ... make it possible for representations of violence ... to eras[e] not only the victim's body but his or her pain ... [T]he manipulation of words, images, and literary figures ... often function to efface ... the materiality of the victimized body.[12]

In a variation of standpoint theory, Tanner proposes that in order to counter aestheticization of violence in literature, the point of view (or standpoint) of the victim needs to be restored. Following Elaine Scarry's interpretation of Marx, Tanner proposes that in his critique of capitalism, Marx restored the absent referent of the worker's physical suffering, which was obscured by capitalist ideology. Marx's critique, she asserts, may thus serve as a model for an ethical approach to literature.

> Marx's unveiling of the way in which the laborer's suffering body is rendered invisible by the machinery of capitalism thus provides a critical model for understanding representations which obscure the materiality of bodily violation ... acts of representation that reinscribe violation within a magical system devoid of ... suffering and pain. As the victim's body disappears beneath the force of narrative abstraction ... narrative may implicitly endorse a vision of violence that divorces an act of violation from its consequences. (8)

Such tacit endorsement may be seen in the novels under consideration by Coetzee and O'Brien.

Readers of such novels become complicit with the perpetrators of violence and evil and with the authors who construct such scenes, because the only point of view that is available to the reader is that of the violator, not the victim. The reader thus becomes a witness

---

[12]Laura E. Tanner, *Intimate Violence: Reading Rape and Torture in Twentieth-Century Fiction* (Bloomington: Indiana University Press, 1994), p. 9.

(as opposed to a wit(h)ness), whose "perspective," Black notes, is necessary to the "construct[ion of] an aesthetic of murder" (62).

In her critique of the scene of rape in William Faulkner's novel *Sanctuary*, Tanner observes how the reader is "pressure[d]... to perceive the rape from the perspective of the violator" (19) and because of a "desire for narrative closure" (Adorno's "synthesis," which is prescripted by Pollock's "mythic troping"), "the reader is pressured into... impatiently awaiting the promised violence" (21). "[W]ithin the frame" of the text's "imaginative construct," "the reader identifies with (imaginatively becomes) the violator while the victim remains an object of imaginative manipulation, her body merely the text on which the crime is written" (28).

In "Reading the Unspeakable" (2003), a study of rape in Coetzee's *Disgrace*, Lucy Graham argues that the absence of the women victims' point of view in that novel reduces those episodes to an "aesthetic encounter"[13]; the final episode of animal sacrifice is likewise, I propose, in the end to be seen as an aesthetic construction.

Black argues that as a distanced onlooker to violent acts, the reader experiences a voyeuristic thrill, "a peak aesthetic experience" (3), "that is not of this world, and that cannot coexist with any world familiar to ethical beings" (52). Through the participation in mimetic transgressive acts "the individual transcends his mundane social identity" (209). Viewing the violent events thus ritualistically "evoke[s] in the reader a vivid aesthetic experience of the sublime" (73).

The term *sublime* as an aesthetic category was first developed in the modern era by Edmund Burke in his *Philosophical Inquiry into the Origin of Our Ideas of the Sublime and Beautiful* (1757) and Kant in his *Observations on the Feeling of the Beautiful and Sublime* (1763). Both view the experience of the sublime as an intense emotional high comprised of awe, terror, and thrill. Both also characterize the experience as essentially masculine. Kant conceived of the sublime largely as a response to powerful displays of nature that are seen as life-threatening but which one can view in security from a distance. In *Critique of Judgment*, Kant proposed that the experience of the sublime, because we are not directly threatened by the natural event, gives us a sense of surviving or overcoming or transcending nature.

---

[13]Lucy Valerie Graham, "Reading the Unspeakable: Rape in J. M. Coetzee's *Disgrace*," *Journal of Southern African Studies* 29, no. 2 (2003):440.

> While making us recognize our own physical impotence, considered as beings of nature, [the sublime] discloses to us a faculty of judging independently of and a *superiority over nature*, on which is based a kind of self-preservation entirely different from that which can be attacked and brought into danger by external nature (Kant *Critique of Judgment*, sec. 28, as cited in Black 70–71, emphasis added)

Thus the aesthetic experience of the sublime is seen to signify humans' dominance over the natural world, echoing the aspirations of early modern scientists and philosophers like Bacon, Boyle, and Descartes.

In his elaboration of Kant's conception, "On the Sublime," the German poet Friedrich Schiller conceived the sublime as an experience that lifts one out of the natural, physical order, which is feminized, into a pure spiritual masculine transcendence. "The sublime opens to us a road to overstep the limits of the world of sense, in which the feeling of the beautiful would forever imprison us."[14] Unlike an aesthetics of care under which one engages lovingly with the natural world, the Germanic sublime enables an escape from it, "wrench[ing] our spiritual and independent nature away from the net which feeling has spun round us, and which enchains our soul" (200). Nets, chains, imprisonment: Schiller's sublime seems but another enactment of the masculine flight from the feminine, once again identified with the material world and mortality.

Many feminist critics have noted the misogyny inherent in these masculinist notions of the sublime. Barbara Claire Freeman, for example, observes that "the canonical theories [of the sublime]... domesticate, and ultimately exclude an otherness that, almost without exception, is gendered as feminine."[15] As seen in the O'Brien and Coetzee novels discussed above, where sacrifice is seen to enable the establishment of male identity, "scapegoating a

---

[14]As cited in Cornelia Klinger, "The Concepts of the Sublime and the Beautiful in Kant and Lyotard," in *Feminist Interpretations of Immanuel Kant*, ed. Robin May Schott (University Park, PA: Pennsylvania State University Press, 1997), p. 199. Further references follow in the text.

[15]Barbara Claire Freeman, *The Feminine Sublime: Gender and Excess in Women's Fiction* (Berkeley: University of California Press, 1997), p. 3. Further references follow in the text.

feminine figure," Freeman maintains, "guarantee[s] discursive unity and the formation of autonomous, centered selves" (69), pointing up "the misogyny that lies at the heart of the sublime's theorization and remains implicit in so many novels" (69).

Schiller emphasizes that the sublime comes as a sudden "shock" (200), which as Cornelia Klinger points out, lays the groundwork for the "modern aesthetics [of] shock and cruelty" (200)—articulated most recently by French critic Jean-François Lyotard, who, in "L'intérêt du sublime" (1988), claimed "violence, force is necessarily linked to the sublime, that breaks free and rises."[16]

English essayist Thomas De Quincey extended Kant's notion of the masculine sublime from a reaction to the violence of nature to human acts of violence. In a 1827 satirical essay "On Murder Considered as One of the Fine Arts," De Quincey "brought Kant's concept of the natural sublime to its 'logical' conclusion in the spectacle of murder" by proposing that "the most brutal killings can be appreciated as works of art if only they are viewed from an aesthetic or disinterested, amoral perspective" (Black 15). Such appreciation De Quincey labeled the "dark sublime" (69) and Joel Black the "transgressive sublime" (72). Ritual enactments of human violence are therefore seen to afford the spectator/participant with "ecstatic acts of transcendence" (209) that constitute the experience of the "transgressive sublime," "whereby the individual transcends his mundane social identity" (209).

Both Black and Adorno, along with Paul Virilio and other critics of modernity, consider that the supersession of the ethical by the aesthetic—a hallmark, as we have seen, of modernity—has created a culture that habitually views atrocity aesthetically.

Once murder was aestheticized in modernist works of art, actual murder in all its brutality was free to flare up on an unprecedented scale in the form of fascist genocide. One of the most tragic aspects of the mass killings of the 1930s and 1940s was that, thanks in part to the aestheticization of violence by

---

[16]As cited in Klinger, "Concepts," p. 202. Lyotard presents his theory through a bizarre rape fantasy, which has been criticized by feminists. See Joanna Zylinska, *On Spiders, Cyborgs and Being Sacred* (Manchester, England: Manchester University Press, 2001), pp. 21–23. Further references to Zylinska follow in the text.

the ... modernists, the brutal reality of murder went unnoticed for far too long by all but the victims (Black 93).

There are those, however, who argue that the depiction of violence in literature and art serves to purge violent tendencies in readers or spectators, harking back thus to Aristotle's *katharsis* theory, which holds that theater-goers' "fear" and "pity" are purged through the vicarious experience of violence and death presented on the stage. (In actuality, in Greek tragedy the actual violence took place off-stage so spectators didn't actually see it.)

But fear and pity are not violent emotions; indeed they are emotions generally gendered female (including by Aristotle). Therefore, while "the dominant modern trend has been to take *katharsis* as a process of emotional release or OUTLET—a harmlessly pleasurable means of expending pent-up emotions,"[17] this is an erroneous extrapolation from Aristotle.

A reexamination of Aristotle's concept enables us to reconsider the aesthetic experience from a different perspective. Why, for example, is it that the emotions Aristotle deems it necessary to purge are those typically associated with femininity and weakness? Elsewhere in the *Poetics*, for example, Aristotle specifies that as "valour in a woman"[18] is an improbability, playwrights are enjoined to avoid such characterization, according to the doctrine of decorum that the poet should concern himself with probabilities. As John McCumber notes, "courage is the manly virtue. Fear is then the manly vice, and it is fear (with ... its displacement, pity) which tragic catharsis cleanses from the soul" in the *Poetics*.[19] The connection between pity and fear is specified by Aristotle himself in the *Rhetoric* (1382b26f, 1386a27f): "that which arouses fear when we think of it happening to ourselves arouses pity when we see it happening to others" (McCumber 60). Pity, in short, is the experience of caring compassion and sympathy which is at the heart of an aesthetics of care.

---

[17]Stephen Halliwell, *Aristotle's Poetics*, 2nd ed. (Chicago: University of Chicago Press, 1998), p. 353.

[18]Aristotle, "*Poetics* 15.4," in *Criticism*, ed. Walter Jackson Bate (New York: Harcourt, Brace & World, 1952), p. 28.

[19]John McCumber, "Aristotelian Catharsis and the Purgation of Women," *Diacritics* 18, no. 4 (Winter 1998):57. Further references follow in the text.

Why does Aristotle establish as tragedy's definitional purpose the purgation of these feelings? Partly, of course, to establish the societal worth of the genre as against Plato's critique and dismissal. But more fundamental issues are at play.

In his analysis, McCumber notes how Aristotle associated tragedy with urban upper classes and with free high-status citizens (unlike comedy which concerns lower classes in domestic locales). For this reason, the experience of "tragic catharsis," McCumber maintains, is restricted to the "freeborn and educated" (61); "women and slaves" were seen as "unfit to experience catharsis" (61). The audience therefore that Aristotle had in mind—whose "fear and pity" are to be purged—is composed of elite men.

Why is it desirable that these feminine emotions be purged from these men? McCumber suggests that the underlying fear these men harbored was of a relapse into the women's world of the *oikos*—the household (62); in other words, like the protagonists of the Coetzee and O'Brien novels, their underlying fear was of "becoming women."

The model tragedy upon which Aristotle based his theory was Sophocles' *Oedipus Tyrannus*. That work concerns the lifting of a plague and natural disasters that have befallen the city of Thebes because of Oedipus' abominable deeds. The underlying logic of the mythic script is that in order for the plague to be lifted, Oedipus must be punished and expelled as a scapegoat.

While Oedipus' original transgression was the slaying of his father and marrying of his mother, this occurs offstage, so to speak, before the events of the play begin. The play itself concerns Oedipus' relentless search for the murderer of his father and research into the origins of the plague; his intellectual drive and ambition not unlike that of a modern hubristic scientist. In that his downfall and self-mutilation establish him as an abject, feminized figure, Oedipus himself thus "becomes woman."

"The entire plot of the play," then, McCumber proposes, "depicts a catharsis—one by which the suffering body of Thebes, the Theban earth, rids herself of the cleverness of Oedipus...The catharsis is completed when Oedipus...returns to the house—to the domain of necessity" (64). The action of the play follows "a natural process of catharsis: that by which the suffering mother, the earth of Thebes, is...cleansed of the cleverness and daring of Oedipus" (66). "The cathartic process [is] that [of]...mother-earth. Hence, Oedipus the stateman and political healer...becomes Oedipus the quasi-female natural being" (66). The *katharsis* for the male spectator, then, involves being cleansed of the fear and pity of, like Oedipus, "becoming woman."

Insofar as contemporary versions of *katharsis* hew to this original meaning, it may be proposed that much of the artifacts of contemporary culture are still designed to purge male readers and spectators of the fear of becoming women, that is, abject victims, prey to mortality. (To the extent that women might also wish to avoid such a fate, the *katharsis* afforded in contemporary literature and visual arts is available thus to them, insofar as they model themselves as the transcending male.)

An ecofeminist aesthetics, an aesthetics of care, offers an alternative interpretation of *Oedipus Tyrannus*. Building on McCumber's thesis,, one may see the play as concerning a confrontation between the natural world—"mother-earth"—and the male intellect, *res cogitans*, which would dominate and control her through the exertion of rationalist and violent methodologies. The "suffering mother" brings to account the hubris-filled arrogant son, restoring the natural world to health and balance. For, as the wise seer Teiresias tells Oedipus, "you are the land's pollution."[20] It is not difficult to extrapolate from *Oedipus Tyrannus*, thus construed, to contemporary ecological crises such as global warming, industrial and chemical pollution of the earth, or various epidemics and plagues unleashed as the result of human rationalistic and violent intervention in the natural order.

The experience to be gleaned from the play, then, from an ecofeminist point of view would be not to have one's pity and fear expunged but rather to have them intensified, so that one's appreciation of the interconnectedness and relatedness of all natural things might be enhanced and enriched, making one loathe to condone the sort of detached aestheticized operations enacted in modern Cartesian science and Kantian art. Instead, one's *pity*—caring love—for the earth and her creatures—and *fear* for their fate would deepen.

---

[20]Sophocles, "Oedipus the King," trans. David Grene, in *The Complete Greek Tragedies*, ed. David Grene and Richmond Lattimore, vol. 2 (Chicago: University of Chicago Press, 1959), p. 25, l. 353.

In critiquing and rejecting Kantian masculinist conceptions of the sublime feminist critics have developed an alternative "feminine or feminist sublime" that is rooted in an aesthetics of care, reflecting, Barbara Freeman notes, an "ethics and aesthetics of attachment rather than detachment" (112).

> Unlike the masculinist sublime that seeks to master, appropriate, or colonize the other ... the feminine sublime involves ... a position of respect in response to an incalculable otherness ... [requiring] receptivity and constant attention. (11)

The feminine sublime, nearly all its theorists agree, involves a recognition of the interconnectedness of all beings and an openness to "a chance of communion and relatedness," Patrick Wright notes, "with Otherness in all its forms" (97). Anne K. Mellor connects the feminine sublime to the "ethic of care," defining it as "a heightened sensibility ... of love, reverence, and mutual relationship ... an ecstatic experience of co-participation in a nature ... gender[ed] female."[21] Patrick D. Murphy suggests that a feminine or ecofeminist sublime is "*participatory* or *integrational*" seeing "other parts of the biotic community as speaking subjects" through a "partnership ethic of caring."[22]

Bonnie Mann identifies a "feminist sublime" that is rooted in acknowledgment of "intersubjective vulnerability" and the resulting ethic of care where "value" is bestowed on those "cared for" and "moral obligation on those in the position to care."[23] Such an ethic therefore recognizes human dependency—unlike the "fantasy of independence" at the heart of the masculine sublime (seen most prominently in Schiller)—and indeed of the interdependency of all natural beings. This alternative sublime is "rooted in and disclosive of our relations of dependence" (145) and a recognition of "the deep entanglements of our natural and intersubjective dependencies"

---

[21]Anne K. Mellor, *Romanticism and Gender* (New York: Routledge, 1993), pp. 105, 97.

[22]Patrick D. Murphy, "An Ecological Feminist Revisioning of the Masculinist Sublime," *Revista Canaria de Estudios Ingleses* 64 (April 2012):90, 91.

[23]Bonnie Mann, *Women's Liberation and the Sublime Feminism, Postmodernism, Environment* (New York: Oxford University Press, 2006), p. 135. Further references follow in the text.

(161). For, she warns, there is "a violation of the sacred at the heart of our disregard for relations of dependency" (139).

Like other theorists of the aesthetics of care, as discussed in earlier chapters, many of these theorists emphasize the importance of localized, qualitative *place* in feminine experiences of the sublime. This reconceptualization of an "aesthetics beyond grandeur and might" looks "for wonder in the most minuscule spaces of the quotidian," Joanne Zylinska proposes (5). The feminine sublime focuses on "microspaces" (151), "an instance of presence" (38), "a singular event, immersed in the local perspective" and "resistant to theorisation" (152). It is a matter of paying ethical and aesthetic attention "as listeners rather than conquerors" to "the particles of being ... [W]e can ... open to the particles of being and listen to their story" (153).

Sophocles' final play in the Theban trilogy, *Oedipus at Colonus*, invites an ecofeminist interpretation in its thematic enactment of the ethic of care, reinforcing, thus, such an interpretation of *Oedipus Tyrannus*. Twenty years have passed since the events of the earlier play. Oedipus, now "old, blind, bearded and ragged,"[24] arrives at the sacred grove of the matriarchal Eumenides, "Daughters of darkness and mysterious earth: (p. 81, l. 40), the "Gentle All-seeing ones" (ll. 42–43), a sanctuary where Oedipus is prophesied to die. The grove is "shady with vines and olive trees and laurel;/Snug in their wings within, the nightingales make a sweet music" (p. 80, ll. 16–18).

In order to elicit the Eumenides' protection, Oedipus is instructed by the Chorus to make a ritual sacrifice, while uttering the following suppliant prayer.

That as we call them Eumenides,
Which means the gentle of heart,
May they accept with gentleness
The suppliant and his wish. (p. 101, ll. 486–88)

The sacrifice, be it noted, is not of an animal but of spring water, "libations" (l. 469), mixed with honey, which is poured on "the leaf-dark earth" (p. 101, l. 482), upon which are to be laid twenty-seven

---

[24]Sophocles, "Oedipus at Colonus," trans. Robert Fitzgerald, in *Complete Greek Tragedies*, ed. Grene and Lattimore, vol. 2, p. 79, stage direction. Further references follow in the text.

olive shoots. The ritual thus is one deriving from an agricultural cult, likely that of Demeter, the ancient goddess of vegetative life. For, in his final ritual bathing, Oedipus' daughters, Antigone and Ismene, bring him libation water from "the hill of Demeter, Freshener of all things" (p. 148, ll. 1600–01).

By dint of his suffering, Oedipus has achieved a kind of grace, which gives him the power to bless and to prophesy. The main events of the play concern his preparation for proper burial and his enactment through blessings and curses of his last will and testament.

Throughout his years of exile and suffering, Oedipus has been accompanied by his loyal care-giving daughters, Antigone and Ismene, who are also his sisters, all having the same mother, Jocasta—the blood link here being thus strongly matriarchal. Antigone is described as "forever tending" Oedipus, "leading a beggar's/Life" (p. 113, ll. 751–52) for years in order to devote herself to him. Oedipus gratefully acknowledges their care: "Only by grace of these two girls unaided/Have I got food or shelter or devotion" (p. 99, ll. 446–47).

By contrast, Oedipus' feckless sons, Polyneices and Etiocles, have deserted him. "These were the two/Who saw me in disgrace and banishment/And never lifted a hand for me" (p. 98, ll. 427–29). On the contrary, they have occupied themselves with fighting each other over Thebes' throne. Instead of peace and care: war and violence. In his final wisdom, Oedipus has become a pacifist who honors the *via feminina* of care and love over masculine arrogance and violence, rejecting those who "grow hard and push their arrogance to extremes" (p. 146, ll. 1534–35), an apt characterization of his younger self. In his final actions, Oedipus disowns and curses his sons (p. 139, ll. 1375, 1383), while Antigone vainly attempts to persuade her brother Polyneices to avoid war (p. 141, l. 1416). After damning his war-driven sons, Oedipus blesses his caring daughters. In recompense for their years of loving service, Oedipus negotiates with Theseus, king of Athens, for his daughters' perpetual care and protection in exchange for his blessing of Athens.

In the final scenes, Oedipus seems linked in some primal way with the natural order. Thunder and lightning signal that his death is nigh. After the bathing ritual with Demeter's holy water, Oedipus embraces his daughters and gives thanks for their years of devotion.

> I know it was hard, my children.—And yet one word
> Makes all those difficulties disappear:
> That word is love. (p. 148, ll. 1615–17)

Then, "They clung together/And wept, all three" (p. 149, ll. 1620).
Oedipus death is peaceful and loving—not shock-and-awe, yet awe-inspiring.

> It was not lightning,
> Bearing its fire from God, that took him off;
> No hurricane was blowing.
> But some attendant from the train of Heaven
> Came for him; or else the underworld
> Opening in love the unlit door of earth (p. 131, ll. 1157–63)

Theseus, the witness, is overwhelmed and cowed, "his hands before his face,/Shading his eyes as if from something awful,/Fearful and unendurable to see" (p. 149–50, ll. 1650–52); he is moved to "do reverence to Earth and to the powers of the air" (p. 150, ll. 1653–54). The final wisdom seems to be summed up by Antigone: "Now the finish/Comes, and we know only … Bewildering mystery" (pp. 150–51, ll. 1675–77).

Thus, in *Oedipus at Colonus*, fear and pity (which the Chorus expresses throughout) are not expunged through violent sacrifice. Rather they are embraced as feelings of humbling reverence before the mysteries of life and death. The experience of the sublime which Theseus has and which spectators share is not the transgressive one of violent violation but rather one of reverential submission before the awesome powers of the universe. It is an articulation of the feminine sublime.

Oedipus at Colonus is not a tidy play that follows an identifiable sacrificial script, a synthesis with clear beginnings, middles, and ends. Rather it is an evocation of a mood, that of caring solicitude, which is exuded in the protective nurturance of the Eumenides' sanctuary.

> In the god's untrodden vale
> Where leaves and berries throng,
> And wind-dark ivy climbs the bough,
> The sweet sojourning nightingale

Murmurs all day long. (p. 110, ll. 672–75)
The crocus like a little sun
Blooms with its yellow ray;
The river's fountains are awake,
And his nomadic streams that run
Unthinned forever, and never stay;
But like perpetual lovers move
On the maternal land

(p. 111, ll. 686–92)

One of the foundational texts of Western literature thus forswears the script of violent sacrifice characteristic of so much subsequent literature in favor of a vision of a maternal land that nourishes life. Vaunted throughout the play is an ethic of care, linked to the earth as the ultimate nurturer and sanctuary. Spectators are not invited to distance themselves from abject objects of derision from whose demise they may expunge their own fears of being similar, experiencing thereby the transgressive sublime and establishing themselves as superior to the abjection of mortality. Rather, in this play the viewer or reader is a participant, invited to share in the "bewildering mystery" of existence and enjoined to experience with those who share that lot heartfelt compassion. It is an aesthetics of care.

10

Caring to hear, caring to see: Art as emergence

"All creation or passage of non-being into being is poetry or making" declares Diotima to Socrates in Plato's *Symposium*.[1] In contemporary philosophical terms, "the passage of non-being into being" is *emergence*. One of the greatest philosophical and scientific mysteries remaining today is the phenomenon of *emergence*: how nonlife forms emerged and emerge into life and consciousness, how unified organisms emerge from micro units or parts, how mind emerges from body and/or body from mind, how certain situations and relationships bring out potential aspects of something, so that it "becomes" or emerges into something else. Love between two persons brings out latent aspects in each, thus effecting their emergence into something new. Relationship between a human and an animal changes both. In quantum physics, an observer brings out the particle aspect of a wave-particle phenomenon. Under an aesthetics of care, the phenomenon of emergence may be seen as the prototype for art.

In describing a medieval account of a boy raised by wolves, Karl Steel notes how both wolves and boy emerge differently from the experience, exhibiting atypical behavior (un-wolflike, on the one hand, and un-human, on the other) that is provoked by their encounter: "otherwise sleeping or withdrawn qualities in boy, wolves, and trees have been activated or made apparent in this odd event."[2] (The wolves had placed the boy in a pit in winter

---

[1] Plato, "Symposium," in *The Dialogues of Plato*, ed. B. Jowett, vol. 1 (New York: Random House, 1937), p. 330, l. 205.
[2] Karl Steel, "With the World, Or Bound to Face the Sky: The Postures of the Wolf-Child of Hesse," in *Animal, Vegetable, Mineral*, ed. Cohen, p. 28. Further references follow in the text.

and covered him with leaves and other plants for warmth, which enabled his survival.) Steel concludes, provocatively, "subjects are objects that are cared about" (33).

Caring attention, in other words, brings out—*causes to emerge*—potential aspects of entities that might otherwise remain unseen or un*real*ized. The presence of the boy brought out latent caring-for-humans behavior in the wolves; the boy conversely developed an ability to run in a "wolf-like" fashion. Through their encounter, the boy and wolves emerged into qualitatively different beings.

"Everything," Steel proposes, echoing Lee Smolin, "is always at once a subject and an object" (29). The subjective aspect—or the "within" side—is realized or comes alive or emerges only when recognized or attended to or intuited—whatever epistemological term one chooses to use—by another subject. Meditative caring attentiveness, as discussed in previous chapters, thus enables the emergence of subjectivity in entities otherwise deemed by ideological construction to be inert, lifeless, deanimated, and mechanical objects.

Art, I propose in this chapter, picking up on ideas introduced in Chapter 3, replicates nature's *emergence*, whereby the viewer and reader, along with the author, participate in this transfigurative resurrectory process, the bringing forth into recognition what is not otherwise seen or realized. Art enacts *mimesis*—not in the traditional sense of an imitation of a surface reality—but in the sense here intended: as a recognition of and a representation of the spiritual power that inheres in physical reality and which comes to life in the phenomenon of aesthetic emergence. Such *mimesis* is nature reflecting back on herself; nature in her spiritual dimension becoming aware of herself.[3]

That spiritual, nonphysical, or mental dimension may come in many forms and exist on qualitatively different ontological levels. The mind of a human or a frog or a heron is not to be equated ontologically or ethically with the vibrancy of electrons in a park bench, as I noted in my critique of the New Materialists. Yet the park bench—or, for example, a family quilt or hand-made pot—even though, per se, inert nonliving entities may exude emotional qualia which a sensitive artist or photographer might pick up. Where such qualia come from and how they are perceived is a mystery we do not have the answer to. But

---

[3]By spiritual I mean non-physical or mental—the realm of mind, consciousness, and qualia, of the anima or soul: what Eddington terms "mind-stuff" (276).

that we cannot understand the physical dynamics of the phenomenon does not mean that we should deny its existence. The theorists treated here hold that there is a sub-surface nonphysical communicative medium through which such emotional qualia are transmitted. That communication is transcribed by the artist or writer via words, notes, paint, giving it substantial form— enabling it to emerge in a concrete apprehensible state. There is, as Virginia Woolf put it, "some real thing behind the appearances, and I make it real by putting it into words" ("Sketch" 72).

The matter of art—whether paint on a canvas, sound-notes in a symphony, or words on a page—are but surface signposts then that lead the viewer/reader to apprehend the spiritual nonphysical reality they represent. The reader/viewer dissolves those signposts as he follows the author/composer into the ineffable realm she is attempting to represent. So the artistic or literary text is but a surface object— "an outpicturing of consciousness," as Candace Pert put it (257)— that communicates the unreifiable, subjective, and qualitative realm beneath the surface. In this sense, all art—all language—is symbolic of some "other" dimension that is ultimately uncategorizable in human symbolic forms. Great art—like *Oedipus at Colonus*—points to, leads into, this hidden spiritual or mental dimension but under an aesthetics of care does not access it through the violence of sacrifice, the transgressive sublime. In short, the matter in art (paint, notes, words) is the medium through which spirit is accessed and transmitted to spirit, and the transfigurative process in art whereby matter yields spirit replicates the emergence phenomenon in nature.

The French poet Paul Valéry once proposed that we live therefore in a *poetic universe* (relying on the Greek sense of poetry—seen in Diotima's comment—as ποιεῖν or making; that is, enabling life or spirit to emerge from nonlife). To explain his concept, Valéry analyzes how we understand meaning in language.

I speak to you, and if you have understood my words, these very words are abolished...the *language* is transformed into *nonlanguage*...In other terms...the physical, the concrete part, the very act of speech—does not last.[4]

---

[4]Paul Valéry, "Poetry and Abstract Thought," in *Critical Theory Since Plato*, ed. Hazard Adams (New York: Harcourt, Brace, Jovanovich, 1971), p. 914. Further references follow in the text.

This language, when it has served its purpose, evaporates almost as it is heard. I have given it forth to perish, to be radically transformed into something else in your mind...it has been completely replaced by its *meaning*...transformed into something altogether different (916)

In other words, the physical has been transformed into the nonphysical or spiritual as its meaning is registered.

Valéry sees an analogous process occurring as one hears the notes in a musical composition; the notes—inanimate physical sounds—dissolve as they are transfigured into the spiritual realm of the music itself. "*The sound evokes...the musical universe*" (914). Valéry uses an example of physical emergence to explain the concept.

The musical universe, therefore, was within you...as in a saturated salt solution a crystalline universe awaits the molecular shock of a minute crystal in order to *declare itself*. (915)

In an essay on Valéry included in his *Notes to Literature*, Theodor Adorno interprets the French poet's emergence theory as a theory of *mimesis*. "Art is imitation," Adorno explains, "but not of something material;...[it is rather] the imitation of the *language of things* themselves."[5] In another essay, "The Handle, the Pot, and Early Experience," in *Notes to Literature*, vol. 2, Adorno comments on Ernst Bloch's animist view of an item of pottery (in *Spirit of Utopia*), proposing that for the artist and the appreciator it is a matter of trying to know "what the pot in its *thing-language* is saying" (219 emphasis added)—a knowledge that "the discipline of civilizing thought, climaxing in the authority of Kant, has forbidden consciousness to ask" (219). "Art," Adorno concludes, "is an imitation not of what has been created but of the act of creation itself" (*Notes* 1:171). The "mimesis" is therefore of "something that precedes objectness" (171).

Seventeenth-century philosopher Margaret Cavendish sketched out a literary theory of *mimesis* in a panpsychist universe that points in the direction of the aesthetic theory of emergence

---

[5]Theodor W. Adorno, "Valéry's Deviations," *Notes to Literature* 1:170, emphasis added. Further references follow in the text. See also Adorno's defense of Valéry in "The Artist as Deputy," *Notes to Literature* 1:106–7.

proposed here. In *The World's Olio* (1655), Cavendish observes how the transfigurative process of emergence occurs in art, music, and literature.

> As eight notes produce innumerable tunes, so twenty-four letters produce innumerable words ... which marks produce innumerable imaginations ... which imaginations ... begets another soul ... a soul in communitie.[6]

Throughout her writing, Cavendish insisted that writers should not follow aesthetic rules—"the Rules of Art"—in their creations but rather follow the "Rules of Nature"; since "the Rules of Art cannot be the Rules of Nature ... for though Art proceeds from Nature, yet Nature doth not proceed from Art."[7] By "Rules of Nature" Cavendish does not mean "Nature methodized" in the Cartesian-Newtonian view so aptly characterized by Alexander Pope (*Essay on Criticism*, ll. 88–89), but nature in panpsychic animation.

"There is no part of Nature," she proclaims in her *Philosophical Letters* (1664), "that hath not life and knowledge" (99). "Can anyone believe that Nature is ignorant and dead ...?" (59). On the contrary, "the earth is not ... a dull, dead, moveless and inanimate body but ... is ... internally active" (*Observations* 114). "Nature hath infinite more ways to express knowledg [sic] than men can imagine ... Nature is neither blind nor dumb" (*Philosophical Letters* 151).

Not only humans have *res cogitans* but also animals, plants, the elements, minerals, and cosmic bodies. "For the Sun, Stars, Earth, Air, Fire, Water, Plants, Animals, Minerals ... all have sense and knowledg" (*Philosophical Letters* 167).

> A stone has reason [and] doth partake of the rational soul of nature, as well as man doth, because it is part of the same matter man consists of; but *yet it has not an animal or human sense and reason ... but ... a mineral sense and reason.* (*Observations* 221, emphasis added)

---

[6]Cavendish, *World's Olio* (London: J. Martin and J. Allestrye, 1655), p. 100.

[7]Cavendish, *Philosophical and Physical Opinions* (London: William Watson, 1663), p. d2. Further references follow in the text.

Note here how Cavendish is allowing for ontological distinction among the various forms of "reason"—a perspective that honors the diversity of nature's different voices. "Other creatures," thus, "*in their kinds* are as knowing and wise, as man *in his kind*" (*Observations* 219, emphasis added).

> Wherefore though other Creatures have not speech, nor Mathematical rules and demonstrations, with other Arts and Sciences, as Man, yet may these perceptions and observations be as wise as Man's, and they may have as much intelligence and commerce betwixt each other, *after their own manner and way*, as men have theirs. (*Philosophical Letters* 114, emphasis added)

Cavendish holds that there is an organic sympathy that operates within the body, a cosmic sympathy that operates throughout nature through a submerged communicative medium. "[A]ll parts of the body have their particular knowledges and perceptions...when one part of the body is oppressed, or in distress, all the other parts endeavour to relieve that distressed or afflicted part" (*Observations* 152). "Each part hath its sense and reason,...and although they cannot talk or give intelligence to each other by speech, each has its own peculiar and particular knowledge" (*Philosophical Letters* 114). And throughout nature, as in the body, "there is perpetual commerce and intercourse between parts and parts" (*Observations* 140). That that "commerce" is one of "cosmic sympathy" is suggested in "A Dialogue of Birds," a long poem, where Cavendish has the swallow declare, "Love is *Natures* chiefest *Law*" (*Poems, and Fancies* 86).

Cavendish's concept of *mimesis* therefore must be understood within the context of this animist cosmos, one that is governed by love and sympathy. Her epistemological theory, which sees perception as an imitative operation, undergirds her aesthetics of care. "Perception," she writes, "is an action of figuring or patterning" (*Observations* 55). "The sensitive motions in the eye...pattern out the figure of the object" (79) by imitation. In *Philosophical Letters*, she gives as an example:

> the perception of foreign objects is made by patterning them out: as for example, the sensitive perception of foreign objects is *by making or taking copies* from these objects, so the sensitive corporeal motions in the eyes *copy out* objects of sight. (127, emphasis added).

Throughout her work, as noted, Cavendish counters the Cartesian/Newtonian objectifying and dominative approach to nature—indeed, one senses that such opposition to the growing influence of early modern science is her prime motivation. Literary practice, in Cavendish's view, must engage in an alternative manner to the violative, distortive approach seen in the sciences. The writer should instead imitate nature directly without prescripted constructs or distortive "rules." That imitation involves—as seen in her theories of perception—an empathetic modeling of nature—Adorno's mimetic comportment. Such imitation or mimesis is accomplished, she writes in *Philosophical Letters*, through attentive empathy or "Sympathy," which, she maintains, is "but a conforming of the actions of one party to the actions of the other, as by way of *Imitation*" (292, emphasis added). Since the natural world is animate in Cavendish' view and interconnected by networking waves of sympathy, with "love as its chiefest Law," the writer must comport to this medium in her work, thus enabling the "beget[ting]" or emergence "of another soul" (*World's Olio* 28). Such a vision conceives of literature and art therefore as transfigurative, enabling the emergence of "soul" from otherwise reified matter.

In order to further amplify this revitalized theory of *mimesis* we need to turn to contemporary philosophy and science, which provide alternatives to the Cartesian/Newtonian model, upon which, as we have seen and as Adorno notes, Kantian aesthetics is based.

The question of how and/or if mind emerged or emerges from matter—or how *res cogitans* relates to or emerges from *res extensa*—has plagued Cartesian theory from the onset, as noted in Chapter 1. Likewise the question of how nonphysical qualities (or *qualia*), such as color, taste, and sound emerge or relate to physical *quanta* remains unexplained in the Cartesian/Newtonian epistemology of classical physics, wherein *qualia* are relegated to secondary or inessential status, as Descartes dismissed all but quantitative properties in his analysis of the bees' wax. "Physics," philosopher Charles Hartshorne remarked, "describes the ... spatio-temporal outline of things, but says nothing about the qualitative stuff."[8] Nor does it say anything about *meaning*.

---

[8] Charles Hartshorne, *Beyond Humanism: Essays in a New Philosophy of Nature* (Chicago: Willett, Clark, 1937), p. 178. Further references follow in the text.

We may identify words on the page quantitatively—by their shape, size, etc.—for example, but quantitative analysis will not yield their meaning.

Jakob von Uexküll, an early twentieth-century biologist, in his panpsychist theory of natural life, emphasized "meaning bridges the gap between physical and nonphysical processes."[9] In other words, like Valéry—as well as Eddington, Virginia Woolf, Cavendish, and others—von Uexküll intuits a communicative nonphysical substrate or dimension—a "poetic universe"—in which conscious creatures communicate and connect. Von Uexküll maintains that all creatures live in a subjective "dwelling world" (*Umwelt*) (139) wherein everything is subjectified according to the meaning it has for the creature. "*The question as to meaning*," he writes, "*must therefore have priority in all living beings*" (151). How meaning and qualia emerge from physical properties remains, however, as noted, an unexplained mystery.

Panpsychists propose that for emergence to occur there has to be a latent capacity or quality in the entity wherein emergence occurs. *Ex nihilo, nihil fit.* To explain the phenomenon of qualitative emergence in terms of panpsychism, contemporary theorist Patrick Spät points to a naturally occurring phenomenon not unlike the one highlighted by Valéry. Consider, he suggests, the quality of saltiness and its relation to the physical molecule of sodium chloride. The molecule by itself is not salty. Saltiness only emerges or occurs when experienced by a tasting subject. "For there to be something having the property of saltiness one needs something that experiences this property."[10] But there also has to be something in the molecule that can emerge as saltiness in the encounter with a taster. The saltiness "really *is* in the sodium chloride as an unrealized disposition—and with the intervention of an experiencing subject this *disposition becomes realized*" (163). The panpsychist explanation of this otherwise inexplicable communicative ontology is that there is a mental substrate to all

---

[9]Uexküll, *A Foray into the Worlds of Animals and Humans*, p. 157. Further references follow in the text.

[10]Patrick Spät, "Panpsychism, the Big-Bang Argument and the Dignity of Life," in *Mind That Abides: Panpsychism in the New Millennium*, ed. David Skrbina (Amsterdam: John Benjamins, 2009), p. 162. Further references follow in the text.

reality, that "mind, or some mind-like quality, is present in all parts of the natural world, even in matter itself."[11]

As we have seen, Sir Arthur Eddington similarly proposed in *The Nature of the Physical World* (1928) that there is an "unknown background" within which and from which nonphysical communicative information is transmitted (259). All of our human symbolic forms (Eddington is mainly focused on mathematics) are but "pointers" that register quantitative data "resting on a shadowy background that lies outside the scope of physics" (152) or other symbolic indicators.

Eddington maintains that the shadowy background behind the pointer images is accessible through the mental phenomenon of consciousness, which is "the only avenue to what I have called *intimate* knowledge of the reality behind the symbols of science" (340). Indeed, "it is in this background that our own mental consciousness lies" (282), for "consciousness has its roots in this background" (330). Eddington contends, therefore, that the unknown background is mental, "mind-stuff" (276), "something of spiritual nature of which the prominent characteristic is *thought*" (259). "[L]et us accept the only hint we have received as to the significance of the background—namely that it has a nature capable of manifesting itself as mental activity" (260). The phenomenon of emergence as explained by panpsychism is then that there is in all reality a latent "mind-stuff" that comes to life in certain communicative encounters but is transmitted through representative physical pointer images, such as words, sound-notes, etc.

Another contemporary panpsychist, Freya Mathews, proposes in *For Love of Matter: A Contemporary Panpsychism* (2003) that "external reality...[is] the exoskeleton of subjectival process."[12] "The universe...is a subjectival field that manifests to observers as an order of extension" (55). "The world 'speaks' through symbolic constellations that are...uniquely apposite to the situation at hand" (66). We are thus immersed in a "poetic order" (67) in which "communication...[is] a process whereby subjects...disclose aspects of their nonmanifest interior states to one another" (40).

---

[11]Skrbina, *Panpsychism*, p. 2.
[12]Mathews, *For Love of Matter*, p. 41. Further references follow in the text.

Mathews urges a mode of loving, caring openness as the means by which we access the "poetic order" of the spiritual dimension.

> To adopt a panpsychist outlook is to enter the terrain of "spirituality," since it opens up the possibility of communicative engagement with a responsive world that invites us to assume an attitude of eros in relation to it ... To encounter others [in this way] involves recognition of and contact with their independent subjectivity, where such recognition and contact inevitably give rise to a certain respect for their integrity and sympathetic concern for their fate. (10)

Mathews thus advocates an epistemological mode of "being-in-love"; "when the world is our beloved ... we are engaged with [it] via its local modality of land or place, then [we experience] the state of being-in-love" (19).

Charles Hartshorne, like Mathews a process philosopher under the influence of Alfred North Whitehead, proposes that we connect to this poetic universe through a Whiteheadian mode of "aesthetic 'prehension' rather than an intellectual apprehension."[13] We experience, for example, the sounds of nature as direct sensations, which "preserve primitive (or childlike) animism" (89). This prehensive sensation is itself inherently a "caring for, a valuing of things" (88). Both Mathews and Hartshorne thus propose, in effect, an aesthetics of care.

For aesthetic appreciation, Hartshorne stipulates and operates in a caring mode; it occurs when "we are most attentive to experience in its concreteness" (Hartshorne, *Creative Synthesis*, as cited in Dombrowski 75). Through aesthetic caring we are responsive to [emotional] *qualia*. "Qualia are crucial in an aesthetic appreciation of nature" (105), for *qualia* are the "vibrant" manifestation of the spiritual energy or beauty that inheres in all things. Beauty thus inheres in the object, which is communicated to the appreciator through *qualia*; it *emerges* through the interactive emotional encounter. "The subtle aesthetic qualities of the aesthetic object that appear to impart

---

[13]Daniel Dombrowski, *Divine Beauty: The Aesthetics of Charles Hartshorne* (Nashville, TN: Vanderbilt University Press, 2004), p. 101. Further references follow in the text.

aesthetic feeling in us … [must] inhere in the aesthetic object itself *in some way*" (77). We experience an "aesthetic object … because it is vibrant" (101). For there is "*something* in the natural world that is vibrant and with which we can resonate" (110).[14]

Hartshorne conceives the underlying mental "poetic universe" as fundamentally "emotional in character" (293); like Cavendish he holds it to be unified by a "cosmic sympathy" (316). Communication is therefore mediated by love, for, in the end, he maintains, "knowledge is … love"; "that is, sympathetic identification with, living the life of, another rational or sentient being" (19). And "'mind' is that with which some slight degree of imaginative sympathy … is possible" (192).

Hartshorne's definitions of mind and knowledge cue us to the ontological distinction made earlier in our discussion of the New Materialists. In emphasizing that "mind" inheres in any entity with whom "imaginative sympathy is possible" and that knowledge comes from that sympathy with "another rational or sentient being" Hartshorne implies that there is a distinction to be made between living and nonliving forms. It is with the mental dimension of the former that one communicates through sympathetic understanding, through emotional qualia.

If "subjects are objects that are cared about," as Karl Steel proposed, then Hartshorne's stipulation—that subjectivity can only be recognized (one subject for another) where imaginative sympathy is possible—would seem to restrict the type of objects wherein caring attentiveness can enable subjectivity to emerge, or be seen, to living creatures whose subjectivity has been falsely obscured by ideological constructions, such as Cartesian science, Kantian aesthetics, capitalism, and speciesism.

---

[14]Hartshorne would seem here to anticipate the view of the New Materialists; however, the latter, unlike Harshorne and Mathews, do not conceive of there being an emotional aspect to material "vibrancy." Thus, while the New Materialists grant agency to physical matter, they conceive that agency somewhat mechanistically, ignoring emotional qualia; the universe is seen as a complex assortment of impersonal apathetic actants that exude vibrations but they remain *whats*. There is no *who* there, no subjectivity. "Matter," Bennett states, is "intrinsically lively but not ensouled" (*Vibrant*, xvii). This becomes ethically problematic, as noted in Chapter 1, when living beings are placed on the same ontological level as commodities (see Chapter 1, n. 56). Hartshorne, however, as noted, implicitly adopts an ontological distinction between living and nonliving forms.

The concept of emergence indeed necessarily implies that there is an ontological distinction to be made between conscious, living subjects, and nonliving entities. As noted, some panpsychists contend that there must be a living quality in the nonliving for the emergence of life to occur. Regardless of the answer to these ultimate questions, the point of relevance here is that while classical formalist aesthetics, as well as classical science, deadens and objectifies material in order to manipulate it in accordance with aesthetico-mathematical "laws," an aesthetics of care, on the contrary, enables the livingness—the subjectivity—of entities otherwise conceived as dead, inert objects to emerge and shine forth as alive. An aesthetics of care thus perceives "behind the appearances"—behind objectified forms—revealing an entity's inner subjectivity, rather than deadening that subjectivity, crucifying it on a mathematically constructed aesthetic cross.

That it is ethically insupportable to objectify living creatures, such as animals, for aesthetic purposes has been the central contention of this book, wherein alternative modes of *mimesis* have been identified in writers from Cather to Tolstoy, from Sophocles to Woolf—writers who were able to respond to the emotional qualia emanating from their subjects, bringing out and/or enabling the emergence of their subjectivity rather than objectifying that subjectivity aesthetically. Through ecosympathy and an aesthetics of care they were able "to hear over there … that ewe who is crying" and to comport through their work to "a sound like a vast breath, as though it were the very inspiration of the earth herself, and all the living things on her."

Conclusion

The fundamental dualism of Enlightenment ontology, which undergirds the Kantian aesthetics of modernity, mandates a division between mind and matter, self and other, and subject and object. Perhaps the most grievous of these divisions, however—and the besetting sin, one might say, of the Enlightenment mindset—is the divorce between the ethical and the aesthetic.

Developments in twentieth-century quantum physics have brought into question, as noted in Chapter 3, these dualisms, such that new configurations and understandings are called for, which recognize that such binary oppositions are a falsification, that there are linkages, entanglements, and interconnections—set in an interactive communicative medium—that are unseen and unaccounted for in the classical Enlightenment conception.

Because of its relegation to the status of "negligible" or secondary all that is nonquantifiable, the Enlightenment view strips the world of its animating qualia. "What is reflected in aesthetic transcendence is the disenchantment of the world," Theodor Adorno observed, (*Notes* 1:32). For, as he and Horkheimer note in *Dialectic of Enlightenment* (1944), "the disenchantment of the world is the extirpation of animism" (5). Much modern literature seeks to reenchant by means of mimetic violence, inducing the experience of the transgressive sublime.

In this study, I have argued for different ontological and aesthetic conceptions, ones that abjure the mythic troping of male narcissism and the mimetic violence of animal sacrifice in favor of an ecosympathetic vision that recognizes and honors the spiritual/mental, nonphysical qualitative dimension in all living things—and perhaps in all matter. Literature conceived under an aesthetics of care does not objectify animal subjects for aesthetic purposes nor does it aestheticize animal cruelty. Such literature moreover recognizes and honors the unscripted diversity of the world, refusing to shepherd it into the neat pens of aesthetic synthesis.

Modeled on the precepts of early modern science, the aesthetics of modernity, in contradistinction, is reductive and exclusionary. Excluded or "culled" is whatever is anomalous to the prescripted anthropocentric grid, "mythic troping." What is excluded, in short, in the aesthetico-scientific view is the messy suffering body of animality. Its features must be purged in order for the pure aesthetic object—Virginia Woolf's nuggets of gold—to take shape.

Some may argue that Kantian aesthetics applies more to the visual arts than to literature, but the dominant strain in modern literary criticism—culminating in "New Criticism" of the mid-twentieth century and deconstructionism thereafter—has conceived of literature in terms of aesthetic form, a largely mechanical notion. Jonathan Bate notes, "New Criticism [which] reached its zenith in the aftermath of the Second World War and was transformed into deconstruction during the Cold War...typically treated texts as mechanisms" (*Song* 179). Literary works in this essentially Kantian view are viewed as autotelic objects that operate in terms of the interrelations of "images," "figures of speech," "motifs," etc., which the writer manipulates "disinterestedly" into aesthetic shape. Ethical concerns are deemed irrelevant because the matter being manipulated is inanimate, drained of its vital qualitative juices and extracted from its social, historical, personal, and emotional context, which is simply ignored or deemed aesthetically irrelevant, as the beeswax's qualities were deemed irrelevant to its essential character by Descartes. The aesthetic process in this conception thus is one of purification according to discriminatory criteria that exclude whatever does not conform to the aesthetic ideal— "everything that is heterogenous to [its] form" (Adorno, *Aesthetic Theory* 109). It is a dominative culling process guided by an ideal of "aesthetic correctness." Cast in this light it may be seen as a totalitarian operation that operates by means of the purge, expelling or nullifying all entities that do not fit into the prescribed form.

The aesthetics of care, by contrast, holds that these deviant "different" voices must be heard, must be included, on the theory that, as Adorno noted, "the need to give a voice to suffering is a condition of all truth" (*Negative Dialectics* 17–18).

An especially troubling aspect of the modern cultural perspective is how the formalist distancing aesthetics of modernity enables ethical distancing, a disavowal of ethical responsibility toward the subjects being framed, objectified, and aestheticized—whether in art, in scientific experimentation, or in other cultural practices wherein the suffering of the victim is not seen or heard but instead silenced, trivialized, and excluded from the picture. An aesthetics of care hopes to restore ethical awareness to the suffering subject so as to enable compassionate ethical treatment of those otherwise excluded from moral consideration.

The artist's principal function under an aesthetics of care is to direct ethical caring attention to the living reality of the natural world. The attention of consciousness confers sacrality upon its objects; or more accurately, the attention of the writer's consciousness sees the sacred being that exists in the natural world and through her aesthetic engagement enables that being to become apparent and to be communicated—through her art—to other conscious minds. "I make it real by putting it into words," Virginia Woolf concluded ("Sketch" 72). Indeed by abjuring a dominative mentality, by looking at the natural world *as it is*, much that is otherwise unseen *emerges* and comes to life, just as when a rock is turned over and removed from its place tiny pale yellow and white shoots rise up and emerge into full-fledged greenery.

The seasonal cycle of nature itself reflects the emergence phenomenon—spirit emerging out of matter, life out of death. In replicating the emergence phenomenon, great art therefore responds to the natural resurrectory cycle of the seasons, where life emerges out of death—as seen so brilliantly in Tolstoy's great story "Three Deaths." Death is not cut off and expelled as in scapegoat sacrifice and the masculine sublime but is integrated and accepted as part of the natural processes of transformation—the insight intuited by Bradley Alexander in Cather's novel *O Pioneers!* when he heard the entropic "sound of the rushing water underneath" or as dramatized in *Oedipus at Colonus*.

As a medium where something spiritual emerges out of the physical, art mimics the mysterious emergence of mind out of matter that defines natural life. *Mimesis* in this conception is an imitation of the most fundamental process of life. And as in the natural process, the "emergence" that occurs in art is largely a matter of allowing to shine forth what is already there, enabling the spirit in the material to come to life, assuming an animate panpsychic universe. Art is thus a revelation of ensoulment.

This is perhaps why beauty is thrilling, why our hearts and spirits are lifted when we behold a colorful flower, certain writings, paintings, or music; it is because our spirits respond to their spiritual being—their *geistige Wesenheiten*—which enters into our spirit, enriching, enlivening, companioning it. This is why the loss of her canary companion was so grievous for the woman in "A Jury of Her Peers." He was her only connection to the life-spirit.

Literature and art that does not allow the living spirit of its subjects to flourish, which blocks it with dominative ideological and aesthetic form, fails to perform the consoling office Adorno expected of great literature under an aesthetics of care: that it connect us to the sacred being that inheres in all creatures, to our "soul in communitie."

BIBLIOGRAPHY

Adams, Carol J. *The Sexual Politics of Meat: A Feminist-Vegetarian Critical Theory*. New York: Continuum, 1990.

Adorno, Theodor. "Reconciliation under Duress." In *Aesthetics and Politics* by Ernst Bloch et al., pp. 151–76. London: Verso, 1980.

———. "Parataxis on Holderlin's Late Poetry." *Notes to Literature*, edited by Rolf Tiedemann; trans. Sherry Weber Nicholsen. New York: Columbia University Press, 1961, 2:109–79.

———. "Valéry's Deviations." *Notes to Literature*, edited by Rolf Tiedemann; trans. Sherry Weber Nicholson. New York: Columbia University Press, 1962, 1:137–73.

———. *Minima Moralia: Reflections from Damaged Life*, trans. E. F. N. Jeffcott. London: Verso, 1954.

———. *Aesthetic Theory*, edited by Gretel Adorno and Rolf Tiedemann; trans. Robert Hullot-Kentor. Minneapolis: University of Minnesota Press, 1997.

———. *Negative Dialectics*, trans. E. B. Ashton. New York: Continuum, 2007.

Adams, Carol J. and Lori Gruen, eds. *Ecofeminism: Feminist Intersections with Other Animals and the Earth*. New York: Bloomsbury, 2014.

Armstrong, Philip. *What Animals Mean in the Fiction of Modernity*. London: Routledge, 2008.

Attwell, David, ed. *Doubling the Point: Essays and Interviews*. Cambridge: Harvard University Press, 1992.

Auerbach, Berthold. "Der Lauterbacher." In *Samtliche Schwarzwälder Dorfgeschichten*, vol. 2, pp. 57–130. Stuttgart, Germany: F. E. Cotta'chen, 1884.

———. "Ivo der Hajrle." In *Samtliche Schwarzwälder Dorfgeschichten*, vol. 1, pp. 155–255. Stuttgart, Germany: F. E. Cotta'chen, 1884.

Baier, Annette C. "The Need for More Than Justice." In *Science, Morality, and Feminist Theory*, edited by Marsha Hanen and Kai Nielsen. Calgary, Canada: University of Calgary Press, 1987.

Baker, Steve. *Picturing the Beast: Animals, Identity, and Representation*. Urbana: University of Illinois Press, 2001.

Bakhtin, Mikhail. *Problems of Dostoievsky's Poetics*, trans. R. W. Rotsel. N.p.: Ardis, 1973.

Barad, Karen. *Meeting the Universe Half-Way: Quantum Physics and the Entanglement of Matter*. Durham, NC: Duke University Press, 2007.

Bate, Jonathan. *The Song of the Earth*. Cambridge, MA: Harvard University Press, 2000.

Battigelli, Anna. *Margaret Cavendish and the Exiles of the Mind*. Lexington: University Press of Kentucky, 1998.

Beers, William. *Women and Sacrifice: Male Narcissism and the Psychology of Religion*. Detroit: Wayne State University Press, 1992.

Bell, Clive. *Art*. New York: Frederic A. Stokes, 1913.

Bennett, Jane. "Powers of the Hoard: Further Notes on Material Agency." In *Animal, Vegetable, Mineral: Ethics and Objects*, edited by Jeffrey Jerome Cohen, pp. 237–69. Washington, DC: Oliphaunt Books, 2012.

———. *Vibrant Matter*. Durham, NC: Duke University Press, 2010.

Bigwood, Carol. *Earth Muse: Feminism, Nature and Art*. Philadelphia: Temple University Press, 1993.

Black, Joel. *The Aesthetics of Murder: A Study in Romantic Literature and Contemporary Culture*. Baltimore: Johns Hopkins University Press, 1991.

Bloch, Ernst. *The Utopian Function of Art and Literature*. Cambridge, MA: MIT Press, 1988.

Bloch, Maurice. *Prey into Hunter: The Politics of Religious Experience*. Cambridge: Cambridge University Press, 1992.

Bohls, Elizabeth. *Women Travelers and the Language of Aesthetics, 1716–1818*. Cambridge: Cambridge University Press, 1995.

Bolaño, Roberto. "The Insufferable Gaucho," *The New Yorker*, October 1, 2007.

Broad, Jacqueline. *Women Philosophers of the Seventeenth Century*. Cambridge: Cambridge University Press, 2002.

Brown, E. K. *Willa Cather: A Critical Biography*. New York: Knopf, 1953.

Buber, Martin. *Between Man and Man*, edited by Ronald Gregor Smith. New York: Macmillan, 1965.

———. *I and Thou*, trans. Walter Kaufman. New York: Scribner's, 1970.

Buchon, Max. "Le Matachin." In *En Province: Scènes Franc-Comtoises*. Paris: Michel Lévy, 1858.

Buell, Lawrence. *The Environmental Imagination: Thoreau, Nature Writing, and the Formation of American Culture*. Cambridge, MA: Harvard University Press, 1995.

Burtt, Edwin Arthur. *The Metaphysical Foundations of Modern Physical Science*, rev. ed. 1931. Garden City, NY: Doubleday Anchor, n.d.

Cameron, Kenneth Walter. *Young Emerson's Transcendental Vision*. Hartford, CT: Transcendental Books, 1971.

Camus, Albert. *L'Homme Révolté*. Paris: Gallimard, 1951.

Carleton, William. "Phil Purcel: The Pig Driver." In *Traits and Stories of the Irish Peasantry*, vol. 1, pp. 407–27. Savage, MD: Barnes and Noble, 1990.

Cary, Richard, ed. *Sarah Orne Jewett Letters*, enl. and rev. ed. Waterville, ME: Colby College Press, 1967.

Cather, Willa. "A Resurrection." In *Willa Cather's Collected Short Fiction, 1892–1912*, rev. ed., edited by Virginia Faulkner, pp. 425–40. Lincoln: University of Nebraska Press, 1970.

———. "*Alexander's Bridge*." In *Willa Cather: Stories, Poems, and Other Writings*, edited by Sharon O'Brien. New York: Library of America, 1992.

———. *O Pioneers!*. Boston: Houghton Mifflin, 1941.

———. *One of Ours*. New York: Knopf, 1922.

———. Interview. *Philadelphia Record*, 9 Aug. 1913. In *The Kingdom of Art: Willa Cather's First Principles and Critical Statements, 1893–1896*, edited by Bernice Slote, pp. 448–49. Lincoln: University of Nebraska Press, 1966.

———. Preface to *The Country of the Pointed Firs and Other Stories* by Sarah Orne Jewett. New York: Doubleday Anchor, 1956.

———. *The Professor's House*. New York: Knopf, 1925.

———. *The Song of the Lark*. Lincoln: University of Nebraska Press, 1978.

Cavendish, Margaret. *Poems, and Fancies*. London: J. Martin and F. Allestrye, 1653.

———. *Philosophical and Physical Opinions*. London: William Watson, 1663.

———. *Philosophical Letters: Or, Modest Reflections upon Some Opinions in Natural Philosophy*. London: n.p., 1664.

———. *Observations upon Experimental Philosophy* (1666), edited by Eileen O'Neill. Cambridge: Cambridge University Press, 2001.

———. *The World's Olio*. London: J. Martin and J. Allestrye, 1655.

Chaon, Don. "I Demand to Know Where You're Taking Me." In *The Pushcart Prize XXVII*, edited by Bill Henderson, pp. 227–48. Wainscott, NY: Pushcart Press, 2003.

Cheney, Jim. "Postmodern Environmental Ethics: Ethics as Bioregional Narrative." *Environmental Ethics* 11 (1989):117–34.

Cladel, Leon. *Le Bouscassié*. Paris: Alphonse Lemerre, 1869.

Clark, George. *The Seventeenth Century*, 2d ed. New York: Oxford University Press, 1961.

Coetzee, J. M. *Boyhood: Scenes from a Provincial Life*. New York: Viking, 1997.

———. *Disgrace*. New York: Viking, 1999.

———. *Elizabeth Costello*. New York: Viking, 2003.

————. *The Life and Times of Michael K*. New York: Viking, 1983.

————. "The Narrative of Jacobus Coetzee." In *Dusklands*. New York: Penguin, 1996.

————. *Waiting for the Barbarians*. 1980. New York: Penguin, 1982.

Coetzee, J. M. et al. *The Lives of Animals*, edited by Amy Gutmann. Princeton. NJ: Princeton University Press, 1999.

Collins, Margery L. and Christine Pierce. "Holes and Slime: Sexism in Sartre's Psychoanalysis." In *Women in Philosophy*, edited by Carol C. Gould and Mary W. Warshofsky, pp. 112–27. New York: Putnam's 1976.

Conway, Anne. "The Principles of the Most Ancient and Modern Philosophy (1692)." In *Women Philosophers of the Early Modern Period*, edited by Margaret Atherton. Indianapolis: Hackett, 1994.

Cooke, Rose Terry. "Dely's Cow." In *How Celia Changed Her Mind and Other Stories*, pp. 182–95. New Brunswick, NJ: Rutgers University Press, 1986.

————. "Miss Lucinda." In *How Celia Changed Her Mind and Other Stories*, pp. 151–81. New Brunswick, NJ: Rutgers University Press, 1986.

Coole, Diana and Samantha Frost, eds. *New Materialisms: Ontology, Agency, and Politics*. Durham, NC: Duke University Press, 2010.

Crawford, Jennifer. *Spiritually-Engaged Knowledge: The Attentive Heart*. Aldershot, Hampshire, England: Ashgate, 2005.

Danta, Chris. "'Like a dog...like a lamb': Becoming Sacrificial Animal in Kafka and Coetzee." *New Literary History* 38 (2007):721–37.

Derrida, Jacques. "'Eating Well,' or the Calculation of the Subject." In *Points...Interviews 1974–1994*, trans. Peter Conor and Avital Ronell, pp. 255–87. Stanford, CA: Stanford University Press, 1995.

Descartes, René. "Discourse on the Method." In *Descartes Selections*, edited by Ralph Eaton. New York: Scribner's, 1927.

Detienne, Marcel and Jean-Pierre Vernant. *The Cuisine of Sacrifice*, trans. Paula Wissing. Chicago: University of Chicago Press, 1989.

Dombrowski, Daniel. *Divine Beauty: The Aesthetics of Charles Hartshorne*. Nashville, TN: Vanderbilt University Press, 2004.

Donovan, Josephine. "Aestheticizing Animal Cruelty." *College Literature* 38, no. 4 (Fall 2011):207–22.

————. *After the Fall: The Demeter-Persephone Myth in Wharton, Cather, and Glasgow*. University Park, PA: Pennsylvania State University Press, 1989.

————. "Breaking the Sentence: Local-Color Literature and Subjugated Knowledges." In *The (Other) American Traditions*, edited by Joyce Warren, pp. 226–43. New Brunswick, NJ: Rutgers University Press, 1993.

————. "Ecofeminist Literary Criticism: Reading the Orange." *Hypatia* 11, no. 2 (Spring 1996):161–82.

————. *European Local-Color Literature: National Tales, Dorfgeschichten, Romans Champêtres*. New York: Bloomsbury Continuum, 2010.

————. "Everyday Use and Moments of Being: Toward a Nondominative Aesthetic." In *Aesthetics in Feminist Perspective*, edited by Hilde Hein and Carolyn Korsmeyer, pp. 53–67. Bloomington: Indiana University Press, 1993.

————. "Feminism and the Treatment of Animals: From Care to Dialogue." *Signs* 31, no. 2 (2006):305–29.

————. *Gnosticism in Modern Literature: A Study of Selected Works of Camus, Sartre, Hesse, and Kafka*. New York: Garland, 1990.

————. "Interspecies Dialogue and Animal Ethics: The Feminist Care Perspective." In *The Oxford Handbook of Animal Studies*, edited by Linda Kalof. New York: Oxford University Press, 2015.

————. "Jewett and Swedenborg." *American Literature* 65, no. 4 (1993):731–50.

————. "'Miracles of Creation': Animals in the Work of J. M. Coetzee." *Michigan Quarterly Review* 43, no. 1 (Winter 2004):78–93.

————. *New England Local Color Literature*. New York: Continuum Ungar, 1983.

————. "Participatory Epistemology, Sympathy, and Animal Ethics." In *Ecofeminism: Feminist Intersections with Other Animals and the Earth*, edited by Carol J. Adams and Lori Gruen, pp. 75–90. New York: Bloomsbury, 2014.

————. "Provincial Life with Animals." *Society & Animals* 21, no. 1 (2013):17–33.

————. "The Voice of Animals: A Response to Recent French Care Theory in Animal Ethics." *Journal of Critical Animal Studies* 11, no. 1 (2013):8–23.

————. "Tolstoy's Animals." *Society & Animals* 17, no. 1 (2009):38–52.

————. *Women and the Rise of the Novel, 1405–1726*, 2d. rev. ed. New York: Palgrave Macmillan, 2013.

Donovan, Josephine and Carol J. Adams, eds. *The Feminist Care Tradition in Animal Ethics*. New York: Columbia University Press, 2007.

Dunayer, Joan. *Animal Equality: Language and Liberation*. Derwood, MD: Ryce, 2001.

Eagleton, Terry. *The Ideology of the Aesthetic*. Oxford: Blackwell, 1990.

Eddington, A. S. *The Nature of the Physical World*. New York: Macmillan, 1928.

Edgeworth, Maria. *Ormond*. New York: Penguin, 2000.

Eggers, Dave. "Measuring the Jump," *The New Yorker*, September 1, 2003.

Ehrenreich, Barbara. *Blood Rites: Origins and History of the Passions of War.* New York: Metropolitan, 1997.

Eliot, T. S. "Tradition and the Individual Talent." In *Criticism: The Major Texts,* edited by Walter Jackson Bate, pp. 525–29. New York: Harcourt, Brace & World, 1952.

Elisabeth of Bohemia. "Correspondence with Descartes." In *Women Philosophers of the Early Modern Period,* edited by Margaret Atherton, pp. 11–21. Indianapolis: Hackett, 1994.

Fabre, Ferdinand. *Le Chevrier.* Paris: Bibliothèque-Charpentier, 1913.

Ferry, Luc. "Neither Man nor Stone." In *Animal Philosophies: Essential Readings in Continental Thought,* edited by Matthew Calarco and Peter Atterton, pp. 145–56. New York: Continuum, 2004.

Fielding, Henry. *Joseph Andrews.* In *The Theory of the Novel,* edited by Philip Stevick, pp. 387-88. New York: Free Press, 1967.

Fields, Annie Adams, ed. *Letters of Sarah Orne Jewett.* Boston: Houghton Mifflin, 1911.

Freeman, Barbara Claire. *The Feminine Sublime: Gender and Excess in Women's Fiction.* Berkeley: University of California Press, 1997.

Fry, Roger. *Vision and Design.* London: Chatto and Windus, 1920.

Fudge, Erica. Introduction to "Reading Animals." *Worldviews* 4 (2000):101–13.

———. *Perceiving Animals: Humans and Beasts in Early Modern Culture.* Urbana: University of Illinois Press, 2002.

Gaard, Greta, ed. *Ecofeminism: Woman, Animals, Nature.* Philadelphia: Temple University Press, 1993.

Galt, John. *Annals of the Parish: Or the Chronicle of Dalmailing during the Ministry of the Rev. Micah Balwhidder Written by Himself.* London: Oxford University Press, 1967.

Gilligan, Carol. *In a Different Voice: Psychological Theory and Women's Development.* Cambridge, MA: Harvard University Press, 1982.

———. "Moral Orientation and Moral Development." In *Women and Moral Theory,* edited by Eva Feder Kittay and Diana T. Meyers, pp. 29–32. Totowa, NJ: Rowman & Littlefield, 1987.

———. "Une voix différente: un regard prospectif à partir du passé." In *Carol Gilligan et l'éthique du "care,"* edited by Vanessa Nurock, pp. 19–38. Paris: Presses Universitaires de France, 2010.

Girard, René. *Things Hidden since the Foundation of the World,* trans. Stephen Ban and Michael Metter. Stanford, CA: Stanford University Press, 1987.

Glaspell, Susan Keating. "A Jury of Her Peers" (1917). In *American Voices, American Women,* edited by Lee R. Edwards and Arlyn Diamond, pp. 359–81. New York: Avon, 1973.

Gordimer, Nadine. "The Idea of Gardening." *New York Review of Books*, February 2, 1984, 3–6.

Graham, Lucy Valerie. "Reading the Unspeakable: Rape in J. M. Coetzee's *Disgrace*." *Journal of Southern African Studies* 29, no. 2 (2003):433–44.

Hall, S. C. "Jack the Shrimp" and "The Barrow Postman." In *Sketches of Irish Character*, 3rd ed., pp. 88–109 and 166–74. London: Chatto and Windus, 1854.

Halliwell, Stephen. *Aristotle's Poetics*, 2nd ed. Chicago: University of Chicago Press, 1998.

Hardy, G. H. *A Mathematician's Apology* (1940). Cambridge: Cambridge University Press, 2012.

Harman, Graham. *Prince of Networks: Bruno Latour and Metaphysics*. Melbourne: re. press, 2009.

———. *Tool-Being: Heidegger and the Metaphysics of Objects*. Peru, IL: Open Court, 2002.

Hartshorne, Charles. *Beyond Humanism: Essays in a New Philosophy of Nature*. Chicago: Willett, Clark, 1937.

Hedley, Douglas. *Sacrifice Imagined: Violence, Atonement and the Sacred*. New York: Continuum, 2011.

Heilbrun, Carolyn. "The Masculine Wilderness of the American Novel." *Saturday Review*, January 29, 1972, 41–44.

Hein, Hilda and Carolyn Korsmeyer, eds. *Aesthetics in Feminist Perspective*. Bloomington: Indiana University Press, 1993.

Herman, David, ed. *Creatural Fictions: Human-Animal Relationships in 20th- and 21st-Century Literature*. Houndsmills, Basingstoke, England: Palgrave Macmillan, 2016.

Hogg, James. "Duncan Campbell." In *Winter Evening Tales: Collected among the Cottagers in the South of Scotland*, pp. 80–97. Edinburgh: Edinburgh University Press, 2002.

———. "Further Anecdotes of the Shepherd's Dog." *Blackwood's Edinburgh Magazine* 2 (March 1818):621–26.

———. "The Shepherd's Calendar." In *Winter Evening Tales: Collected among the Cottagers in the South of Scotland*, pp. 372–409. Edinburgh: Edinburgh University Press, 2002.

Homans, Margaret. *Bearing the Word: Language and Female Experience in Nineteenth-Century Women's Writing*. Chicago: University of Chicago Press, 1986.

Horkheimer, Max. *Eclipse of Reason*. New York: Continuum, 1987.

Horkheimer, Max and Theodor W. Adorno. *Dialectic of Enlightenment*, trans. John Cumming. New York: Continuum, 1988.

Hubert, Henri and Marcel Mauss. *Sacrifice: Its Nature and Function* (1898), trans. W. D. Halls. Chicago: University of Chicago Press, 1964.

Hunt, Samantha. "Three Days," *The New Yorker*, January 16, 2006.

Hutton, Sarah. "The Riddle of the Sphinx." In *Women, Science and Medicine 1500–1700*, edited by Lynette Hunter and Sarah Hutton, pp. 7–28. Phoenix Mill, England: Sutton, 1997.

Immermann, Karl. "Münchhausen." In *Werke*, edited by Benno von Wiese, vol. 3. Frankfurt am Main, Germany: Athenäum, 1972.

Jacob, Margaret C. "The Materialist World of Pornography." In *The Invention of Pornography: Obscenity and the Origins of Modernity 1500–1800*, edited by Lynn Hunt, pp. 157–202. New York: Zone Books, 1996.

Jameson, Fredric. *Marxism and Form: Twentieth-Century Dialectical Theories of Literature*. Princeton, NJ: Princeton University Press, 1971.

Jay, Nancy. *Throughout Your Generations Forever: Sacrifice, Religion, and Paternity*. Chicago: University of Chicago Press, 1992.

Jewell, Andrew and Janis Stout, eds. *The Selected Letters of Willa Cather*. New York: Knopf, 2013.

Jewett, Sarah Orne. *Deephaven*. Boston: James R. Osgood, 1877.

———. "A White Heron." In *The Country of the Pointed Firs and Other Stories*, edited by Willa Cather, pp. 161–71. New York: Doubleday Anchor, 1956.

———. "A Winter Drive." In *Country By-Ways*, pp. 163–85. Boston: Houghton Mifflin, 1881.

———. "River Driftwood." In *Country By-Ways*, pp. 1–33. Boston: Houghton Mifflin, 1881.

Johnson, Samuel. "Rasselas." In *Criticism: The Major Texts*, edited by Walter Jackson Bate, pp. 206–07. New York: Harcourt, Brace & World, 1952.

Jonsen, Albert R. and Stephen Toulim. *The Abuse of Casuistry: A History of Moral Reasoning*. Berkeley: University of California Press, 1988.

Kant, Immanuel. "Analytic of the Sublime." In *The Critical Tradition*, edited by David H. Richter, pp. 261–71. New York: St. Martin's Press, 1989.

———. "Critique of Judgment." In *Kant Selections*, edited by Theodore Meyer, pp. 373–432. New York: Scribner's, 1929.

Kappeler, Susanne. *The Pornography of Representation*. Minneapolis: University of Minnesota Press, 1986.

Karahasan, Dzebad. "Literature and War." *Agni* 41 (1995):1–13.

Karelis, Charles. Introduction to *Hegel's Introduction to "Aesthetics,"* trans. T. M. Knox. Oxford: Oxford University Press, 1979.

Keller, Evelyn Fox. *A Feeling for the Organism: The Life and Works of Barbara McClintock*. San Francisco: W. H. Freeman, 1983.

Kepnes, Steven. *The Text as Thou: Martin Buber's Dialogical Hermeneutics and Narrative Theology*. Bloomington: Indiana University Press, 1992.

Kermode, Frank. *The Sense of an Ending: Studies in the Theory of Fiction*. Oxford: Oxford University Press, 1966.

Kheel, Marti. "License to Kill: An Ecofeminist Critique of Hunters' Discourse." In *Animals and Women: Feminist Theoretical Explorations*, edited by Carol J. Adams and Josephine Donovan, pp. 85–125. Durham, NC: Duke University Press, 1995.

———. *Nature Ethics: An Ecofeminist Perspective*. Lanham, MD: Rowman & Littlefield, 2008.

Kim, Junse. 2003, "Yangban." In *Pushcart Prize XXVII*, edited by Bill Henderson, pp. 448–62. Wainscott, NY: Pushcart Press, 2003.

Klinger, Cornelia. "The Concepts of the Sublime and the Beautiful in Kant and Lyotard." In *Feminist Interpretations of Immanuel Kant*, edited by Robin May Schott, pp. 191–212. University Park, PA: Pennsylvania State University Press, 1997.

Kowalsky, Gary. *The Souls of Animals*. Walpole, NH: Stillpoint, 1991.

Kristeva, Julia. *Powers of Horror: An Essay on Abjection*, trans. Leon S. Roudiez. New York: Columbia University Press, 1982.

Kuzniar, Alice. *Melancholia's Dog*. Chicago: University of Chicago Press, 2006.

Laurence, Elizabeth. "Hunting the Wren: A Sacred Bird in Ritual." In *A Communion of Subjects: Animals in Religion, Science, and Ethics*, edited by Paul Waldau and Kimberley Patton, pp. 406–12. New York: Columbia University Press, 2006.

Leadbeater, Mary. "*Annals of Ballitore*." In *The Leadbeater Papers*, vol. 1. London: Routledge/Thoemmes, 1998.

Lederman, Leon M. and Christopher T. Hill. *Quantum Physics for Poets*. Amherst, NY: Prometheus, 2011.

Lukács, Georg. *History and Class Consciousness: Studies in Marxist Dialectics*, trans. Rodney Livingstone. Cambridge, MA: MIT Press, 1971.

Luke, Brian. *Brutal: Manhood and the Exploitation of Animals*. Urbana: University of Illinois Press, 2007.

Malamud, Randy. "Poetic Animals and Animal Souls." *Society & Animals* 6, no. 3 (1998):263–77.

Mann, Bonnie. *Women's Liberation and the Sublime: Feminism Postmodernism, Environment*. New York: Oxford University Press, 2006.

Marais, Michael. "The Hermeneutics of Empire: Coetzee's Post-colonial Metafiction." In *Critical Perspectives on J. M. Coetzee*, edited by Graham Huggan and Stephen Watson, pp. 61–81. New York: St. Martin's Press, 1996.

Mathews, Freya. *For Love of Matter: A Contemporary Panpsychism*. Albany: State University of New York Press, 2003.

Mausch, Richard. "The Weight." In *Pushcart Prize XXVII*, edited by Bill Henderson, pp. 562–78. Wainscott, NY: Pushcart Press, 2003.

May, Brian. "J. M. Coetzee and the Question of the Body." *Modern Fiction Studies* 47, no. 2 (Summer 2001):391–420.

McCumber, John. "Aristotelian Catharsis and the Purgation of Women." *Diacritics* 18, no. 4 (Winter 1998):53–67.

Mellor, Anne K. *Romanticism and Gender*. New York: Routledge, 1993.

Merivale, Patricia. "Audible Palimpsests: Coetzee's Kafka." In *Critical Perspectives on J. M. Coetzee*, edited by Graham Huggan and Stephen Watson, pp. 152–67. New York: St. Martin's Press, 1996.

Mills, Patricia Jagentowicz. *Women, Nature and Psyche*. New Haven, CT: Yale University Press, 1987.

Moir, D. S. *The Life of Mansie Waugh, Tailor in Dalkeith, Written by Himself*. Edinburgh: William Blackwood, 1828.

Morgan, Lady. *Florence Macarthy: An Irish Tale*, vol. 1. New York: Garland, 1979.

———. *The Wild Irish Girl*. London: Pandora, 1986.

Morson, Gary Saul and Caryl Emerson. *Mikhail Bakhtin: Creation of a Prosaics*. Stanford, CA: Stanford University Press, 1990.

Mortensen, Peter. "Taking Animals Seriously: William Wordsworth and the Claims of Ecological Romanticism." *Orbis Litterarum* 55, no. 4 (2000):296–311.

Munro, Alice. "Runaway," *The New Yorker*, August 11, 2003.

Murdoch, Iris. *Metaphysics as a Guide to Morals*. New York: Viking Penguin, 1993.

———. "Negative Capability." *Adam International Review* 284–86 (1960):172–73.

———. *The Sovereignty of Good*. New York: Schocken, 1971.

———. "The Sublime and the Good." *Chicago Review* 13 (Autumn 1959):42–55.

Murphy, Patrick. "Ground, Pivot, Motion: Ecofeminist Theory, Dialogics, and Literary Practice." *Hypatia* 6, no. 1 (1991):146–61.

———. "An Ecological Feminist Revisioning of the Masculinist Sublime." *Revista Canaria de Estudios Ingleses* 64 (April 2012):79–94.

Nagel, Thomas. *Mind and Cosmos: Why the Materialist Neo-Darwinist Conception of Nature Is Almost Certainly False*. New York: Oxford University Press, 2012.

Najmi, Samina. "Naomi Shihab Nye's Aesthetic Smallness and the Military Sublime." *MELUS* 35, no. 2 (Summer 2010):151–71.

Norris, Margot. *Beasts of the Modern Imagination: Darwin, Nietzsche, Kafka, Ernst, and Lawrence*. Baltimore: Johns Hopkins University Press, 1985.

O'Brien, Sharon. *Willa Cather: The Emerging Voice*. New York: Oxford University Press, 1987.

O'Brien, Tim. *The Things They Carried*. New York: Broadway, 1990.

O'Connor, Maureen. *The Female and the Species: The Animal in Irish Women's Writing*. Bern, Switzerland: Peter Lang, 2010.

Page, Frederick, ed. *Letters of John Keats*. London: Oxford University Press, 1965.

Panofsky, Erwin. "Die Perspektive als Symbolic Form." In *Vorträge der Bibliothek Warburg Institut 1925–25*. Berlin: B. G. Tuebner, 1927.

Patton, Kimberley. "Animal Sacrifice: Metaphysics of a Sublimated Victim." In *Communion of Subjects: Animals in Religion, Science, and Ethics*, edited by Paul Waldau and Kimberley Patton, pp. 391–405. New York: Columbia University Press, 2006.

———. "'He Who Sits in the Heavens Laughs': Recovering Animal Theology in Abrahamic Traditions." *Harvard Theological Review* 93, no. 4 (2000):401–34.

Perkins, David. *Romanticism and Animal Rights*. Cambridge: Cambridge University Press, 2003.

Perlina, Nina. "Mikhail Bakhtin and Martin Buber: Problems of Dialogic Imagination." *Studies in Twentieth-Century Literature* 9, no. 1 (1984):13–28.

Pert, Candace B. *Molecules of Emotion: Why You Feel the Way You Feel*. New York: Scribner's, 1997.

Pick, Anat. *Creaturely Poetics: Animality and Vulnerability in Literature and Film*. New York: Columbia University Press, 2011.

Plato. "Symposium." In *The Dialogues of Plato*, edited by B. Jowett. Vol. 1, pp. 301–48. New York: Random House, 1937.

Plumwood, Val. "The Concept of a Cultural Landscape: Nature, Culture and Agency in the Land." *Ethics and the Environment* 11, no. 2 (2006):115–49.

———. "Decolonising Australian Gardens: Gardening and the Ethics of Place." *Australian Humanities Review* 36 (July 2005):1–5.

Pollock, Griselda. "Dying, Seeing, Feeling: Transforming the Ethical Space of Feminist Aesthetics." In *The Life and Death of Images: Ethics and Aesthetics*, edited by Diamuid Costello and Dominic Willsdon, pp. 213–35. Ithaca, NY: Cornell University Press, 2008.

Pope, Alexander. "Essay on Criticism." In *Alexander Pope: Selected Poetry and Prose*, edited by William K. Wimsatt Jr., pp. 63–84. New York: Holt, Rinehart & Winston, 1961.

Quincey, Christian de. *Radical Nature: Rediscovering the Soul of Matter*. Montpelier, VT: Invisible Cities Press, 2002.

Rabuzzi, Kathryn Allen. *The Sacred and the Feminine: Toward a Theology of Housework*. New York: Seabury, 1982.

Rayfield, Donald. "Orchards and Gardens in Checkhov," *SEER* 67, no. 4 (October 1989):530–45.

Regan, Tom. *The Case for Animal Rights*. Berkeley: University of
California Press, 1983.

Rubin, Gayle. "The Traffic in Women: Notes on the 'Political Economy'
of Sex." In *Towards an Anthropology of Women*, edited by Rayna R.
Reiter, pp. 157–210. New York: Monthly Review, 1975.

Ruddick, Sara. "Maternal Thinking," *Feminist Studies* 6, no 2 (1980):342–67.

Sand, George. *La Mare au diable*. Paris: Nelson/Calmann Lévy, 1931.

———. *La Petite Fadette*. Paris: Livre de Poche, 1973.

———. *Le Meunier d'Angibault*. Paris: Calmann Lévy, 1888.

———. *Mauprat*. Paris: Calmann Lévy, 1930.

Scholtmeijer, Marian. "Animals and Spirituality: A Skeptical Animal
Rights Advocate Examines Literary Approaches to the Subject." *LIT*
10, no. 4 (2000):371–94.

———. *Animal Victims in Modern Fiction: From Sanctity to Sacrifice*.
Toronto: University of Toronto Press, 1993.

Schor, Naomi. *Reading in Detail: Aesthetics and the Feminine*. New York:
Methuen, 1987.

Scott, James C. *Seeing Like a State: How Certain Schemes to Improve the
Human Condition Have Failed*. New Haven, CT: Yale University Press,
1998.

———. *Weapons of the Weak: Everyday Forms of Peasant Resistance*.
New Haven, CT: Yale University Press, 1985.

Sherman, Sarah Way. *Sarah Orne Jewett: American Persephone*. Hanover,
NH: University Press of New England, 1989.

Simons, John. *Animal Rights and the Politics of Literary Representation*.
Houndsmills, Basingstoke, England: Palgrave, 2002.

Skrbina, David. *Panpsychism in the West*. Cambridge, MA: MIT Press,
2005.

Slosson, Annie Trumbull. "Anna Malann." In *Dumb Foxglove and Other
Stories*, pp. 85–117. New York: Harper, 1898.

Smith, Adam. *The Wealth of Nations*. New York: Bantam Dell, 2003.

Smolin, Lee. *Time Reborn*. Boston: Houghton Mifflin, 2013.

Sokel, Walter. *The Writer in Extremis: Expressionism in Twentieth-
Century German Literature*. Stanford, CA: Stanford University Press,
1959.

Sontag, Susan. *Regarding the Pain of Others*. New York: Farrar, Straus &
Giroux, 2003.

———. "Regarding the Torture of Others." *New York Times Magazine*,
May 23, 2004, 22–29, 42.

Spät, Patrick. "Panpsychism, the Big-Bang Argument and the Dignity of
Life." In *Mind That Abides: Panpsychism in the New Millennium*, edited
by David Skrbina, pp. 159–76. Amsterdam: John Benjamins, 2009.

Spiegel, Marjorie. *The Dreaded Comparison: Human and Animal Slavery*.
Philadelphia: New Society, 1988.

Steel, Karl. "With the World, Or Bound to Face the Sky: The Postures of the Wolf-Child of Hesse." In *Animal, Vegetable, Mineral: Ethics and Objects*, edited by Jeffrey Jerome Cohen, pp. 9–34. Washington, DC: Oliphaunt Books, 2012

Stifter, Adalbert. "Die Mappe meines Urgrossvaters." In *Gesammelte Werke*, vol. 1, pp. 441–674. Wiesbaden, Germany: Insel-Verlag, 1959.

Stowe, Harriet Beecher. *Oldtown Folks*. Boston: Houghton Mifflin, 1894.

———. *The Minister's Wooing* (1859). Ridgewood, NJ: Gregg, 1968.

———. *The Pearl of Orr's Island: A Story of the Coast of Maine*. Boston: Houghton Mifflin, 1896.

———. "Rights of Dumb Animals." *Hearth and Home* 1 (January 2, 1869):24.

Sullivan, Marnie M. "Shifting Subjects and Marginal World: Revealing the Radical in Rachel Carson's Three Sea Books," in *Feminist Ecocriticism: Environment, Women, and Literature*, edited by Douglas A. Vakoch. Blue Ridge Summit, PA: Lexington, 2012.

Tanner, Laura E. *Intimate Violence: Reading Rape and Torture in Twentieth-Century Fiction*. Bloomington: Indiana University Press, 1994.

Taylor, Paul W. *Respect for Nature: A Theory of Environmental Ethics*. Princeton, NJ: Princeton University Press, 1986.

Tchekov, Anton. *The Cherry Orchard*. In *The Plays of Anton Tchekov*, trans. Constance Garnett. New York: Modern Library, n.d.

———. *Uncle Vanya*. In *The Plays of Anton Tchekov*, trans. Constance Garnett. New York: Modern Library, n.d

Thomas, Keith. *Man and the Natural World: A History of the Modern Sensibility*. New York: Pantheon, 1983.

Thompson, E. P. *Customs in Common*. New York: New Press, 1991.

Tolstoy, Leo. *Anna Karenina*, trans. Constance Garnett. New York: Random House, 1939.

———. "Esarhaddon, King of Assyria." In *Collected Shorter Fiction*, vol. 2, trans. Louise Maude, Aylmer Maude, and Nigel J. Cooper, pp. 741–47. New York: Knopf, 2001.

———. "The First Step." *The New Review* (1892):23–41.

———. "Master and Man." In *Collected Shorter Fiction*, vol. 2, trans. L. Maude, A. Maude, and Cooper, pp. 541–96. New York: Knopf, 2001.

———. "Snow Storm." In *Collected Shorter Fiction*, vol. 1, trans. L. Maude, A. Maude, and Cooper, pp. 227–60. New York: Knopf, 2001.

———. "Strider: The Story of a Horse." In *Collected Shorter Fiction*, vol. 1, trans. L. Maude, A. Maude, and Cooper, pp. 583–626. New York: Knopf, 2001.

———. "Three Deaths." *Collected Shorter Fiction*, vol. 1, trans. L. Maude, A. Maude, and Cooper, pp. 565–82. New York: Knopf, 2001.

———. *What Is Art?* trans. Aylmer Maude. Indianapolis: Bobbs-Merrill, 1960.

Trevor, William. "Folie à Deux." *The New Yorker*, July 24, 2007.

Troyat, Henri. *Tolstoy*. Garden City, NY: Doubleday, 1967.

Uexküll, Jakob von. *A Foray into the Worlds of Animals and Humans*, trans. Joseph D. O'Neil. Minneapolis: University of Minnesota Press, 2010.

Valéry, Paul. "Poetry and Abstract Thought." In *Critical Theory Since Plato*, edited by Hazard Adams, pp. 909–19. New York: Harcourt, Brace, Jovanovich, 1971.

Virilio, Paul. *Art and Fear*. New York: Continuum, 2006.

Vyvyan, John. *In Pity and in Anger: A Study of the Use of Animals in Science*. Marblehead, MA: Micah Publications, 1988.

Walker, Alice. "Everyday Use." In *Women and Fiction*, edited by Susan Cahill, pp. 364–72. New York: Mentor, 1975.

———. "In Search of Our Mothers' Gardens." *Ms.* 2, no. 11 (May 1974).

Waller, Elizabeth L. "Writing the Real: Virginia Woolf and the Ecology of Language." *Bucknell Review* 44, no. 1 (2000):137–57.

Watson, Stephen. "Colonialism and the Novels of J. M. Coetzee." In *Critical Perspectives on J. M. Coetzee*, edited by Graham Huggan and Stephen Watson, pp. 13–36. New York: St. Martin's Press, 1996.

Webb, Stephen H. *On God and Dogs: A Christian Theology of Compassion for Animals*. New York: Oxford University Press, 1998.

Weil, Simone. "Classical Science and After." In *On Science, Necessity, and the Love of God*, edited by and trans. Richard Rees, pp. 3–43. London: Oxford University Press, 1968.

———. "Fragment: Foundation of a New Science." In *On Science, Necessity, and the Love of God*, edited by and trans. Richard Rees, pp. 79–84. London: Oxford University Press.

———. *La Pesanteur et la grâce*. Paris: Librarie Plon, 1948.

———. "Reflections on the Right Use of School Studies with a View to the Love of God." In *The Simone Weil Reader*, edited by George A. Panichas. New York: McKay, 1977.

Wilkins, Mary E. "Christmas Jenny." In *A New England Nun and Other Stories*, pp. 160–77. New York: Harper, 1891.

Willey, Basil. *The Seventeenth-Century Background*. Garden City, NY: Doubleday Anchor, n.d.

Wilson, Edward O. "Biophilia and the Conservation Ethic." In *The Biophilia Hypothesis*, edited by Stephen R. Kellert and Edward O. Wilson, pp. 31–41. Washington, DC: Island Press, 1993.

Wint, Callan. "Breathariano," The New Yorker, October 22, 2012.

Wolfe, Cary. "Human, All Too Human: 'Animal Studies' and the Humanities." *PMLA* 124, no. 2 (2009):567–8.

Wolin, Richard. "The De-Aesthetization of Art: On Adorno's *Aesthetische Theorie*." *Telos* 41 (1979):107–27.

Woolf, Virginia. "The Death of a Moth." In *Collected Essays*, vol. 1, pp. 359–61. London: Chatto & Windus, 1966.

———. "Modern Fiction." In *Collected Essays*, vol. 2, pp. 103–110. London: Chatto and Windus, 1966.

———. *A Passionate Apprentice: The Early Journals 1897–1909*, edited by Mitchell A. Leaska. New York: Harcourt, 1990.

———. *A Room of One's Own*. New York: Harcourt Brace, 1957.

———. "The Russian Point of View." In *Collected Essays*, vol. 1, pp. 238–46. London: Chatto and Windus, 1966.

———. "A Sketch of the Past." In *Moments of Being*, edited by Jeanne Schulkind, pp. 61–160. San Diego, CA: Harcourt Brace Jovanovich, 1985.

Wright, Patrick. "A Timeless Sublime? Reading the Feminine Sublime in the Discourse of the Sacred." *Angelaki* 15, no. 2 (August 2010):85–100.

Youngs, Amy. "Creating, Culling and Caring." In *The Aesthetics of Care?: The Artistic, Social and Scientific Implications of the Use of Biological/ Medical Technologies for Artistic Purposes*, Symposium, Perth Institute of Contemporary Arts, August 5, 2002, edited by Oron Cutts, pp. 68–73. Perth: University of Western Australia, 2002.

Zola, Emile. "The Experimental Novel." In *The Experimental Novel and Other Essays*, trans. Belle M. Sherman, pp. 1–23. New York: Haskell House, 1964.

Zylinska, Joanna. *On Spiders, Cyborgs and Being Sacred*. Manchester, England: Manchester University Press, 2001.

INDEX

Note: Literary works are listed under the author where known.